THE ENGLISH NOVEL.

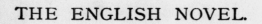

THE
ENGLISH NOVEL

A SHORT SKETCH OF ITS HISTORY
FROM THE EARLIEST TIMES
TO THE APPEARANCE
OF *WAVERLEY*

By SIR WALTER RALEIGH

LATE PROFESSOR OF ENGLISH LITERATURE IN GLASGOW UNIVERSITY

LONDON
JOHN MURRAY, ALBEMARLE STREET

FIRST EDITION . . . *October*, 1894.
Thirteenth Impression . *January*, 1929.

PRINTED IN GREAT BRITAIN BY
WILLIAM CLOWES AND SONS, LIMITED, LONDON AND BECCLES.

To

MY PUPILS

who have shown themselves willing

to tolerate

Parts of this Book,

I inscribe

the Whole of it

with Gratitude and Esteem.

PREFACE.

THIS is a little book on a great subject. Its aim is critical and historical; to furnish studies of the work of the chief English novelists before Scott, connected by certain general lines of reasoning and speculation on the nature and development of the novel. Much material has been omitted, and many works silently passed over, in the effort to attain a fair perspective and a reasonable continuity of treatment within a narrow compass. I much regret that my limited opportunities of access to a great library forbid my attempting a bibliography of the English Novel. Such a work would be the best companion to the present history.

My warmest thanks are due to Mr. John Sampson, librarian of University College, Liverpool, for many valuable criticisms, and for the gift of an index.

W. A. R.

UNIVERSITY COLLEGE,
  LIVERPOOL,
    June, 1894.

CONTENTS

THE ENGLISH NOVEL.

CHAPTER I.

THE ROMANCE AND THE NOVEL.

Time and again, in the world's history, where East meets West, the spirit of romance has been born. Herodotus on his travels, Heliodorus carrying Ethiopian traditions to his bishopric, Apuleius the Carthaginian sojourning at Rome, are all parents of prose romance; and in mediæval legend, Alexander in correspondence with the Brahmins, Charlemagne in conflict with the Moors, furnish the same unfailing inspiration. But the late Greek and Latin writers of prose fiction have little enough to do with the beginnings of story-telling in English. There exists an Anglo-Saxon version of the story of Apollonius of Tyre; for the rest, it was the noble army of Elizabethan translators who first brought these early prose romances within the domain of English literature. The earlier English romances, like the word *Romance* itself, are mediæval and French in origin.

The Celtic races of Europe are almost singular in

their early preference for telling their traditional stories in prose. The Normans, like the Teutonic races, narrated in verse, and their stories reappeared in English verse, alliterative or rhymed, long before they were redacted, in the fifteenth century, into English prose. From the time of Layamon onwards, throughout the thirteenth and fourteenth centuries the work of translation and adaptation went on, and the establishment of the English language in its own country, about the middle of the fourteenth century, gave a fresh impetus to the process. In this way the four principal mediæval cycles of romance, dealing severally with the legends of Charlemagne, Arthur, Alexander, and Troy, had been made familiar to the English people in their own tongue by the close of the fourteenth century. Fashioned by French and Anglo-Norman poets and reciters from material supplied by popular or literary tradition, modified by each successive generation to suit prevailing tastes, these legends reached the English-speaking people of England for the most part in late and elaborately wrought forms. There is no English version of any of the Charlemagne legends that reproduces the grave and unadorned simplicity of the French *chansons de geste* of the eleventh century. Religious and severe in spirit, as monotonous in theme and phrase as in metre, the *Chanson de Roland* has nothing in it of the marvellous adventures or of the love-interest that came to be regarded later as constituting the essence of romance. The fair Aude, the sister of Oliver, betrothed to Roland, is the only woman who figures in this poem, and her name is never mentioned by Roland. Only when he is

dead, she comes to Charlemagne. " 'Where is the Lord
Roland who swore that I should be his bride?' she
asked the king. Full of grief and pain, weeping and
tearing his white beard, Charles replied, 'My sister, my
dear friend, you ask for one who is dead; but in his
place I will give you one who is more mighty, Louis,
my son, who rules my marches, better man I know
not.'

"Then answered Aude, 'Strange to me seems your
speech. God and his angels and saints forbid that I
should live now when Roland is dead.' Her colour
fled, she fell forthwith dead at the feet of Charles. May
God have mercy on her soul. The French barons wept
and lamented her." *

The severity and restraint of this may be taken as
typical of the earliest monuments of mediæval romantic
literature. But the influence of the Crusades, and the
development of early feudal manners into the richly
decorative chivalry of the later Middle Ages, transformed
and elaborated the romances before they became
English. When Sir Thomas Malory, Caxton, and Lord
Berners gave to the Arthur and Charlemagne romances
their first English prose dress, it was from late French
versions that they worked. The history of English
prose fiction begins with those three names, at precisely
the point where the researches of folk-lore reach their
conclusion. The age of the nameless minstrel is over,
that of the responsible prose author has begun.

The greater part of the story-telling of Chaucer's time
was done by the minstrel, the descendant of the early

* Translated in the *Dublin Review*, July, 1890.

jongleur. But not only was the minstrel degenerate
since the days of Taillefer, when he shared in heroic
exploits; he was also in danger of eclipse from purely
literary rivals. In the towns, growing wonderfully in
number and importance, the annual performance of
the dramatic cycles of "Mysteries" by the trade gilds
formed the principal literary diversion of the people.
At the court, the new poetry of Geoffrey Chaucer was
putting to shame, by its high artistic finish, the ambling
monotony of the chanted recitations concerning Sir
Eglamour, Sir Perceval, and Sir Isembras. But in the
baronial hall in the country, especially "when folk were
feasted and fed," and willing to stifle conversation for a
little, the minstrel was sure of a welcome and gifts. His
usual method of performance, still common in Eastern
countries, was to chant the stanzas of his long narrative
poem to the droning accompaniment of the *vielle*,
played with a short bow. In this way gentle and simple
were made familiar with—

> " What resounds
> In fable or romance of Uther's son,
> Begirt with British and Armoric knights,"

with the exploits of Roland and Oliver, or the adventures of those unattached knights whose names were, for
the most part, ultimately connected with one or other of
the great cycles.

The examples that have been preserved of this immense body of metrical literature are not without their
characteristic merits. They are epical in spirit, although
not in form; they frequently begin with the genealogy

of their hero, and carry him through the actions and adventures of his life, concluding with his epitaph and a general doxology. They display a marked preference for deeds done, and attempt no character-drawing. Knights are brave and ladies are fair, and the actions of both are directed by honour and love, in the highly conventional sense put upon these motives in the later days of chivalry. If a mediæval minstrel had been requested to embody all the novels of Mr. Henry James in his narrative, he would have put them into a single line,—

> " When twenty years were come and gone,"—

and hurried on to the next giant. The broad outlines of such a scheme work their own effect, and the deeds of the doughtiest of heroes are often saved from exaggeration by the largeness of the background behind. A sense of the instability of human life, very present to the minds of men familiar with battle and plague, is everywhere mirrored in these romances; some of them end, like a modern novel, with a marriage, but the chronicler rarely forgets to add the few additional lines of doggerel to the effect that—

> " They lived and died with good intent,
> And sithen all to heaven they went,
> When that they dead were.
> Pray we now to heaven's King,
> He give us all His dear blessing
> Now and evermore ! "

When the great story-teller of his age came, in the maturity of his powers, to build up the fabric of the

Canterbury Tales, he put into his own mouth a parody of the current metrical romances :—

> " Al of a knight was fair and gent
> In batail and in tornament,
> His name was Sir Thopas."

Chaucer the artist—perhaps the purest artist of all great names in English poetry—despised the otiose epithets, and the metre, so lacking in emphasis and distinction, of the verse romances ; Chaucer the humourist, familiar with the witty and spirited tales of the South, found the languors of the ministrels' chronology intolerable. He commits the task of criticism to the host, who interrupts the tale with curses on its dulness, and orders its narrator to tell something in prose, containing matter either of mirth or doctrine. The host, that is to say, positively invites Chaucer to produce the first English novel. Here was the opportunity to naturalize in English prose the brief jocular *fabliau* of France, already perfected by Boccaccio in Italian prose under the name of the *novella*. For reasons best known to himself Chaucer lets slip this opportunity, and elects to narrate unto edification. In the *Tale of Melibeus*, with which he responds to the host's invitation, he chooses to treat of doctrine, and of doctrine in the dreariest mediæval manner of allegory. The stories in the Latin *Gesta Romanorum*, well known to Chaucer, can be stripped of their allegorical and moral tags, and thoroughly enjoyed by the profane reader; in the *Tale of Melibeus* the allegory permeates and curdles the story. It would seem as if Chaucer, who had emancipated his verse so completely from mediæval allegory and abstraction,

were unable in his prose to save his ear from obsession
by the cadences of the pulpit. His treatise on the
Astrolabe is learned matter reduced to English for the
instruction of a child, the *Parson's Tale* and the translation of Boethius, his other prose works, are bald sermons,
with none of the glitter and melody of his poorest line of
verse. English prose had really no standing in an age
when there were few readers who could not read Latin.

The original work done by Chaucer on the themes of
the old romances was more deadly than his ridicule to
the supremacy of the ministrel. In the *Knight's Tale*
and *Troilus and Cressida* he showed what could be
made of the legends of Thebes and Troy. In the
handling of his material as well as in the new elevation
of every syllable of his verse to value and dignity, he
superseded for ever the artless garrulity and tumbling
periods of the ministrel poets. The Chaucerians of the
fifteenth century, from Lydgate onwards, appropriated
more and more legendary material, keeping generally in
their longer poems to the two famous metres of their
master, the seven-lined "Troilus" stanza and the deca-
syllabic couplet. These are measures intended to be
read rather than sung; their adoption marks the triumph
of the written over the spoken word, and heralds the
later conquests of prose.

Although his prose writing merits no particular notice,
it is difficult to pass over the name of Chaucer without marking the high pitch of perfection to which he
brought the art of narration in verse. Not until centuries after his time could there be found in English
prose the equivalent of his spirited incident, his delicate

characterization, his dramatic realism, his sly gentle
humour. It is not merely that he succeeded, alone among
the writers of his age and nation, in ridding himself of
the allegorical fetters that cramped the growth of English
literature even in the fifteenth century. It is not only
that he had an unexampled dramatic genius, which
prompted him to substitute for the statical scheme of the
Decameron a brilliant dynamical scheme of his own,
instinct with life and grace. The greatness of Chaucer's
dramatic power has left its impress on his story-telling
in a hundred subtleties of inspired observation, to be
equalled only by the sudden startling dramatic felicities
of the great romantic playwrights. But first of all he
was a great narrative artist, incomparably the greatest of
an age that loved story-telling and knew nothing of the
drama. He is a master of all those effects, beyond the
scope of the dramatist proper, to be obtained from the
apposite intrusion of himself as narrator, pointing a
moral or interposing a reflection, laughing or criticizing,
expressing incredulity or sympathy. Thus, in the *Prologue*, he hastens to dissent from the Sumpnour's cynical
contempt for the archdeacon's curse, and adds, with
humorous ambiguity, his own conviction—

> " For curs wol slee right as assoillyng saveth."

In the *Knight's Tale*, he refuses, on the ground that he
is no "divinister," to speculate on the fate of the soul
of Arcite :—

> " His spirit chaunged was, and wentè ther
> As I cam never, I can nat tellen wher."

In *Troilus and Cressida* he is constantly at the reader's

elbow, disclaiming skill in love, discussing the conduct
of the heroine, defending her from the charge of im-
modesty in the ready bestowal of her affections, pleading
for her even in her infidelity,—

> " For she so sory was for hir untrouthe,
>   Y-wis, I wolde excuse hir yet for routhe."

And some of the most beautiful of his reflective passages
are interpolated as his own criticisms on the narrative;
thus, in the *Franklin's Tale*, he tells of the marriage of
Arviragus and Dorigen, adding the thought that it
suggests to him,—

> " For o thing, syres, saufly dar I seye,
>   That frendes everich other motte obeye,
>   If they wille longè holdè companye.
>   Love wol nought ben constreyned by maystrie.
>   When maystrie cometh, the god of love anon
>   Beteth on his winges, and fare wel, he is gon."

Yet when he comes, in the *Clerk's Tale*, to tell of a love
that was cruelly " constrained by mastery" and survived
it, he is at no loss for a criticism; after the heart-
rending pathos of the story of Griselda, he turns lightly,
in the inimitable *Envoy*, on the " arch-wives" of his own
day, satirically counselling them against taking Griselda
for a model, and warning their husbands that the story
is an insecure precedent.

The illuminative play of his own thought and humour
around the incidents of the stories he tells so tersely and
vividly gives to Chaucer much of his greatness as a
narrator. But he wrote in verse, and prose was slow to
learn from him. Here and there in his compilation Sir
Thomas Malory took leave to indulge his own knightly

thoughts. In the chapter entitled "How True Love is likened to Summer" (book xviii. ch. 25) such a passage occurs, and the sentiments sound strangely reminiscent of Chaucer. But the earlier prose romances for the most part kept to the beaten path, and chronicled deeds; nothing like the consciousness and freedom of Chaucer's treatment, nothing of his vigilantly critical attitude towards his own art, is to be found in the dream-like formal cavalcade of early prose romance.

In the fifteenth century both of the ancestors of the modern novel—that is, the *novella* or short pithy story after the manner of the Italians, and the romance of chivalry—appear in an English prose dress. But it was not a translation of Boccaccio, or of any of the approved masters of the Italian type, that first found favour with the English people. Direct prose translations of the chief Italian novels were plentiful in the reign of Eliza-beth; for the two preceding centuries the influence of Boccaccio was felt only by scholars and poets, and the reputation of his Latin works overshadowed the merits of the *Decameron*, which was more esteemed as a store-house of tractable material than as a model for imitation. Thus two of the most famous of his novels, the stories of Tancred and Ghismonda, and of Titus and Gisippus, were rendered in English at the beginning of the six-teenth century by William Walter, servant to Sir Henry Marney, and printed by Wynkyn de Worde. Both stories are given in Chaucerian metres, and the translator works, not from the Italian original, but from the Latin versions of Leonardo Aretino and Bandello respectively. The direct influence of Boccaccio belongs to the later sixteenth century. His secular zest and his satires on the clergy would hardly commend his works for translation by a mediæval clerk, or obtain him credit with readers accustomed chiefly to the grave prose of sermons or lives of the saints. It was the *Gesta Romanorum*, a Latin collection of stories, largely of Oriental origin, compiled probably about the beginning of the fourteenth century, that was translated into English prose in the reign of Henry VI., and printed by Wynkyn de Worde at the beginning of the next century.

In this work, allegory, which flourished all through the Middle Ages like some deadly carnivorous plant, entrapping all bright careless forms of life, and converting them to nutriment for its own vegetable substance, appropriated to itself the most volatile of the jests and anecdotes of mediæval society. The stories are drawn from very diverse sources; some of them are characteristically Oriental; some of them contain incidents of Roman history, refracted through the mediæval imagination; some record only a witty response or wise saying, others again bear the mark of an original homiletic intent. All alike are applied, in the lengthy and violent "moralizations" that are appended, to the uses of pastoral theology and the illustration of Christian mysteries. A single moralization may serve as a sample. In the original Latin *Gesta* is preserved the story, told by Cicero, of the man whose friend begged for a sprig of the tree on which his three wives had hanged themselves. The tree, it is stated in the moral, is the cross of Christ. The three wives are pride, lust of the heart, and lust of the eye. He who begged for a sprig is any

good Christian. The implication that a man does well to hang his three wives is not perceived, or, if perceived, does not abash this fearless moralizer.

To trace the history of the stories of the *Gesta Romanorum*, to chronicle their re-appearances in European literature, and to discuss their origin, would be an endless task. Some of the individual tales had honourable destinies in store for them. In form the book was the precursor of the numerous jest-books of the sixteenth and seventeenth centuries, wherein there is no allegorical application and scant narrative interest, the "gests" of knights and emperors tending more and more to give way to the "jests" of the tavern-lounger, popular comedian, or court fool. Rescued from the toils of allegory, the early short prose story had a tendency to degenerate into the mere anecdote. It was saved from this fate by the elements which it assimilated in the course of centuries from the romance, the drama, and the epic.

In the mean time, before the Revival of Learning had made much progress in England, the interest of these brief stories was centred, it is important to observe, not in any light they threw on individual human character and destiny, but in the theology or the dialectic to which they were subordinated. Human beings in them are mere puppets, inhabiting the great fabric of mediæval thought and mediæval institution; playing many parts, standing for virtues, doctrines, or ideas, never for themselves. And it was the work of the Renaissance to recover the literal and obvious sense of human life, as it was the work of the closely allied Reformation to recover

the literal sense of the Bible, overlaid and obliterated by
metaphysical subtleties.   Even Wiclif elaborates at great
length the meaning of the "two fishings that Peter
fished" as betokening the two takings of men into
Christ's religion, finding strange parallels for the net, the
water, and the "void places between knots."   But Colet
and the earlier scholars of his time cast aside the "tro-
pological, allegorical, and anagogical" senses of Scripture, and insisted that Scripture had "only one sense,
and that the most true one."

In much the same way the Renaissance promoted
interest in human life and human character, freed from
the arbitrary domination of the universals to which they
had been enthralled.   The power to see the world in a
detached light, to enjoy the infinite and inexplicable
variety that life and character offer, was acquired only
by degrees.   Even Spenser, restless with delight in the
sensuous world, saddles himself with a double allegory.
And before the full flood of the Italian influence—that
is, in the fifteenth and early sixteenth centuries—the
short prose story remained domesticated with the
preacher, or, dismissed from clerical service and un-
frocked, went the round of the taverns so graphically
described by Langland.

It was otherwise with the romance.   On that, too, the
Church had laid its hand, spiritualizing and refining the
early Celtic legends with marvellous effect.   But the
wild instincts of the romance were too strong to permit
of its complete affiliation.   The interest of the people in
incident and adventure for their own sake kept it independent.   And in the reign of Edward IV. there arose,

in Sir Thomas Malory, an artist conscious of his art, who gave to the scattered Arthur legends a unity and a beauty of presentment that secured for them their supreme place in English prose literature.

The scholars who are unwilling to admit that the Arthur legends grew up on Breton soil have also claimed Sir Thomas Malory, on the authority of Bale, for a Welshman. It is quite certain, at least, that he was, as Bale calls him, "heroici spiritus homo," a man of a heroic temper; the facts of his life are lacking. His book, *Le Morte Darthur*, a compilation mainly from French sources, was finished, as he himself states, in the ninth year of the reign of King Edward IV., that is to say, either in 1469 or 1470. It was secured for posterity by Caxton, who printed it in 1485.

In the preface which he contributed to his edition of the work, Caxton discusses at some length the existence of an historical Arthur. He had delayed printing the noble history of King Arthur because, like Milton later, he was troubled with the doubt whether such a king had ever existed. Divers gentlemen of this realm of England had attempted to conquer his scepticism, alleging, among other things, that in the castle of Dover "ye may see Gawaine's skull." He concludes by remarking that, true or not, the book is exemplary and profitable. "And for to pass the time this book shall be pleasant to read in, but for to give faith and belief that all is true that is contained herein, ye be at your liberty; but all is written for our doctrine, and for to beware that we fall not to vice ne sin, but to exercise and follow virtue; by the which we may come and attain to good fame and renown

in this life, and after this short and transitory life to come
unto everlasting bliss in heaven."

The words are memorable as marking the beginning
of prose fiction; history and fable, so long inextricably
entangled, are here drawing apart from one another;
literature is proclaiming itself as an art, and declaring a
purpose beyond the scope of the humble chronicle.

To attain to a finely ordered artistic structure was
beyond Malory's power; the very wealth of legend with
which he had to deal put it beyond him, and he is too
much absorbed in the interest of the parts to give more
than a passing consideration to the whole. His simple
forthright narrative is admirably lucid and effective, and
makes amends for an inevitably rambling structure,
while his flashes of chivalrous feeling illuminate the
plains through which his story wanders. He is a master
in the telling use of the Saxon speech, although he
translates from the French. When Queen Guinevere
escaped from the insolent overtures of Sir Mordred, she
took the Tower of London and suddenly "stuffed it,"
says Malory, "with all manner of victual, and well
garnished it with men, and so kept it." Sir Launcelot,
after her death, "dried and dwined away . . . and ever
he was lying groveling on the tomb of King Arthur and
Queen Guenever." The Holy Grail descends amidst
"cracking and crying of thunder." Sir Bedivere, when
he was sent to throw away Excalibur, "saw nothing but
the waters wap and the waves wan." And this fascinat-
ing simplicity of diction is matched by the clearness of
outline that distinguishes Malory's pictures; the figures
he employs, few in number, are of the natural and

unsought kind dear to Saxon speech. A knight appears in the lists as "bright as an angel," two combatants rush together "like two rams," the children that King Arthur finds the giant roasting are broached on a spit, "like young birds." The allegorical habit has left traces here and there on Malory's work, but indeed it may be said for allegory that it fosters simplicity in prose narration. Where words are to bear a double meaning it is important that the first should be clearly defined, and perfectly distinguished from the second ; the elaborated metaphorical style of a later and more sophisticated age mingles the fact and its figurative associations as early narrative prose never does. The Renaissance troubled the waters, and it was long ere prose ran clear again. There is no better prose style for the purposes of simple story-telling than that which many English writers have at command from Malory to Latimer.

The human emotions enshrined in this style have an irresistible appeal. Pity, anger, love, and pride, speak straight to the heart. The passionate and rebellious cry of Queen Guinevere, "I trust through God's grace after my death to have a sight of the blessed face of Christ, and at doomsday to sit at His right side, for as sinful as ever I was are saints in heaven," has parallels in modern literature. Burns expresses the same hope, but his surmise that after all he may—

> "Snugly sit among the saunts
>   At Davie's hip yet,"

has lost more in pathos than it can make good by its gain in humour.

The work of Sir Thomas Malory became for the

following age the embodiment of the ideas of chivalry
and the well-head of romance. It was twice reprinted
by Wynkyn de Worde, in 1498 and 1529, and again by
William Copland in 1557. The demand continued,
and there are later reprints, belonging to the reigns of
Elizabeth and Charles I. respectively, by Thomas East
and William Stansby. But in the Elizabethan age, as in
our own, it became the feeder of poetry rather than of
prose; Spenser knew it well and Shakespeare read it;
traces of its influence on the greater prose writers, even
on Sir Philip Sidney, are scant enough.

When William Caxton, not later than the year 1477,
set up his press at Westminster, he retained the tastes
that had made him a printer. He had been first a
translator of romances, and he tells how his attention
was directed to the new art of printing by the large
demand for his translation of the mediæval tale of Troy,
made in Bruges for the Duchess of Burgundy, sister to
Edward IV. In England he and his pupils devoted
themselves largely to popularizing the old romances,
and most of those he printed were translated from the
French by himself. His attention was early turned to
the Nine Worthies. Of these, three were Pagans, and
three were Jews; but versions of the Lives of the
three Christians, Arthur, Charlemagne, and Godfrey of
Bouillon, were printed by Caxton, two of them being
his own translations. In the prologue to the earliest,
Godefrey of Boloyne (1481), translated from William of
Tyre, he gives as his reason for preferring the least of
the Christian worthies that the acts and histories of the
other two are well known, "in Latin, French, and

English, and other language." Nevertheless, he went
on to these, and, while he was printing Malory's work,
finished his own translation of the *Lyf of Charles the
Grete*, which appeared later in the same year (1485).
The Foure Sonnes of Aymon followed about 1489, and
the only other translations by Caxton himself that need
be mentioned here are his versions of the unaffiliated
romances of *Paris and Vienne* (1485), and *Blanchardyn
and Eglantyne*, about 1489.

Caxton's humility forbade him to claim any literary
skill. He almost apologizes for his admirable industry
in printing and translating by the repeated plea that
idleness must be avoided at all costs. And in the same
spirit he beseeches the Duchess of Somerset, in the
dedication of *Blanchardyn*, to pardon him for his "rude
and common English," and continues, "I confess me
not learned, ne knowing the art of rhetoric, ne of such
gay terms as now be said in these days and used; but
I hope it shall be understonden of the readers and
hearers, and that shall suffice." To reach a wide
audience rather than to please scholars was plainly
Caxton's aim, and his style is well suited to his purpose.
He has less freedom of movement than Malory, and a
less poetical expression; his renderings are pedestrian
and extremely literal, but they are always clear. His
frequent quaintnesses of diction and logic, which endear
him to the modern reader, were probably unperceived
by his contemporaries. The great work he did was
twofold. In the first place, by printing the best of the
earlier writers, he secured to English literature continuity of development; and Spenser, when he appeared,

appeared as the pupil of Chaucer. The Renaissance
brought a crowd of new models, that, but for Caxton's
labours, would have ousted the old. In the second
place, as translator and printer, he established the
romances of chivalry so firmly in the favour of the
reading public, that, in spite of the Renaissance, they
were reprinted for centuries.

The immediate successors of Caxton followed on his
lines in the choice of books to print. Wynkyn de
Worde, besides reprinting several of the romances
originally printed by Caxton, produced many more on his
own account. Among others, he set forth the romances
of *Ponthus of Galyce* (1511), *Hilyas Knight of the
Swanne* (1512), *Olyver of Castylle and the fayre Helayne*
(1518), and *Sir Degore.* The finest of the contributions
to romance literature attributed to his press is the work
of Sir John Bourchier Lord Berners, the translator of
Froissart, who diverted his leisure in the later years of
his life, from 1520 onwards, by manifold literary labours.
His version of the story of *Huon of Bordeaux*, printed
by Wynkyn de Worde about 1534, is the best English
prose specimen of the Charlemagne cycle of romances,
as Malory's work is the best of the Arthur cycle. The
book is remarkable for having introduced Oberon, the
fairy king, for the first time to English readers. Oberon
lives in a wood on the way to Babylon, and, in the
words of Berners, "is of height but of three foot, and
crooked shouldered, but yet he hath an angelic visage,
so that there is no mortal man that seeth him but that
taketh great pleasure to behold his face. And ye shall
no sooner be entered into that wood, if ye go that way,

he will find the manner to speak with you; and if ye
speak to him, ye are lost for ever.   And ye shall ever
find him before you, so that it shall be in manner
impossible that ye can scape fro him without speaking
to him, for his words be so pleasant to hear that there is
no mortal man that can well scape without speaking to
him.   And if he see that ye will not speak a word to
him, then he will be sore displeased with you, and ere
ye can get out of the wood he will cause rain and wind,
hail and snow, and will make marvellous tempests with
thunder and lightnings, so that it shall seem to you that
all the world should perish.   And he shall make to seem
before you a great running river, black and deep.   But
ye may pass it at your ease, and it shall not wet the feet
of your horse, for all is but fantasy and enchantments."

This description may serve to illustrate the excellence
of the narrative prose of Lord Berners' time.   In the
leisurely unfolding of his theme and in his fearless
repetitions Berners resembles Malory and Caxton; he
must be ranked with Malory, rather than with Caxton,
for his effective arrangement of sentences and his frequent
felicities of phrase.   All three writers exhibit a prose
style as yet undeformed by a straining after the ex-
cellences proper to verse, a full stream of narrative, easy,
deliberate, and vigorous.   With them the mediæval
romance attains its noblest expression in English prose.

Its supremacy in the literary world was of short
duration.   The press of Wynkyn de Worde, which put
forth so many romances, was also engaged in supplying
aid to the New Learning.   The renewed interest of the
age in the classics is witnessed by the enormous number

of editions of grammatical treatises that issued from this press, especially of the Latin accidences and vocabularies of Masters Stanbridge and Whittington. The New Learning, if not actually hostile to the mediæval romance, was certainly contemptuous of it. And when the Protestant Reformation of the reign of Henry VIII. broke about the ears of the English people, the division between the new and the old schools of thought was deepened, and the romance was relegated to the old. Few romances issued from English presses during the later years of Henry VIII. and the reign of Edward VI. ; religious controversy and homiletic, on the other hand, occupied much of the energy of the printers. The Protestant form of religion was established : it had to be supplied, at somewhat short notice, with a literature, and the task was heartily undertaken. It is perhaps something more than a coincidence that the romances printed by William Copland, who inherited the traditions of Caxton and Wynkyn de Worde, fall (such of them as are dated) within the reign of Mary. Treatises on the *Understanding of the Lord's Supper* and *Blasphemies of the Mass*, with which he had been busied in the previous reign, give way, as soon as Mary comes to the throne, to folio reprints of the *Recuyell of the Hystories of Troy*, *the Four Sons of Aymon*, and *Kynge Arthur*.

When the history of literature shall be written by a competent bibliographer, the full extent of the popularity of the romances in the sixteenth and early seventeenth centuries will be made apparent. Besides the romances enumerated above, William Copland put forth, during the comparatively short period of his activities as a printer, versions of the stories of *Syr Isenbras*, *The Knyght of the Swanne*, *Valentyne and Orson*, *Syr Degore*, *Syr Tryamore*, *Syr Bevys of Hampton*, *Guy Earl of Warwick*, and *Syr Eglamoure of Artoys*, all in quarto. Reprints are extant of *Blanchardyn and Eglantyne* and *Huon of Bordeaux*, belonging respectively to the years 1595 and 1601. Licenses for the reprinting of *The Four Sons of Aymon* were granted in 1582 and 1598. *Paris and Vienne*, a late Catalonian romance, which had found its way into France not very many years before Caxton rendered it from French into English, had a lasting vogue; it was reprinted in 1620 and four times later. Nor were all the later editions of the romances reprints. The Amadis and Palmerin cycles, which in their extant forms are late artificial Spanish imitations of the natural Arthurian growth, were first given to English readers in the hey-day of the Elizabethan age by the indefatigable Anthony Munday. And references in Fynes Moryson's *Itinerary* (1617) and Burton's *Anatomy of Melancholy* (1621) have often been cited to prove that the prose romances enjoyed an unflagging popularity.

But although their popularity persisted, it changed in character, and they never regained the position they held in Caxton's time as the highest imaginative training of the educated classes. Their gradual passage from the folio to the chap-book might exemplify Hamlet's moral, "how a king may go a progress through the guts of a beggar." At the beginning of the sixteenth century they had held high sway in the world of letters. Gavin Douglas, whose respect for Caxton was not excessive, yet gives to Paris and Vienne a place among the lovers, classic and romantic, that follow Venus in *The Palice of Honour*. Sir David Lyndsay, in the epistle to the King's Grace prefixed to his *Dreme*, enumerates the antique stories that he was wont to recite for the delectation of the youth of James V. Besides some Scottish folk-tales, these consist chiefly of mediæval redactions of classical stories, tales of the Nine Worthies,

" And siegis all of Tyir, Thebes, and Troy."

Even half a century later, in the catalogue of the private library of Mary Queen of Scots, there figure the *Romance of Perceforest*, *Amadis de Gaule*, *The Lyf of Charles the Grete*, *King Alisaunder*, and *Lancelot de Laik*. And then the new influences drove the romances from their head-quarters. Milton, in speaking of the "lofty fables and romances" whither his younger feet wandered, makes it clear that Ariosto, Tasso, and Spenser are the marks of his eulogy. When a new literature was created by the great artists of the Renaissance, the mediæval romance was driven either to seek low society, or to maintain a supremacy that based its claim on style and not on theme. The age of the despotism of the artist had come, and, in the eyes of the artist, King Arthur himself is only a subject.

The survival of romantic themes, therefore, is not the survival of mediæval romance. Roger Ascham may have been too hasty when he made a taste for romance a mark of "Papistry" and obscurantism. But his instinct led him aright in identifying the romance with the old order of things. Like Catholicism, the romance is essentially mediæval. The marvellous cycles of legend that were fashioned by forgotten workers around the names of mythical or historical heroes are as beautiful, as impressive, as unintelligible to modern fashions of thought, as the cathedral of the Middle Ages. And if the romances may be compared to masterpieces of the great mediæval art of architecture, the novel, with which the future lay, has its closest parallel in the art of painting, the outcome of the Renaissance. Even the *Fabliaux* of the thirteenth century, the remote ancestors of the novel, have come down to us with the names of their makers attached. They are the conscious expression of aspects of real life, as it is seen in the light of the temperament of an individual artist. But the great cycles of romance were built by members of an order, impersonal in their aims and methods, whose names have perished, while their work remains, a haunted ruin.

CHAPTER II.

THE English Renaissance of the reign of Elizabeth, in so far as it can be traced to foreign sources, owed its being to Italy. Linacre, Grocyn, Colet, Wyatt, Surrey, all brought from Italy what they were to contribute to English science and English literature. But the full tide of the Italian Renaissance was not felt on these shores until after the settlement under Elizabeth of the religious troubles which had disturbed the reigns of Henry, Edward, and Mary. And when at last it was felt, and England, thoroughly roused to intellectual activity, proved that she would not only set herself to learn all that Italy had to teach, but would go far to better the instruction, many of the older school of humanists, as well as of the newer school of Puritans, showed themselves intensely averse to the dominant foreign influence. Among these, Roger Ascham, living as he did in a period of real transition, found himself a belated supporter of what was once the new learning. Literature had cast off the sober livery of More and Colet, and was borrowing from Italy the works, not of Savonarola, but of Boccaccio and the novelists. The novel was as distasteful to Ascham as the older romance which it supplanted, so he bravely engaged both enemies, and in the *Scholemaster* he attacks on the one hand *Morte Darthur* and the books which were read "when Papistry as a standing pool covered and overflowed all England," on the other the wanton and vain novels that were beginning to be imported from Italy. Ascham's position was a curious one; falling between two generations, he lost his influence with both, and while the older reactionaries, who still regretted the order that had passed away, looked upon him as a hot-headed reformer, the younger gallants, who carried rapiers and "dags" (*i.e.* pistols) instead of the old-fashioned sword and buckler, would no doubt remember that this decrier of Italian love-stories carried his patriotic conservatism to the pitch of championing the antediluvian long-bow as the national weapon.

The history of prose fiction in the time of Elizabeth is the history of the triumph of the Italian novel, long before introduced into England in the verse of Chaucer, over its natural rival the romance. A singular unanimity of scorn for the older romances is displayed by the men of the later sixteenth century. Shakespeare, who drew most of his plots from the Italian, has curt and scanty references to them. Francis Meres, M.A., in his *Palladis Tamia* (1598), after bestowing on all contemporary writers alike a praise that bespeaks a catholic taste, turns in his closing section to the books that are to be avoided or censured. His list is almost entirely made up of romances of chivalry, the most

notable exception being the *Gargantua* of Rabelais.
And similarly Montaigne, a genial critic enough, in
speaking of his own education, tells how Ovid was his
first love, while as for *Lancelot du Lac, Amadis, Huon
of Bordeaux*, and "such-like trash," he knew nothing of
them, not even their names.

These opinions are exactly what might be expected
of scholars in an age when classical literature was first
recovered, or at least first studied aright. The romances
of chivalry were doomed from the very beginning of the
new movement, and the greatness of Cervantes' achievement is not that he killed a dying man by ridicule.
Rather he found the romances rapidly passing away,
and, loving them, put forth his hand just in time to save
as much of the perishable stuff of which they were composed as he could put to new and lasting uses. It was
the literatures of Greece and Rome, rising from the
grave, that pushed the romances from their seats.

But it was not only the literatures of Greece and
Rome that profited by the deposition. Italian literature
exercised a stronger and stronger attraction on the
enfranchised mind of England. The first twenty years
of Elizabeth's reign, though not distinguished by any
very great creative work, are remarkable for the number
of translations that they witnessed, chiefly from the
Latin and Italian. And among these the numerous
translations from the Italian novels of Boccaccio,
Bandello, Cinthio, and others, as well as from French
adapters or imitators, hold a conspicuous place. These
translations need not be exhaustively enumerated; the
chief of them are Painter's *Pallace of Pleasure* (1566–7),

Fenton's *Tragicall Discourses* (1567), Pettie's *Petite Pallace of Pettie his Pleasure* (1576), and, later, Whetstone's *Heptameron of Civill Discourses* (1582). But incomparably the most important, both as giving the lead to other translators, and as furnishing a rich storehouse for later story-tellers and playwrights, is the first, compiled in the intervals of his official employment by William Painter, clerk of the ordnance in the Tower. The Puritan assailant of plays, poetry, and the fine arts, Stephen Gosson, was right when he put Painter's compilation in the forefront of the sources that had been "ransacked to furnish the playhouses in London." Shakespeare and Marston borrowed much, Peele, Beaumont and Fletcher, Webster, Massinger, and many others, borrowed something, from this treasury. And indeed Painter's pages are crammed with the raw material of poetry; neither is it always wholly raw. The monotonous language of the romances, unfolding themselves leisurely and interminably, must have seemed pallid indeed beside the pathos and passion, the vividness and beauty of these transcripts of the very spirit of the South, wherein love lightens and death thunders and the air is clear and the sky blue again, within the magic compass of a few pages. Many critics have called attention to the success of Shakespeare in setting his characters in an Italian atmosphere in such plays as *Romeo and Juliet* or the *Merchant of Venice,* and some have even thought that he must have visited Italy. But the truth is Italy visited England in the days of his youth, and it was not necessary to go further than Cheapside to meet with men whose costumes, manners, conversation, and let it be added morals, were borrowed directly from Italy. The enormous proportion of Italian names among the *dramatis personæ* of the Elizabethan dramatists bears forcible witness to the overpowering vogue of the Italian fashion.

At the time that Painter's book was published the romantic drama in England was not born, nothing but heavy imitations of Seneca and Plautus had been acted, and the *Pallace of Pleasure* had to wait twenty years for the first of the playwrights who rifled it. In the mean time it certainly had a success among readers, and it ought not to be denied a place among the forces that helped the romantic drama, when it was struggling against the formidable and influential array of classicists. But before it helped to create the Elizabethan drama, Painter's book, along with the rest that followed it, had called the Elizabethan novel into being. It was the success of these compilations, no doubt, that prompted Lyly to write his *Euphues*. And as this was, strictly speaking, the first original prose novel written in English, the book and its author may well receive a somewhat exact consideration.

John Lyly was a Kentish man, born about 1553. He was educated at Magdalen College, Oxford, where, according to Wood, he "did in a manner neglect academical studies, yet not so much but that he took the degrees in arts, that of master being compleated 1575. At which time, as he was esteemed at the university a noted wit, so afterwards was in the court of Q. Elizabeth, where he was also reputed a rare poet, witty, comical, and facetious." Of Lord Burleigh Lyly says, " This nobleman I found so ready, being but a stranger, to do me good, that neither I ought to forget him neither cease to pray for him ;" and perhaps he held some minor office about the court, where his plays, *Campaspe, Endymion*, and the rest, were acted during the ten years immediately preceding the appearance of Shakespeare as an original author. But the success of his plays does not seem to have led to any substantial preferment, and Lyly led the life of an indigent hanger-on of the court for many years, until he had long outlived his successes, and died in retirement and obscurity in 1606. He had hoped for the post of Master of the Revels, and when it was given to Edmund Tylney in 1579 still lived in hopes of its reversion. Two pathetic petitions, addressed by him to the Queen, remain to furnish another illustration of Spenser's lines—

> " So pitiful a thing is suitors' state ;
> Most miserable man, whom wicked Fate
> Hath brought to Court to sue for ' Had I wist,'
> That few have found, and many one hath missed."

They are written in the style that would appear to have become a second nature with Lyly, and set forth how he has waited ten years with an unwearied patience, and "suffered shipwreck of my time, my wits, my hopes." "I know not what crab took me for an oyster that in the midst of your sunshine of your most gracious aspect hath thrust a stone between the shells to eat me alive that only live on dead hopes." He beseeches "some land, some good fines, or forfeitures that should fall by the just fall of these most false traitors ; that seeing nothing will come by the Revels, I may prey upon the

Rebels." And his last request is marked by a witty freedom that calls to mind the boldness that moved Sir Philip Sidney to offer advice to the Queen concerning her marriage—" That if I be born to have nothing, I may have a protection to pay nothing, which suit is like his that, having followed the court ten years, for recompense of his service committed a robbery and took it out in a pardon."

Lyly scored the great literary success of his life while he was still a "noted wit" of the university, by the publication of his *Euphues, the Anatomy of Wit*, in 1579. This was followed in 1580 by the second part, called *Euphues and his England;* and of the two there were six editions in the space of two years. It was frequently reprinted until 1636, when it finally passed out of vogue. But on its appearance it took the fashionable world of ladies and courtiers by storm, so that "our nation was in his debt for a new English which he taught them." Euphuism, as it was called, became the language of the court, until it was driven out in 1590 by a new affectation, and the Euphuized gentlewomen gave place to the Arcadian, who were complimented by their gallants in " pure Sir Philip Sidney."

The story of *Euphues* is its least part, and may be briefly told. Euphues (a name borrowed by Lyly from Ascham) is a youth of quick parts and generous impulses, who comes from the academy of Athens, where he has been educated, to see the world in Naples. There he meets with an aged gentleman called Eubulus, who offers him much counsel and warning on the conduct of life; but Euphues rejects it with scorn. He finds a more congenial companion in a young man called Philautus, and strikes up a romantic friendship with him of so close a kind that "they used not only one board but one bed, one book (if so be it they thought not one too many)." By Philautus he is introduced to Lucilla, the lady to whom Philautus is betrothed, and they all sup together. During supper Euphues attracts the admiration and affection of Lucilla by the ingenuity and wit which he displays in discoursing on the topics whether beauty or wit move men most to love, and whether man or woman be most constant in love. He falls in love with Lucilla, as she with him; but he conceals his passion from his friend Philautus by pretending that another lady is the cause of it. In the mean time he opens his heart to Lucilla, and becomes her accepted lover. A rupture naturally ensues between Euphues and Philautus, and between Lucilla and her father Don Ferardo, who had designed her for Philautus. A solution of the entanglement is found in the conduct of Lucilla, who crowns her inconstancy by forsaking Euphues for Curio, introduced for this sole purpose. Euphues regains the friendship of Philautus, "both abandoning Lucilla as most abominable," and goes back, a wiser man, to study philosophy in his scholarly retirement at Athens, where he writes "a cooling card for all fond lovers," a treatise on education, and a refutation of atheism—all duly appended to the first part of the novel.

In the sequel, produced a year later, Euphues and Philautus visit England; they discourse on love and state-craft with an old beekeeper in Kent, called Fidus; they visit the court; there Philautus, after being long tossed on the waves of love, finds the haven of marriage, and Euphues, leaving him and England, retires, tormented in body and grieved in mind, to his cell at Silexsedra.

Euphues, since its brief triumph, has met with little but abuse at the hands of critics. Berkenhout, writing in 1777, calls it "a contemptible piece of affectation and nonsense;" and Sir Walter Scott's parody of a Euphuist in *The Monastery* even misses the most conspicuous features of the style. Yet the book deserves to be approached with respect, if only for this reason, that it exercised an enormous influence on greater men than Lyly—Greene and Shakespeare among them—and set the first fashion in novel-writing.

The main characteristics, then, of the style, which is vastly more important than the story, are three—

1. The structure of the sentences is based on anti-thesis and alliteration, or cross-alliteration, almost every sentence being balanced in two or more parisonic parts, chiming in sound, changing in sense. Thus Naples is a place "of more pleasure than profit, and yet of more profit than piety." Euphues is "a young gallant of more wit than wealth, yet of more wealth than wisdom," who, "seeing himself inferior to none in pleasant conceits, thought himself superior to all in honest conditions." All the characters alike speak or preach in this form of sentence, sometimes with oppressive monotony and prolixity, sometimes, again, with a certain approach to epigram. When Euphues is asked at supper to contribute to the company's entertainment by discoursing either of love or of learning, he begins the speech that von Lucilla's heart in this manner—"For me to intreat

D

of the one, being a novice, or to discourse of the other, being a truant, I may well make you wearier, but never the wiser, and give you occasion rather to laugh at my rashness than to like of my reasons; yet I care the less to excuse my boldness to you who were the cause of my blindness. And since I am at mine own choice either to talk of love or of learning, I had rather for this time be deemed an unthrift in rejecting profit, than a stoic in renouncing pleasure;" and he elects to speak of love accordingly.

It is this artificial character of the style, as much as anything, that has led the critics into a unanimity of scorn, and made them declare (to euphuize the burden of their observations) that they would sooner be content to forego the author's wisdom than constrained to undergo his wit; that they esteem the style more wordy than worthy, and judge Lyly to be rather a profligate dissipator of sound among his companions, than a prudent dispenser of sense to his heirs.

Yet Lyly can use the device at times with a force that goes far to justify it. Addressing his friend Philautus in the *Cooling Card*, Euphues exclaims—

"How curious were we to please our lady, how careless to displease our Lord! How devout in serving our goddess, how desperate in forgetting our God! Ah, my Philautus, if the wasting of our money might not dehort us, yet the wounding of our minds should deter us; if reason might nothing persuade us to wisdom, yet shame should provoke us to wit."

And Shakespeare, before he parodied the style of *Euphues* in *Henry IV.*, had felt the infection of Lyly's

cadences. In *Richard II.*, the Duke of Norfolk, after
receiving his sentence of banishment, thus invokes the
king—

> " A dearer merit, not so deep a maim
> As to be cast forth on the common air,
> Have I deserved at your Highness' hands."

This is a better example of the formal characteristics
of Euphuism than Falstaff's speech—" For, Harry, now
I do not speak to thee in drink, but in tears; not in
pleasure, but in passion; not in words only, but in woes
also."

But, besides a love for stricter form than consists with
the variety and flexibility of prose-writing, there is to be
found in Lyly a wasteful and pointless redundance of
ornament, a love of ornament for its own sake, which is
accountable for two more features of his style.

2. In *Euphues* there is an amount of classical allusion
and reference to classical authority which passes the
borders of the ludicrous. Thus Lyly cannot mention
friendship without incontinently quoting the cases of Titus
and Gisippus, Damon and Pythias, Pylades and Orestes,
Theseus and Pirithous, Scipio and Lælius; in his story
lovers argue their own constancy by the examples of
Troilus and Dido, or accuse each other of faithlessness
by quoting the instances of Cressida, Demophoon, or
Æneas. Lucilla justifies her fickleness by citing, for
her own reassurance, long extracts from the mythological
dictionary, in the course of which it appears that Helen,
the pearl of Greece, first took Menelaus, then Theseus,
and last of all Paris, and that (if Curio be not comely to
look upon) Venus herself was content to desert the

handsome god of war for "a blacksmith with a polt foot." Moreover, an appeal to classical authority often encroaches on the domain of daily experience, and Lyly's work marks a step in the development of that style which was to find its culmination and masterpiece in Burton's *Anatomy of Melancholy*. "Is it not true which Seneca reporteth, that as too much bending breaketh the bow, so too much remission spoileth the mind?" And Euphues and Philautus, on approaching the coast of England in order to visit the court of Queen Elizabeth, gravely refer to Cæsar as the principal authority on the habits of the people of Britain. This tendency, common to many writers, is instanced by Sir Thomas Browne from the works of an author to whom, more than to any other, Lyly was indebted. "Antonius Guevara," says Sir Thomas, "that elegant Spaniard, in his book entituled *The Dial of Princes*, beginneth his epistle thus : 'Apollonius Thyanæus, disputing with the scholars of Hiarchas, said, that among all the affections of nature, nothing was more natural than the desire all have to preserve life.' Which being a confessed truth, and a verity acknowledged by all, it was a superfluous affectation to derive its authority from Apollonius, or seek a confirmation thereof as far as India." The same disease of style, to which scholars will always be specially liable, is ridiculed by Shakespeare, not only in the passage in *Henry IV.* already referred to ("this pitch, *as ancient writers do report*, doth defile"), but also in *Love's Labour's Lost*, where Armado, addressing his page, says—

"Comfort me, boy ; what great mén have been in love ?

"*Moth.* Hercules, master.

"*Arm.* Most sweet Hercules! More authority, dear boy, name more; and, sweet my child, let them be men of good repute and carriage."

Moth mentions Samson, but Armado will hardly be comforted until he has " exampled his digression " by some mightier precedent.

3. Lastly, Lyly further cumbered the movement of his style, and weakened its force, by a pulpit employment of a real or fictitious natural history. Many of his curiosities in this sort are found in Pliny, but many others no doubt lay ready to his hand in the plentiful animal and plant lore that has always been preserved by tradition, or in the long line of bestiaries that preceded biological handbooks. So late as the middle of the seventeenth century, an ostensibly scientific work would moralize all its instances, and impart a lesson in parental affection from the whale, in the use of pleasures from the dogs of Egypt who lap running, an emblem from the hedgehog concerning the safety of mean estates, or from the hare who can run faster up hill than down— besides including the basilisk, dragon, unicorn, salamander, lamia, scolopendra (" a fish of strange property, and how we ought to resemble this fish "), and many others unknown to modern research.* Lyly could without difficulty find masses of this lore, and, caring nothing for it as truth, he cared greatly for it as illustration, and plastered it extravagantly on his discourse by way of adornment.

" I have read that the bull being tied to the fig-tree

---

* Swan's *Speculum Mundi.* Cambridge, 1635.

loseth his strength, that the whole herd of deer stand at the gaze if they smell a sweet apple, that the dolphin by the sound of music is brought to the shore. And then no marvel it is that if the fierce bull be tamed with the fig-tree, that women, being as weak as sheep, be overcome with a fig; if the wild deer be caught with an apple, that the tame damosel is won with a blossom; if the fleet dolphin be allured with harmony, that women be entangled with the melody of men's speech, fair promises, and solemn protestations."

An interminable procession of figures of this kind runs throughout the book, and the crucial situations are sometimes determined by the comparative masses of opposed groups of similes. Thus Lucilla, arguing with herself on her purpose to forsake Philautus for Euphues, is afraid that her new lover may despise her, remembering " that the glass once crased will with the least clap be cracked, that the cloth which staineth with milk will soon lose his colour with vinegar, that she that hath been faithless to one will never be faithful to any." Yet she comforts herself by the same process, for will not Euphues also remember " that the broken bone once set together is stronger than ever it was, that the greatest blot is taken off with the pummice, that though the spider poison the fly she cannot infect the bee, that though I have been light to Philautus, I may be lovely to Euphues "? and then, by a dozen more bizarre similitudes, she satisfies herself that she is only following the course of Nature, and rests secure for the time on the precedent of the spaniel and the epicure.

To enumerate one-tenth part of the objects to the

paradoxical properties of which Lyly often reverts with loving assiduity would be tedious, to trace the sources to which he was indebted would in this connection be idle. Perfumes, we learn, refresh the dove and kill the beetle, the elephant liveth upon air, the salamander, the further he lieth from the fire the warmer he is. It was this feature of the Euphuistic style that most incurred contemporary ridicule. Drayton and Sidney condemned it; Nash indignantly disclaimed imitation of it; Shakespeare ridiculed it in the instance of the camomile, which "the more it is trodden the faster it grows;" and the authors of the *Pilgrimage to Parnassus* even more happily parodied the phrases so common in Lyly by the highly probable statement that "there is a beast in India called a polecat, . . . and the further she is from you the less you smell her."

When the crusade against the Albigenses was inaugurated, its extremest severities of persecution were justified by a text of Scripture, drawn from the parable of the wedding-feast—"Compel them to come in."   A not less plausible fanaticism it was that prompted Lyly to make his bold attempt. His instinct was literary, and in the service of the humanities he laid hands on all the scattered scientific statements he could find, hunting many a poor fact or error out of the obscurest nooks, racking them with the powerful engine of simile, affiliating them by force to man and his high interests. Of what possible interest is the unrelated fact, reported by Pliny, that the root of Anchusa is insoluble in water, but dissolves in oil? Let it illustrate the heart of Euphues, which, "though it be hardened with the water of wiliness,

yet will it be mollified with the oil of wisdom." So
cavalier a treatment is opposed, no doubt, to the spirit
of modern science, which has learned to reverence
every solitary fact for its possible uses and destinies.
But in Lyly's time human knowledge was one; and his
attempt may serve in passing to illustrate that oneness,
which was to the Elizabethans both an inspiration and
a snare. "To see this age!" says the clown in *Twelfth
Night*, "a sentence is but a cheveril glove to a good wit;
how quickly the wrong side may be turned outward!"
So Lyly took the whole available store of knowledge for
his wardrobe, and used it to deck his style. Too often,
indeed, the wrong side is turned outward. Yet his
writing is all witty; similes, it is true, are misapplied,
facts are falsified to supply comparisons, classical instance
is ranged after classical instance without purpose or
method, like the crowd in a street, to impress by number
rather than fitness, the display of mediæval physic and
physiology becomes mere ostentation; but all this is
the outcome of the same quick-wittedness and versatility
which marked the Elizabethan gentleman, who made of
the world a whetstone for his wit. All these far-fetched
similes and laboured figures give light of a kind—not
light focussed on the subject, but the flashing desultory
light of a display of fireworks. The classic use of simile,
which might be instanced by Milton's description of
Satan's shield—

> "The broad circumference
> Hung on his shoulders like the moon,"

is far enough removed from the irresponsibility of Lyly's
manner, which gives no real help to the constructive

imagination, and generally tickles the fancy only to cheat the thought, explaining *ignotum per ignotius.* What Ben Jonson said of Shakespeare is a hundred times more applicable to Lyly—" He flowed with that facility that sometime it was necessary he should be stopped. . . . His wit was in his own power; would the rule of it had been so too!" And the cause in Shakespeare's case as well as Lyly's is indicated by the confession inadvertently made in *Euphues,* " I have ever thought so superstitiously of wit, that I fear I have committed idolatry against wisdom."

And yet Lyly was no mere player with words or grand inquisitioner appointed for the torture of sense. Beneath the courtier's slashed doublet, under his ornate brocade and frills, there stood a Puritan; and M. Jusserand has found in Euphues the lineal predecessor of Sir Charles Grandison and Daniel Deronda. The grave reflections and weighty morals that the author has to enforce overload the story, so that the book has rightly been called a collection of essays on friendship, love, education, religion, philosophy, and foreign travel " sowed" (as the author remarks in one of the few figures drawn from what he had seen) " here and there like strawberries, not in heaps like hops." To look, therefore, for any approach to the characterization that is to be found in Richardson or George Eliot would be a mistake; the book is almost devoid of it. Once or twice Lyly seems near the dramatic imagination; thus when Euphues, disappointed by Lucilla, resolves on a course of study, he exclaims—

" I will to Athens, there to toss my books, no more in

Naples to live with fair looks. I will so frame myself as
all youth hereafter shall rather rejoice to see mine amend-
ment than be animated to follow my former life. Philosophy, physic, divinity, shall be my study. Oh, the
hidden secrets of nature, the express image of moral
virtues, the equal balance of justice, the medicines to
heal all diseases, how they begin to delight me! The
Axiomaes of Aristotle, the Maxims of Justinian, the
Aphorisms of Galen, have suddenly made such a breach
into my mind, that I seem only to desire them that did
only erst detest them."

Here the author might certainly fall under the suspicion
of a dramatic and satirical intent, but in the next sentence
he speaks so plainly in his own voice that the doubt is
resolved—

"If wit be employed in the honest study of learning,
what thing so precious as wit? If in the idle trade of
love, what thing more pestilent than wit?"

A plainer instance of those rare occasions where the
story-teller gets the better of the didactic moralist occurs
in the passage describing the voyage to England, where
Euphues tells his friend a long and tedious story, balancing and finishing every sentence, until Philautus, goaded
to the point of abandoning the alliterative convention,
remarks, "In faith, Euphues, thou hast told a long tale,
the beginning I have forgotten, the middle I understand
not, and the end hangeth not together; . . . in the
mean time, it were best for me to take a nap, for I cannot
brook these seas, which provoke my stomach sore."

But generally when the encumbering style is thrown
off for a sentence or two, it is in the interest of didactic

rather than of dramatic effect, and then Lyly is to be found expressing himself in plain pithy English, and coining or adopting homely proverbs like these—

"It is the eye of the master that fatteth the horse, and the love of the woman that maketh the man."

"Thou must halt cunningly to beguile a cripple."

"It is a blind goose that cometh to the fox's sermon."

And when Philautus consults a sorcerer for a love-charm, "C'était là," says M. Jusserand, "une excellente occasion de parler des serpents et des crapauds, et le magicien n'y manque pas." But at the end of the display of lore there follows the pointed comment, "The best charm for an aching tooth is to pull it out, and the best remedy for love, to wear it out."

The fashions and customs of the English on which Lyly spends his gravest invective are those that are also attacked by Ascham, Stubbes, and Howell. During the long period represented by these three names, an Englishman was a by-word for the readiness with which he adopted foreign costumes, airs, manners, oaths, and habits. The "lisping, affecting fantastico," who proved that he had "swam in a gondola" by wearing strange suits and swearing strange oaths, was the stock subject for patriotic satire for fifty years after *Euphues*. It is to the extravagant fashions of women, however, that Lyly chiefly addresses himself. "Take from them their peri-wigs, their paintings, their jewels, their rolls, their bolsterings, and thou shalt soon perceive that a woman is the least part of herself, . . . an apothecary's shop of sweet confections, a pedlar's pack of new fangles." And he wittily excuses himself to the "grave matrons and

honest maidens of Italy," by saying, "You ought no
more to be aggrieved with that which I have said than
the mint-master to see the coiner hanged." One woman
only is raised above all censure, and she, it is needless
to say, is the Queen. Euphues and Philautus come to
England chiefly to see her, and the praises bestowed on
her would be held exceptionally extravagant if they could
not so easily be paralleled from the dramatists.

> " Eliza, that most sacred dame,
> Whom none but saints and angels ought to name,"

who rules over the realm that, by another familiar
conceit, is called Elysium, is spoken of with bated breath
by the court-follower, who excuses himself even for nam-
ing her, whom "neither art nor heart can set forth as
she deserveth. . . . But in this we imitate the old
painters of Greece, who, drawing in their tables the portraiture of Jupiter, were every hour mending it, but durst
never finish it, and being demanded why they began that
which they could not end, they answered, in that we
show him to be Jupiter, whom every one may begin to
paint, but none can perfect. In the like manner mean
we to draw in part the praises of her whom we cannot
throughly portray, and in that we signify her to be
Elizabeth."

There is no more signal instance of the imitative
tendencies that Lyly attacks than his own style, which
has been shown by careful study and research to be a
motley compound made up from many sources. From
Ovid, Plutarch, and Pliny he borrows whole phrases,
passages, or even discourses; the balanced antithetical
sentence is modelled, it is said, on Guevara or the

English translations of Guevara by Berners, North, and others which were popular before Lyly's time, and which lent him also the suggestion of the free employment of comparisons from natural history ; while a fanciful prose alliteration is to be found here and there in several earlier writers.   And yet the style is Lyly's own, although the materials are borrowed, and those who would rob him of originality must rob Shakespeare too.   The immediate popularity of *Euphues* is in itself sufficient evidence that a taste was already formed : the writer who has no pre-decessors will also have no readers.   Lyly's work was to combine and carry to their extreme development the literary fashions that he found in vogue, and to raise them to the dignity of a convention ; hence he is justly called the inventor of a new English.   To make of his style a mere theft is as impossible as to make of it a mere affectation.   And the importance of that style is so great, both as typical of the time, and as marking a crucial point in the history of prose fiction, that a few words will be spent not amiss in the attempt to show its bearings.

The age of Elizabeth is pre-eminently an age of poetry, of which prose may be regarded as merely the overflow. Poetry as an art attained a range and perfection that has never since been reached, and much material that now finds expression in prose forms was then drawn into the main current of verse.   Philosophy, autobiography, his-tory, morals, all found their natural expression in verse form.   A later generation has found cause for wonder or incredulity in the fact that both Shakespeare and Sidney " coined their hearts and dropped their blood for

drachmas" in the form of the sonnet, and were proud to
forego their privacy so they might gain the stamp of art
Yet no one has questioned the trenchant sincerity of
Greene's autobiographical poems; Michael Drayton versi-
fied his historical gazetteer; and Sir John Davies shaped
his philosophy in stanza form. "Seeing," says Nash,
"that poetry is the very same with philosophy, the fables
of poets must of necessity be fraught with wisdom and
knowledge, as framed of those men which have spent all
their time and studies in the one and in the other." And
he even censures some of the inevitable consequences of
this breadth, as well as height, of the scope of poetry,
whereby, he complains, it has come to be thought that
rhyming is poetry. "Hence come our babbling Ballets,
and our new-found Songs and Sonnets, which every red-
nose fiddler hath at his fingers' end, and every ignorant
ale-knight will breathe forth over the pot, as soon as his
brain waxeth hot."

Those instincts of poetry, which cause it to seek
music and form, were no way blunted in consequence of
the diversity of subjects admitted. And so it came
about that the prose of the time (all of which, it may
safely be said, bears the mark of the sovereignty of
poetry) felt the double influence, and approximated to
poetry either in the elaborated figurative method of its
treatment, or in the rhythmical balance of its form, or
in both. Matthew Arnold finds the prose of Chapman
intolerable because of its riotous excess of figure, unrestrained by the coercive means supplied by the rules of
verse. And certainly there is much of the prose of the
time, besides Chapman's, that, lacking the wings of

verse, falls into fantastic chaos. Now, Lyly's experiment
is thus seen to be of the highest interest. The old
verse romances, still chanted among the people, were
contemned as worn-out absurdities by a generation that
had found a new source of inspiration in the classics.
Prose was largely taking the place of verse in the realm of
narrative fiction, and for his didactic and discursive aims
prose suited Lyly best. But he strove, as if by instinct,
to fit prose for the bearing of the weight of figure and
ornament that the age demanded, by lending it more of
definite constructive form, justifying ornament by structure. And his alliteration, which is a convention and
not a trick, is the basis of this structure.* Alliteration
is commonly looked upon as an idle ornament of prose,
and idle it is in the authors from whom Lyly is sometimes
alleged to have borrowed it. But if he borrowed it he
changed its use, and attempted to make of it something
essential—the pillars instead of the crockets of the
building. Alliteration is often condemned as a flaw in
rhymed verse, and it may well be open to question
whether Lyly did not give it its true position in attempting to invent a place for it in what is called prose. It is
not in his alliteration, at any rate, that his chief error lies ;
that alone would no more have hampered and marred
his expression than it marred the most magnificent lines
of William Langland or any other of the early alliterative
poets.

> " Deth cam drivynge after, and al to dust ȝashed
>   Kynges and knyghtes, kayseres and popes." †

---

* How tame the euphuistic balance of sentences becomes without
alliteration may be well seen in F. Meres' *Palladis Tamia*.

† *Piers Plowman*, *Text B.*, xx. 99.

The success of the early alliterative poetry ought to modify the haste with which Lyly is condemned on this score. Rather he made success impossible by adding forced antithesis and simile to his chosen convention until to write Euphuistic prose became a task many times more difficult than to write simple verse, and Lyly himself breaks down oftener from constraint than from taste. His style became as unfit a vehicle for the prolonged expression of weighty matters as the form of nonsense rhymes is for the embodiment of an epic. It is easy to enforce, say, the duties of temperance and patriotism in rhymed verse; it is by no means easy to maintain on these themes an interesting discourse with all the sentences equipoised, all the emphatic words alliterative, and with every point driven home by allusion to the properties of a mineral or the habits of an animal. Dr. Watts was too wise to burden himself thus in all his hymns. The instrument becomes too complicated, as well as too limited in its compass.

Thus *Euphues* serves to mark the transition from verse to prose as the vehicle for narrative romantic fiction. Lyly in his "prose poem" (for so it might rightly be called) devised a kind of compromise, and paid the price of compromise in being quickly superseded. The transition itself took long to accomplish, and was involved with changes of the deepest import in the matter or purport of romance. It was not till Dryden's time that prose ceased to feel the glamour of its greater rival, not till Defoe's or Swift's that poetry at last bowed to prose. And long before either, Lyly's work had become no more than an historical landmark.

CHAPTER III.

THE most notable of the Elizabethan writers of fiction were not imitators of Lyly. With the success of *Euphues* the day of the novel was fully come, and Brian Melbancke, John Dickenson, Barnabie Rich, and many others, told their tales, and followed their progenitor to the cell of oblivion whither he retired. Of Greene and Lodge some few more words are necessary, while Nash and Sir Philip Sidney claim places by the side of Lyly as innovators in the art of prose fiction, and foreshadowers of later schools of romancers.

Yet there is much grace, wit, and vigour buried, for lack of reprint, with these almost forgotten pamphleteers; the very cheapest of them has his share of the zest and spirit of the time. " All the distinguished writers of that period," says Thoreau—and the praise might truly be extended to many of the undistinguished—" possess a greater vigour and naturalness than the more modern, . . . and when we read a quotation from one of them in the midst of a modern author, we seem to have come suddenly upon a greener ground, a greater depth and

E

strength of soil. . . . You have constantly the warrant
of life and experience in what you read. The little that
is said is eked out by implication of the much that was
done." And speaking in particular of Sir Walter
Raleigh, he suggests an explanation of the strength and
grace of his writing in words that have a wider application. "There is a natural emphasis in his style, like a
man's tread, and a breathing-space between the sentences,
which the best of modern writing does not furnish. . . .
Every sentence is the result of a long probation. . . .
The word which is best said came nearest to not being
spoken at all, for it is cousin to a deed which the
speaker could have better done. Nay, almost it must
have taken the place of a deed by some urgent necessity,
even by some misfortune, so that the truest writer will
be some captive knight, after all." How true and happy
a criticism this is of many writers of the time may be
learnt from the annals of their lives. The monasteries
were destroyed, literature as a secular profession had as
yet few followers, and the adventurer was supreme
there as elsewhere. Moreover, that great change in
society which is called the Renaissance had convulsed
the old feudal arrangements, and every man was free at
last to take part in life in its fullest sense, and to store
himself richly with experience. All the writers were, in
one way or another, men of action, as Samuel Johnson
and Thomas Carlyle never were. Lodge in the course
of his life was a scholar of Oxford, a freebooting sailor,
a soldier against Spain, a medical practitioner, playwright,
novelist, and pamphleteer. Whetstone was courtier,
soldier, farmer, and author; moreover, in the preface to

his most famous work, *Promos and Cassandra*, which Shakespeare used in his *Measure for Measure*, he sets forth how his voyage with Sir Humphrey Gilbert has interfered with the correction of the "errors" in his works. Stanihurst, the translator of the *Æneid*, is spoken of thus contemptuously by Barnabie Rich : "First he was a chronicler, then a poet, after that he professed Alcumy, and now he is become a massing priest." Nor is this by any means an exhaustive account of Stanihurst's versatility, which, again, is almost equalled by Rich's own.

The emphasis and sincerity that spring from a first-hand knowledge of life are thus the great virtues of the best of Elizabethan writing. Of Sir Philip Sidney himself, whose *Arcadia* would seem but poorly to illustrate the general thesis, his friend and biographer, Lord Brooke, says, "The truth is, his end was not writing, even while he wrote, but both his wit and understanding bent upon his heart to make himself and others, not in words or opinion, but in life and action, good and great." And if the Arcadian style of writing seem to have little relation to life and action, it yet bears witness in its own way to the tumultuous activity of the time. For literature has constantly the double tendency to negative the life around it, as it were, as well as to reproduce it; the lawlessness and unrest of mediæval society are echoed, with the direction reversed, in the monkish hymns of rest and visions of the endless sabbath, while Browning's strenuous *Epilogue* and Mr. Stevenson's thrilling tales of adventure belong, it is no great cynicism to aver, to an age of sedentary occupation. Literature, that is to say

is an escape from life, its monotony or its distractions, as
well as a grappling with life and its problems. And
although the *Arcadia* has more in it of the first than of
the second, it is nevertheless something more than

> " A shadowy isle of bliss
> Midmost the beating of the steely sea,"

and contains here and there some direct evidence of that
restlessness of a high spirit which is so vividly portrayed
in the *Sonnets* to Stella.

It was by his life, and not by his writings, which were
published posthumously, that Sidney wielded his chief
influence on the age. Even in his lifetime he was something of a romantic hero to his contemporaries, and his
death added a lustre from the dazzling effect of which
it is difficult even now to escape in considering his
writings. He was born at Penshurst in 1554, the son of
Sir Henry Sidney, afterwards Lord Deputy of Ireland
and Lady Mary Dudley, the daughter of Northumber-
land, and sister of Leicester. He was educated at
Shrewsbury, where his name was entered under the same
date as the name of Fulke Greville, Lord Brooke, his
lifelong friend and biographer, who, on his own death,
had it inscribed on his tomb that he was "friend to Sir
Philip Sidney." In 1572, in preparation for courtly
employ, he began a period of three years' travel, and was
sheltered during the massacre of St. Bartholomew in the
house of his future father-in-law, Sir Francis Walsingham,
at Paris. Thence he passed to Frankfort, where he
formed another of his enduring friendships with Hubert
Languet, a ripe scholar and ardent reformer of fifty-four,

who did much to strengthen the lofty gravity that had
always been a note of Sidney's character. Speaking of
him in the *Arcadia*, Sidney says—

> "My skilless youth he drew
> To have a feeling taste of Him that sits
> Beyond the heaven, far more beyond our wits."

In the course of the next two years Sidney visited
Vienna, Venice, Padua, and many other famous European cities, learning foreign languages, and everywhere
winning the golden opinions of grave statesmen, until in
1575 he returned to the English court. Elizabeth called
him "one of the jewels in her crown," and William the
Silent, who was not prone to light eulogy, spoke of him
in 1577 as one of the ripest statesmen in Europe. But
before 1580 he had fallen into disfavour with the queen,
and his public employ was uncertain and intermitted.
Twice he sat in Parliament. In 1583 he married
Frances Walsingham, and at last, having, as an outlet
for his patriotic energy, accompanied Leicester to the
Netherlands in the capacity of governor of Flushing, he
fell at the battle of Zutphen on September 22, 1586.
His body was conveyed to London, and his funeral celebrated at St. Paul's with rich ceremony. Never was
poet's death so splendidly deplored; the elegies written
on him are almost a literature. And the unanimity of
praise is unbroken until the surly Ben Jonson, who never
knew him, thought fit to censure his outward man in
conversation with Drummond by the remark that "Sir
P. Sidney was no pleasant man in countenance, his face
being spoiled with pimples, and of high blood, and long."

The letters of his friends convey a more pleasing impression.

Sidney's literary activity displays the versatility of the time. He wrote a masque for the court, a number of poetical versions of the Psalms, besides the *Arcadia* and those two other works without which his greatness could not adequately be measured, namely, the poems addressed to Stella, which constitute the first truly great sonnet sequence in the English tongue, and the *Apologie for Poetrie*, which remains to this day a piece of criticism showing enthusiasm and insight.

The *Sonnets* express the history of his passion for Penelope Devereux, sister to Essex, whom he first met at Kenilworth in 1575 when she was twelve years old. Some scheme of an alliance between the families was formed, but Sidney's loss of the queen's favour prevented it before his love was fully awake, and in 1580 Penelope, against her will, became Lady Rich.

There is a class of critics who, in view of the fact that the *Sonnets* (posthumously published) were addressed to Lady Rich after her marriage, hold the well-meaning opinion that Sidney never was in love with her, but employed her name as a peg on which to hang graceful fancies. Sidney himself, rising from the grave, could do nothing to convince the man who, having read the sonnets, clings to this belief. From first to last they are struck off at a white heat of glowing emotion, played over at times by the breath of conceit, but shaped with a vividness and minuteness that bespeak their intense sincerity. From the beginning to the end the reader is carried through the stormy vicissitudes of passion in all

its phases, until, by the time he reaches the noble lines,
commonly printed at the close, in which the earthly love
is renounced, he can almost feel the speed and impetuosity with which life was lived in that unexhausted time.

The very prologue to the *Sonnets* strikes their keynote—

" Loving in truth, and fain in verse my love to show,
    That she, dear She, might take some pleasure of my pain.

" I sought fit words to paint the blackest face of woe ;
    Studying inventions fine, her wits to entertain,
Oft turning other's leaves, to see if thence would flow
Some fresh and fruitful showers upon my sunburn'd brain.

" Biting my truant pen, beating myself for spite,
    ' Fool ! ' said my Muse to me, ' look in thy heart and write ! ' "

And before many sonnets have followed, the reader feels
the truth of the poet's further declaration—

" I now have learn'd love right, and learn'd even so
    As they that being poisoned poison know."

The "dictionary's method" of rhyming Sidney ridicules,
and expressly sets aside the poetry of "graceful fancy"
made to order, with no real goad in the occasion.   There
is a crowning sincerity and pathos in the two last
sonnets—

" Desire !   Desire !   I have too dearly bought,
    With price of mangled mind, thy worthless ware
Too long, too long, asleep thou hast me brought,
    Who shouldst my mind to higher things prepare.

" Leave me, O Love, which reachest but to dust ;
    And thou, my mind, aspire to higher things ;
Grow rich in that which never taketh rust ;
    Whatever fades, but fading pleasure brings.

" Then farewell, world ; thy uttermost I see.
Eternal Love, maintain thy life in me."

The contention that the "worthless ware" that Sidney
purchased had no individual existence save in his own
mind is at the root of a criticism that dishonours art
by robbing it of its strongest inspiration, and makes of
literature a bauble. It must never be forgotten that
Sidney's *Sonnets* were not written originally for publication ; poetry was chosen in this as in many cases at that
day for the expression of the deepest personal throes and
feelings, because for those feelings it was felt to be the
fittest exponent. Moreover, the vindication of Sidney's
sincerity is important for this reason, that his novel lacks
what his poems are thus seen to contain. There can be
little doubt that had Sidney chosen to write novels in the
autobiographical vein of Greene and Nash, he would have
produced works equal at least to the best of either. He
trod a very different path in his prose, and his *Sonnets*
remain to furnish another instance of how hard it was
for prose fiction to maintain itself at all in that age of
surpassing poetry. With the still growing drama on the
one side, hungry for material, daily devouring apace the
fair themes that the novelists procured, with the lighter
forms of verse on the other, ready to give their highest
expression to the intensest personal experience, it was no
wonder that the novel did not long succeed in maintaining
itself, or that where it did succeed, it maintained itself on
stilts, to be out of the reach of its adversaries. Plays had
large audiences, but few persons could read, and a
surprisingly large number of those who could preferred
reading poetry. Thus the novel held, in Elizabeth's time,

very much the same place as was held by the drama at
the Restoration; it was an essentially aristocratic
entertainment. And the same pitfall waylaid both, the
pitfall of artificiality. Dryden's audiences and the readers
of the *Arcadia* both sought for better bread than is made
of wheat; both were supplied with what satisfied them
in an elaborate confection of husks.

*The Countess of Pembroke's Arcadia, written by Sir
Philip Sidney*, was published in 1590, but its composition
belongs chiefly to the time of retirement that Sidney
passed with his sister at Wilton in 1580. It was left
unfinished, and Lady Mary had even instructions to
burn it. As the first example in English of a pastoral
romance, it commanded an influence on later writers,
both in England and France, which no other Elizabethan romance attained, so that Sidney's borrowings
and lendings have a real bearing in the development of
the prose story. Setting aside, then, Virgil and Longus
as prototypes in the pastoral kind at too great a
remove, it may be said that Sidney probably borrowed
his title from the *Arcadia* (1502) of Sannazaro; his
treatment and incidents in part from Montemayor's
Diana (published in 1560), and the *Amadis of Gaul*,
which he had probably read in a French translation.
The admixture of adventures modelled on the later school
of the Romances of Chivalry unhappily takes from the
pastoral its justification, which was well enunciated by
Honoré d'Urfé in his *Astrée*, a later and even more
famous work than the *Arcadia*. In noticing the charge
that the language of his shepherdesses was above their
station, he says, "Réponds-leur, ma Bergère, que tu

n'es pas, ni celles aussi qui te suivent, de ces Bergères
nécessiteuses qui pour gagner leur vie conduisent les
troupeaux aux pasturages; mais que vous n'avez toutes
pris cette condition que pour vivre plus doucement et
sans contrainte." *

There is the philosophy of the pastoral romance. To
devise a set of artificial conditions that shall leave the
author to work out the sentimental inter-relations of his
characters undisturbed by the intrusion of probability or
accident, is the problem; love *in vacuo* is the beginning
and end of the pastoral romance proper. And Montemayor had approached this ideal in his device of the
four lovers, two nymphs and two swains, who loved
each other in cyclical order. Their passion is not very
passionate it is true, but it is enough to set up a rotatory
action under a receiver, and the absence of any thwart-
ing reciprocity secures the perpetual motion of the
machine—under the one condition that it does no work.
But the simplicity of such a design was not often un-
impaired. The pastoral convention was found to afford
excellent cover for wilder game than love, and political
or personal satire often took shelter there. Sidney
wisely avoided these, but he fell a victim to the temptation of drama and episode. The long and complicated
plot of the *Arcadia* is overburdened with incident and
action, which swoon into mere dream in the scented
atmosphere of the style. And the author made a worse
mistake when he attempted to relieve the high-strung
monotony of the story by the introduction of comic characters in the clown Dametas and his wife and daughter.

* D'Urfé's *Astrée*, cit. Dunlop, ii. 391.

The Vice of the old Moralities was never naturalized in the English drama until Shakespeare's day, and Sidney had no better models than "Grim, the Collier of Croydon," who plays an irrelevant and tedious part in the *Damon and Pythias* of Richard Edwards. Thus he committed the fault that himself in the *Apologie* condemned, and "thrust in the clown by head and shoulders to play a part in majestical matters, with neither decency nor discretion." The clown is a dull clown, for his creator jokes with difficulty.

Sir Philip Sidney is one of the large body of Shakespeare's creditors. Gloucester and his sons in *Lear*, perhaps Valentine and the outlaws in the *Two Gentlemen*, were lent by him. And Day, Beaumont and Fletcher, and Shirley took from him what they could put to better use in adapting some of his incidents for the drama.

The debt of prose fiction to the *Arcadia* is not so quickly estimated. "Read the Countess of Pembroke's *Arcadia*," says Gabriel Harvey, "a gallant legendary, full of pleasurable accidents and profitable discourses; for three things especially, very notable—for amorous courting (he was young in years); for sage counselling (he was ripe in judgment); and for valourous fighting (his sovereign profession was arms); and delightful pastime by way of pastoral exercises, may pass for the fourth." Of these divisions of praise some may be discounted at once. Harvey was willing to be "epitaphed" as the "Inventor of the English Hexameter;" he was an enthusiastic supporter of the "Areopagus," or school of reformed versifying, and was delighted to find Sidney following in his steps. Hence his admiration for Sidney's "pastoral exercises," or those quaint verses, Asclepiadics, Phaleuciacs, and the like, with which the *Arcadia* is plentifully bestrewn, was no more than a commendation, to use another of his phrases, of " a pig of his own sow." Certainly the song of Dorus, in which every stanza begins—

> " O sweet woods, the delight of solitariness !
> Oh, how much I do like your solitariness !"

does not strike gratefully on a modern ear. Of the other grounds for praise, it may safely be said that the " valourous fighting " jumps better with Sidney's sove reign profession than with the artistic finish of his book, while in " sage counselling " he is no match for Lyly. There remains his greatest merit in the " amorous court- ing," which is his predominant theme, and which he so treated as to leave a lasting bequest to romance-writers. The lovers—and they are many—are the only interest- ing figures in the book. The tender love of the maiden Pamela, the servile love of the old king Basilius, and the guilty and jealous love of Queen Gynecia, are each depicted, in spite of the formal monotony lent them by the interminable " rich conceits and splendour of courtly expressions," with real differences and with real dramatic feeling. The story, with its disguisings, digressions, and cross-purposes, would furnish forth plot enough for twenty ordinary novels ; but it was the sentiment of the work rather than its plot that procured its popularity and influence in the next century. The *Arcadia*, in fact, is in some sort a halfway house between the older romances of chivalry and the long-winded " heroic " romances of the seventeenth century. Action and adventure are already giving way to the description of sentiment, or are remaining merely as a frame on which the diverse-coloured flowers of sentiment may be broidered.

The characteristics of Sidney's style are in a large measure attributable to his conception of the *Arcadia* as a "prose-poem." Like almost all his contemporaries, Sidney defined poetry so as to include any literary work of the imagination, and absolutely refused to make of rhyming or versing an essential. But the instinctive craving of the imagination for some sort of definite form returns upon him, and avenges the dismissal of verse. Hence arise the formal affectations of his style, chief among which is the habit of playing with a word, or pair of words, and tossing it to and fro, until its meaning is more than exhausted. Thus the house in Arcadia to which the two shipwrecked princes who are the heroes of the tale are welcomed is described as "all more last-ing than beautiful, but that the consideration of the exceeding lastingness made the eye believe it was ex-ceeding beautiful." One of the princes, crossed in love, finds himself "not only unhappy, but unhappy after being fallen from all happiness, and to be fallen from all happiness not by any misconceiving, but by his own fault, and his fault"—and so on, the repetition of the same word performing something of the office of the repetition of the rhyme in *terza rima.* This particular trick of style is not, of course, proper to Sidney; it is solemnly classified by his contemporary Puttenham among the figures that adorn verse, and it is common in the old romances, where it is carried to an extreme of unintelligibility—witness that "cartel of love" on the clearness and intricate argument of which Don Quixote doted, "The reason of the unreason which is done to my reason in such manner enfeebles my reason that with reason I lament your beauty."

The other marks of the style are equally poetical. The famous description of the vale of Arcadia will instance them all : " There were hills which garnished their proud heights with stately trees ; humble valleys, whose base estate seemed comforted with the refreshing of silver rivers ; meadows, enamelled with all sorts of eye-pleasing flowers ; thickets, which, being lined with most pleasant shade, were witnessed so too by the cheerful disposition of many well-tuned birds ; . . . here a shepherd's boy piping as though he should never be old ; there a young shepherdess knitting, and withal singing, and it seemed that her voice comforted her hands to work, and her hands kept time to her voice-music." It is difficult not to be reminded of a fine piece of tapestry by this artificial description, which is a good instance of Sidney's love for, and frequent employment of, what Mr. Ruskin has called the " pathetic fallacy." The attributing of human emotions to all senseless things is no artistic fallacy when it is inspired by strong feeling, as in "Clorinda's" beautiful lay on the death of Sidney himself—

> " Woods, hills, and rivers now are desolate,
>   Sith he is gone the which them all did grace ; "

but when it is, as with Sidney, a constant recipe for a picturesque sentence, it is a cloying device. The remainder of the description epitomizes the author's extravagances. " As for the houses of the country, they were all scattered, no two being one by the other, and yet not so far as that it barred mutual succour; a show, as it were, of an accompanable solitariness and a civil wildness." Romeo makes use of this figure, but it is to express his love for Rosaline, not for Juliet—

> "Why then, O brawling love! O loving hate!
> O anything of nothing first create!"

And again, "I pray you" (said Musidorus), "what countries be these we pass through, which are so divers in show, the one wanting no store, the other having no store but of want?" Here is the favourite jingle once more, in a form that recalls more than one line of Shakespeare's. But Sidney wrote in prose, and as the poetical traits of his work passed for its chief glory in his own time, so he has had to pay for them by the neglect of posterity. His influence reached down to the second birth of the novel in England; Paměla, her name shortened to Paměla, came to life again, no longer a princess, but a servant-girl; she was introduced to the public by no knight, but by a Fleet Street bookseller, whose passion was not poetry, but morality; and she has lived on to this day. Richardson is the direct inheritor of the analytic and sentimental method in romance which Sidney had developed before him.*

The rival tendencies of court and town which are so

---

* Richardson perhaps read the *Arcadia* in Mrs. Stanley's "modernized" version (1725), where the above passage is thus rendered:—"The Shepherd-Boys were playing on their Pipes, as they were ignorant they lost the Hours they soothed: a little Distance off sat a young Shepherdess a-spinning, beguiling of her task with rural Songs and Roundelays; the Houses were scattered with a kind of pleasing Irregularity, but yet the Distance was not so great, to bar a mutual Succour, or hinder the Pleasures of Society."

clearly marked in the Elizabethan drama, are no less
conspicuous in the novel. Sidney and Lyly were both
courtiers, and in their novels both cast in their lot with
court tastes and tendencies, just as Sidney in his *Apologie*
praises *Gorboduc*, which he says " climbeth to the height
of Seneca his style," but has no word of praise for the
new romantic drama. Indeed, it would not have gratified
either author to hear his work spoken of as a " novel,"
for the word carried with it in those days something of
evil imputation, of new-fangled Italianate proclivities,
while " novellist " meant nothing but innovator, generally
in religion. And the rest of the notable contributors to
the prose fiction of Elizabeth's reign present a striking
contrast to Sidney in the conditions of their work. On the
one hand, the courtier, dreaming his valorous and amorous
dreams in stately and leisured retirement, and committing
them to paper for the private delight of his noble sister ;
on the other, a group of struggling adventurers, familiar
with the scenes and shifts of penury, seeking for
themselves money and notoriety by means of the
stationers' shops in Paul's Churchyard, where their
" novellets " and " love-pamphlets " would be ranged in
heaps to tempt the young gallants who came for their
daily lounge in the aisles of the church. And yet it was
in the school of necessity that Greene and Nash, and, in
a lesser degree, Lodge, learned to write in their happiest
vein, and to shape out of their private experiences the
beginnings of a true realistic romance.

Of Robert Greene, the facts that are known are chiefly
drawn or inferred from his autobiographical pamphlets.
He was born at Norwich about 1560, and entered St.

John's College, Cambridge, in 1575. There he "con-
sumed the flower of his youth" with riotous companions,
who induced him to travel with them into Italy and
Spain, "in which places I saw and practised such
villainy as is abominable to declare." Imbued with a
spirit of restlessness and discontent, he returned to
Cambridge, where he wrote his first novel, *Mamillia,* and
took his M.A. degree in 1583. Coming up to London,
he soon became known as an "author of plays and a
penner of love-pamphlets," and entered at once on the
impetuous and dissolute career that was to close so early.
In 1586 he married a "gentleman's daughter of good account." If Roberto's brief story in the *Groatsworth of
Wit* may be taken as autobiographical, Greene won his
wife by a trick, when she was betrothed to another ; in
any case he left her in a year, she returning to Lincolnshire,
he to London to his old copesmates and companions.

The romantic novels, with plots adapted or imitated
from the Italian, may now have had a less rapid sale
than formerly, or perhaps Greene himself turned to a
style of writing that had become more congenial to him,
and was probably quite as profitable. However it may
be, the last two years of his life saw the production of
that curious series of pamphlets which describes so
vividly the tricks and habits of the sharpers and criminals
of London. These are written with knowledge, and
were likely enough to be popular except with the
"coney-catchers" or swindlers themselves, who bitterly
resented the exposure. Finally, Greene, sinking lower
and lower in want, pawned his own garments, as it were,
for bread, in those marvellous confessions where he lays

F

his own life and heart as bare as he had laid the practices of his vagabond associates. The last of these was written in 1592, on his very deathbed in the house of a poor shoemaker called Isam, who had given him shelter when he was overtaken by his fatal surfeit of drinking. The last scene of all, familiar though it is, may be related in the words of Greene's bitter enemy, Gabriel Harvey, who visited his lodgings a day or two after his death, with the object, it is to be feared, of making controversial and didactic capital out of Greene's misery. Speaking of Greene, the shoemaker's wife told Harvey "how he was fain, poor soul, to borrow her husband's shirt while his own was a-washing; and how his doublet and hose and sword were sold for three shillings; and beside the charges of his winding-sheet, which was four shillings; and the charges of his burial yesterday, in the new churchyard near Bedlam, which was six shillings and fourpence; how deeply he was indebted to her poor husband, as appeared by his own bond of ten pounds, which the good woman kindly showed me; and beseeched me to read the writing beneath, which was a letter to his abandoned wife in the behalf of his gentle host, not so short as persuasible in the beginning, and pitiful in the ending.

"*Doll, I charge thee by the love of our youth, and by my soul's rest, that thou wilt see this man paid; for if he and his wife had not succoured me, I had died in the streets.*

"Robert Greene."

It is easy to condemn the man, impossible not to love him important to understand him, for his is a typical figure. He may be taken as the very epitome of many writers of the time, wild, profligate Bohemians in their lives, and in their writings earnest and often terrible moralists. Yet it surely is not necessary, with M. Jusserand, to assign to Greene "two separate selves" in order to understand this. Rather, the man who should preach repentance without having felt, as Greene did, all the anguish of self-reproach and self-abasement, all the bitterness of the fruits of his misdoing, is in need of two selves, one for the pulpit, another for the complacent regulation of his private affairs. Greene had but one self, full of impulse, readily kindled to generosity, or carried by sympathy or ridicule into vice, and above all filled with that artistic instinct which compelled him to give expression in poetic or literary form to what he felt and knew. The despairing verses in the *Groats-worth of Wit*, expressing the sorrow and penitence wherewith he breathed out his life, are as perfect in form as they are matchless in intensity. There is a heart-stirring pathos about his retrospect of the love-lyrics and love-romances that he had written :—

> "Oft have I sung of love and of his fire;
> But now I find that poet was advised,
> Which made full feasts increasers of desire,
> And proves weak love was with the poor despised;
> For when the life with food is not sufficed,
> What thoughts of love, what motion of delight,
> What pleasance can proceed from such a wight?"

In the same year the Jesuit priest, Robert Southwell, was thrown into prison, where he was kept for three years and "ten several times was most cruelly racked," for no other crime than belonging to the Society of

Jesus; and he too solaced his extremity by setting his
desire for death, as Greene set his for life, to some of
those clear poetic melodies of which the secret is well-
nigh lost :

> " By force I live, in will I wish to die ;
>   In plaint I pass the length of lingering days ;
> Free would my soul from mortal body fly,
>   And tread the track of death's desirèd ways ;
> Life is but loss where death is deemèd gain,
> And loathèd pleasures breed displeasing pain."

With both men poetry was a passion rather than an
accomplishment ; both poured out their sorrows in verse,
as if verse were not only the most adequate, but also the
easiest speech.   And such verse baffles criticism, for it
is more than verse ; it is the treasured spirit of a man.

It is no wonder, then, that Greene's latest novels (so
to call them) are also his best.   His growth in power
during the nine brief years of his literary activity was
immense.   In *Mamillia* it is difficult to see much more
than an imitation of *Euphues*, and a poor imitation, for
Greene neglects the alliteration and out-Lylys Lyly, if
that were possible, in his idle multiplication of instances
from natural history.   In *Pandosto* (1588), on which the
Winter's Tale was founded, he shows a much matured
power in the art of maintaining interest in a story, and
this art reaches its height in *Menaphon* (1589), or
perhaps in *Philomela* (1592).   But before the last of
these he had eclipsed them in the pamphlets already
mentioned, where he drew from experience, and, casting
Euphuism aside, wrought, save for the sparks that would
fly, directly and simply.   It was an invention on which

Nash modelled his best writings, and, so modelling it, surpassed his teacher. To substitute for a fancied Arcadia, with its quaint mixture of pagan deities, feudal institutions, and Christian ideas, the real London of the time; and to introduce into the story contemporary characters, speaking and acting as in life, was an immense advance; and although Greene and Nash had no disciples, and the novel followed a very different line of development for the next century, yet they deserve the credit of their attempt.

Thomas Lodge, who collaborated with Greene in play-making, escaped the fate that befell his friend. The son of a Lord Mayor of London, he was educated at Oxford, where he seems to have come under Lyly's influence; thence he came to London and took up the study of law, diversified by excursions into literature. A bout that he had with Stephen Gosson shows that Lodge too had lived in Bohemia, if his antagonist may be believed. Gosson speaks of him as "hunted by the heavy hand of God, and become little better than a vagrant, looser than liberty, lighter than vanity itself." But Lodge never fell into that limbo of Bohemia where Greene spent the last years of his life; literature was never his mainstay, and he took to cruising, accompanying Captain Clarke to the Canaries, and Master Thomas Cavendish to the Straits of Magellan and Patagonia. Returned home, he became a physician, and died as late as 1625, having seen the end, as he had seen the beginning, of the first period of English prose fiction.

His first novel, the *Delectable Historie of Forbonius and Prisceria*, published in 1584, is a pallid romance of the

school of Lyly.   The plot is slight.   Two lovers are with-
held from their bliss by nothing more considerable than
the rancorous opposition of the lady's father, but Forbonius disguises himself as a shepherd, and the elder
man, after detecting him, succumbs to that Arcadian
device, and withdraws his hostility.   The style is a
faded and decadent Euphuism ; the balanced sentence
is retained, to the extreme of monotony, but the air of
epigram that alliteration lends, and the colour furnished
by profuse simile, are almost entirely foregone, to the
detriment of a languid theme.

Lodge's most famous novel, the *Rosalynde, Euphues
Golden Legacie,* was written on shipboard, and published
in 1590.   "Room," he says in the preface, "for a soldier
and a sailor, that gives you the fruits of his labours that
he wrought in the ocean, when every line was wet with
a surge, and every humorous passion counterchecked
with a storm."   The romance is written in a style that
often, to its own advantage, forgets *Euphues,* and Lodge
must have the credit of the delightful story of *As You
Like It.*   He must have the credit of it, that is, when
Jaques, Touchstone, and Audrey, who are Shakespeare's
own, have been deducted on the one hand, and when
the part of the plot that is drawn from the older *Tale of
Gamelyn* has been deducted on the other.   This leaves
Lodge with the lion's share of the plot-interest in the
shape of the love-affairs of the Forest of Arden.   Lodge
did well in many diverse kinds of writing, but he never
surpassed the idyllic beauty of this pastoral tale.

An Alarum against Usurers, Lodge's first essay in
the more directly moral and realistic style of writing,

was published in 1584, earlier than Greene's "coney-catching" pamphlets, and dedicated, along with his first novel, to Sir Philip Sidney. As the son of a well-to-do citizen, and the heir to some property, Lodge had doubt-less received overtures from the brokers and usurers whose malpractices he describes. Whether he ran the whole course of the "young novice" of his story, who, "thinking he had God Almighty by the heel, held the Devil by the toe, and by this means was brought to utter wrack and ruin," remains a matter of doubt. He passed away from Bohemia to wider scenes, and never followed up this or kindred subjects.

A year or two before Lodge took his farewell of the "ballet makers, pamphleteers, press-haunters, boon pot poets, and such-like," who were Greene's companions in London, to sail for Brazil with Cavendish, there appeared on the same stage a writer, ten years younger than he in age, ten times greater in force, in the person of "ingenu-ous, ingenious, fluent, facetious Thomas Nash." Nash was born at Lowestoft in 1567, the third son of " William Nash, Minister" (whatever that may mean), and entered St. John's College, Cambridge, as a sizar in 1582. He says he remained there for "seven year together, lacking a quarter," but Harvey alleges that, "fearing he would not attain to the next Degree," he "forsook Cambridge, being Bachelor of the third year." Except on the supposition of some such temporary interruption of his college course, it is difficult to find a place in Nash's brief life for the travels in Germany and Italy to which his works bear almost unimpeachable witness. By the year 1589, at any rate, he was in London with Greene, whose friendship he had made during his first year at college, and to whom he loyally clung until death parted them. In that year he wrote an introductory discourse to Greene's *Menaphon*, and produced his own first original prose tract, the *Anatomie of Absurditie*, a kind of comic counterpart to Stubbes' austere *Anatomie of Abuses* (1583). Stubbes found the "licentious follies of the times" intensely wicked; Nash found them also very ludicrous. Both were agreed on what no one at that time denied, the degeneracy and depravity of the age.

The rest of Nash's known history is little more than a history of his writings and his controversies. Of these latter one was public, the famous Marprelate war, into which, with native impetuosity, Nash seems to have rushed soon after he reached London, as a freelance on the side of the bishops. The other was a private war with Gabriel Harvey, Greene's antagonist, and was waged over Greene's body. The astonishing vigour of Nash's abusive wit reached its zenith in the pamphlet entitled *Have with you to Saffron Walden, or Gabriel Harvey's Hunt is up. Containing a full Answer to the eldest son of the Halter-Maker* (1596). The war had begun about the question of Harvey's pedigree. He was the son of a rope-maker at Saffron Walden, and the various uses to which a rope may be put in the social economy did not fail to figure largely in the attacks on him. This wild war of wit, transcending in power even the ancient Scottish "flytings," makes it clear that Shakespeare, in Kent's abuse of Oswald or Petruchio's apostrophe to the tailor, was merely reproducing what he had seen and heard. Nash's part in it, moreover, proves that Mercutio was no poet's fancy, but walked embodied in the streets of London.

He knew the hardships of his profession and time From the autobiographical fragments scattered at random through his works, it appears that he long indulged vain hopes from the court, and that he had found a patron who sustained him with more than promises in Sir George Carey, afterwards Lord Hunsdon, to whose wife and daughter respectively two of his tracts are dedicated. Perhaps Sir George Carey's connection with Suffolk, where he held the estate of Herstwood in Great Saxham, commended him to the notice of the young wit in search of a protector.   It is certain that in the *Terrors of the Night* (1594) Nash introduces a long digression in praise of that "fortunate blessed island," the Isle of Wight, of which Carey was captain-general, and the "thrice noble and illustrious chieftain" who governed it.   His words leave no doubt that he had received substantial benefits at the hands of the subject of his eulogy :—

"Men that have never tasted that full spring of his liberality, wherewith (in my most forsaken extremities) right graciously he hath deigned to revive and refresh me, may rashly (at first sight) implead me of flattery, and not esteem these my fervent terms as the necessary repayment of due debts."

But therein they are mistaken.   It is not from a lively sense of favours to come that this gratitude proceeds :—

"Whatsoever minute's intermission I have of calmed content, or least respite to call my wits together, principal and immediate, proceedeth from him.   Through him my tender wainscot study door is delivered from much assault and battery; through him I look into and am looked on in the world; from whence otherwise I were a wretched banished exile."

It is a brief but vivid glimpse of the conditions of life in that land of stress and storm where Nash dwelt. "Debt and deadly sin," as he himself cheerfully remarked, "who is not subject to?" Greene had dedicated some of his works to great names, but there was no one to beat back that last onslaught of creditors from the doors of the house where he lay dying. And with Nash the struggle did not last for many years. In August, 1597, he was in the Fleet prison for his unlucky play the *Isle of Dogs*, which is now lost; in 1599 was published his *Lenten Stuffe*, written "because I had money lent me at Yarmouth, and I pay them again in praise of their town and the red herring;" by 1601 he had died—how and where is not known.

It is as a writer of prose that Nash deserves to live. He prided himself on the fact that his style was of his own begetting, owing nothing to Tarlton, Lyly, Greene, or other fashionable models.

"*Euphues* I read when I was a little ape at Cambridge, and I then thought it was *ipse ille* : it may be excellent still for aught I know, but I looked not on it this ten year; but to imitate it I abhor."

This, no doubt, is an extravagant boast; *Euphues* was in the air, and in his earliest work its influence is apparent enough. For instance, to take one out of many passages in the *Anatomie of Absurditie*, there is more than a spice of Euphuism in this criticism on Virgil and Ovid :—

"I commend their wit, not their wantonness, their

learning, not their lust; yet even as the bee out of the bitterest flowers and sharpest thistles gathers honey, so out of the filthiest fables may profitable knowledge be sucked and selected."

So also with the other literary fashions of the time—they have left their mark, slight though it be, on his work. There is a reminiscence of one of Sidney's favourite devices in this lovely description of the anxiety felt for Leander by Hero, whose story is introduced parenthetically in the *Lenten Stuffe:*—

" Hero hoped, and therefore she dreamed (as all hope is but a dream); her hope was where her heart was, and her heart winding and turning with the wind, that might wind her heart of gold to her, or else turn him from her."

But the strongest and best of his writing is his own; or, if a comparison must be found for it, it merits this high praise—it is likest of all others to Shakespeare's prose writing. The same irrepressible inexhaustible wit, the same overpowering and often careless wealth of vocabulary, the same delight in humorous aberrations of logic distinguish both writers. And Shakespeare alone of his sixteenth-century contemporaries can surpass Nash in the double command of the springs of terror and of humour. Like Shakespeare, like Sir Walter Scott, Nash was entirely free from all slavish credulity; astrology and the science of portents he makes a constant theme of his ridicule—with all the greater zest, perhaps, because Richard Harvey, a brother of the pedantic Gabriel, was a professed astrologer; —yet he knows, as Shakespeare and Scott knew, the

reality of the mysterious, and can turn the supernatural
to the best of artistic account.   The *Terrors of the Night*
shows him revelling in all the horrors that his imagination
can draw from the circumstances of darkness and "that
time most fatal and unhallowed."   "As touching the
terrors of the night," he begins, "they are as many as
our sins," and he proceeds to "amplify" them under
many heads, with the whole store of his weirdest imagery.
If any ask why the devil is specially "conversant and
busy in churchyards," it is because a rich man, Nash
replies, "delights in nothing so much as to be incessantly
raking in his treasury, to be turning over his rusty gold
every hour : the bones of the dead the devil counts his
chief treasury, and therefore is he continually raking
amongst them."   But "what do we talk of one devil?"
he breaks off; "there is not a room in any man's house
but is pestered and close packed with a camp royal of
devils."   From the subject of devils he goes on to treat
of dreams, until, tiring of this too, he proclaims, with
characteristic volatility, that those who would read further
on this matter must betake themselves to Artemidorus,
Synesius, and Cardan, "with many others which only I
have heard by their names, but I thank God had never
the plodding patience to read, for if they be no better
than some of them I have perused, every weatherwise
old wife might write better."

In *Christ's Teares over Jerusalem* (1593), a pamphlet
the latter part of which deals with the vices and excesses
of Elizabethan London, his vivid and picturesque handling of terrible themes reaches its height in the description of the torments reserved for those men and women

who "put all their felicity in going pompously and
garishly : they care not how they impoverish their substance, to seem rich to the outward appearance. As
many jags, blisters, and scars shall toads, cankers, and
serpents make on your pure skins in the grave, as now
you have cuts, jags, or raisings upon your garments. . . .
For thy flaring flounced periwigs, low dangled down with
love-locks, shalt thou have thy head side dangled down
with more snakes than ever it had hairs. In the mould
of thy brain shall they clasp their mouths, and, gnawing
through every part of thy skull, ensnarl their teeth
amongst thy brains as an eagle ensnarleth his hook
amongst weeds. . . . In the hollow cave of thy mouth,
basilisks shall keep house, and supply thy talk with hiss-
ing when thou strivest to speak. . . . For thy carcanets
of pearl, shalt thou have carcanets of spiders, or the
green venomous flies cantharides."

And in *Pierce Pennilesse, his Supplication to the Divell*
(1592), a passage describing the ultimate fate of the
usurer, the murderer, the drunkard, and the wanton
anticipates with very singular closeness the description
of the pains of hell given by Ford in the most famous of
his tragedies.

In his most natural vein, when he is writing in a loose,
easy, bantering, conversational style, "*quicquid in buc-
cam venerit*, as fast as my hand can trot," Nash is
perhaps at his best. No pretext is too slight to excuse
a digression, or to introduce an imaginary conversation
between the author and the reader. Fielding introduces himself to the reader, as it were, only between
the acts ; Nash delights in popping up his head in

and out of season, and appearing in full view as the worker of the marionettes. " Methinks I hear one say," he remarks in *Pierce Pennilesse,* "what a fop is this, he entitles his book a Supplication to the Devil, and doth nothing but rail on idiots, and tells a story of the nature of spirits. Have patience, good sir, and we'll come to you by and bye. Is it my title you find fault with? Why, have you not seen a nobleman derive his barony from a little village where he hath least land? So fareth it by me in christening of my book." Then, after continuing the digression for some sentences, he turns on himself in the same abrupt manner: " But what a vein am I fallen into! What, an Epistle to the Readers in the end of thy book? Out upon thee for an arrant block, where learnedst thou that wit? Oh sir, hold your peace; a felon never comes to his answer before the offence be committed. Wherefore, if I in the beginning of my book should have come off with a long apology to excuse myself, it were all one as if a thief, going to steal a horse, should devise by the way as he went what to speak when he came at the gallows. Here is a cross way, and I think it good here to part. Farewell, farewell, good Parenthesis, and commend me to Lady Vanity, thy mistress." And with this subtle turn of his satire against himself, the author is off with one parenthesis only to take up at once with another.

Of Nash's numerous pamphlets only one is written strictly in the form of a novel. *The Unfortunate Traveller, or the Life of Jacke Wilton,* (1594) is remarkable in English literature as the earliest example of a picaresque romance—that is to say, a romance describing realistically the shifts and adventures, perils and escapes, of a light-hearted, witty, spring-heeled knave, who goes through all worldly vicissitudes, thus lending himself to his creator's purpose of gaining the opportunity to describe or satirize all classes of society. The Spanish novel *Lazarillo de Tormes*, which appeared some forty years before Nash's *Unfortunate Traveller*, is, if mediæval allegories like *Reynard the Fox* be set aside, the earliest in this kind, which was especially prolific in England during the eighteenth century. The plot of this class of romance is always slight, often hardly a plot at all, the character of the hero, and the reader's interest in his fortunes, giving to the work the only unity that it attains. Hence it is impossible to set down the *Unfortunate Traveller* as Nash's single contribution to novel literature, when almost all his pamphlets abound in detached scenes, incidents, and character sketches, precisely similar in kind to those that give its chief merit to his more deliberate attempt at fiction-writing. The slender thread of narrative on which these incidental scenes for once are strung may fairly be regarded as unessential.

Yet this narrative itself gives Nash an additional claim on the notice of the genealogist of the novel. For "Jack Wilton," the hero of the book, is made page to the famous Earl of Surrey, of the time of Henry VIII.; and thus a colour of historical interest is lent to adventures, and a semblance of probability thrown over travels, which, in very fact, would seem to have been Nash's own. Certainly the tastes and sympathies of "Jack Wilton" agree very accurately with those that Nash

displays in his other prose works. "God so love me,"
the author of *Pierce Pennilesse* exclaims, "as I love the
quick-witted Italians, and therefore love them the more,
because they mortally detest this surly swinish generation" (viz. the Danes). The account given in the
Unfortunate Traveller of certain academic festivities at
Wittenberg reveals the same antipathy to the Teutonic
races :—

"We were spectators of a very solemn scholastical
entertainment of the Duke of Saxony thither, whom
because he was the chief patron of their University, and
had took Luther's part in banishing the mass and all
like Papal jurisdiction out of their town, they crouched
unto extremely. The chief ceremonies of their entertainment were these : first, the heads of their university
(they were great heads of certainty) met him in their
hooded hypocrisy and doctorly accoutrements, *secundum
formam statuti;* where by the Orator of the University,
whose pickerdevant was very plentifully besprinkled with
rose water, a very learned or rather ruthful oration was
delivered, (for it rained all the while), signifying thus
much, that it was all by patch and by piece-meal stolen
out of Tully, and he must pardon them, for they did
it not in any ostentation of wit, (which they had not),
but to show the extraordinary good will they bare the
Duke, (to have him stand in the rain till he was thorough
wet) : a thousand *quemadmodums* and *quapropters* he
came over him with, every sentence he concluded
with *Esse posse videatur;* through all the nine worthies
he ran with praising and comparing him; Nestor's
years he assured him of under the broad seal of their

supplications, and with that crow-trodden verse in Virgil,
Dum juga montis aper, he packed up his pipes and
cried *dixi*."

The sketch of the "ink-horn orator" who gave a
"broaching double-beer oration" on this occasion is
in the same spirit of burlesque. He had a "sulphurous
big swollen large face, like a Saracen, eyes like two
Kentish oysters, a mouth that opened as wide every
time he spake as one of those old knit trap doors, a
beard as though it had been made of a bird's nest
plucked in pieces, which consisteth of straw, hair, and
dirt mixed together. He was apparelled in black
leather new liquored, and a short gown without any
gathering in the back, faced before and behind with a
boisterous bear skin, and a red night cap on his head."

On the evening after this, Wilton relates, the Duke
was bidden to a dramatic entertainment, where *Acolastus,
the Prodigal child*, was "handled by scholars." "The
only thing they did well was the prodigal child's hunger,
most of their scholars being hungerly kept," he observes ;
and their drama is treated by him with as great a wealth
of humorous scorn as their learning or their drinking.
"The next day they had solemn disputations, where
Luther and Carolostadius scolded level coil.   A
mass of words I wot well they heaped up against the
Mass and the Pope, but farther particulars of their disputations I remember not.   Luther had the louder
voice, Carolostadius went beyond him in beating and
bouncing with his fists, *Quæ supra nos nihil ad nos.*
They uttered nothing to make a man laugh, and so I
will leave them."   And with this reflection, in the true

G

spirit alike of the *picaro* of romance and of facetious
Thomas Nash, the traveller hurries on with his adventures to the point where his master and himself, having
traversed France and Germany, arrive in due course
at Venice.

The description of what the traveller did and saw in
Italy amply vindicates and illustrates the well-known
invectives of Ascham, Harrison, and other grave writers
against the Circe of the nations. If the younger English
gallant of that age was educated in drinking habits, as
Nash and others would seem to believe, by the example
of the Low Countries, from Italy he brought deadlier
lessons. "The sink and drain of hell" is the best name
that Harrison can find for Italy, and he instances one
lesson in particular that was often brought thence, that
"forgiveness is only to be showed when full revenge is
made." The incident of the crimes of Esdras of
Grenada, and the vengeance taken on him by Cutwolf,
related in the latter part of the *Unfortunate Traveller*,
is as lurid and fearful a tale of the *vendetta* as exists in
literature. Esdras, when brought to bay by his enemy,
whose brother he had killed, begs passionately for his
life, offering to undertake any execrable enterprise, to
slaughter his kindred, and to renounce his baptism as
the price of it. Then Cutwolf bethinks himself of a
"notable new Italianism," whereby he may spill the
soul as well as the body of his victim. He promises
life to Esdras on condition that he shall write an obligation of his soul to the devil, and the wretched man
at once pours forth eagerly his blasphemous abjurations.
Then the moment was come—" I shot him full into the

throat with my pistol, so did I shoot him that he might never speak after or repent him. . . . No true Italian but will honour me for it." Then, as if the reader had not supped full of horrors in the description, prolonged through many pages, of this scene, Nash proceeds with unabated zest to as minute an account of the torture and execution of Cutwolf himself.

It was not for nothing that Nash boasted of his admiration for the Italians ; he is perhaps the purest product of the Italian Renaissance to be found among English men of letters. Greene alludes to him as " young Juvenal," but there is no doubt that he owed more to Pietro Aretino, for whose every line he professes an unqualified admiration, than to the Roman satirist, whose English followers wrote in rhymed heroics. And in many points of character and style he recalls to memory that other Italian, who excelled in art and left morals, theoric and practic, to the specialist,—Benvenuto Cellini. So Nash, born further north, loved poetry and hated the Puritans—with the hatred, not of a religious partisan, but of a scholar and a wit. He is always ready for a bout with these enemies of polite learning, and from his earliest work to his latest heaps contempt equally on them and on all "poor Latinless authors," and "lay chronigraphers, that write of nothing but of Mayors and Sheriffs, and the dear year, and the great frost." But of poetry he cannot speak without enthusiasm. "The honey of all flowers, the quintessence of all sciences, the marrow of wit, the very phrase of angels "—these are a few of the phrases he strings together, in his breathless fashion, when the word occurs in his pages.

His style owes much to this unfailing attraction that poetry has for him. In the neglect of any rigid distinction between the functions of prose and verse he only resembles his contemporaries, but the special form which the poetic influence takes in his case, distinguishes him from the rest. Lyly borrowed or adapted the form of verse, Sir Philip Sidney rifled the store of its fancies and conceits.—Nash is attracted chiefly by terse and telling metaphor of a really illuminative kind, permissible enough in prose no doubt, but lending to it a richly decorative and essentially poetic effect when scattered over the page with all a poet's freedom. The fact he has to relate often becomes little better than a model on which he displays one after another the brocaded suits available for its clothing. Yet there is hardly one of these costumes that does not fit the wearer. He will not say that many of the popes are poisoned ; he puts it thus : " In Rome the Papal chair is washed, every five year at the furthest, with this oil of aconitum,"—a grim figure which suggests as much as it says. His satirical intent is, no doubt, in part responsible for the frequent directness and simplicity of his metaphors ; in part his desire for vividness dictates figures such as might be called " natural" figures—of the kind, that is, to be found among the illiterate classes of a people. The Italian executioner in the *Unfortunate Traveller* would, Nash says, "at the first chop with his wood-knife, fish for a man's heart, and fetch it out as easily as a plum from the bottom of a porridge-pot. He would crack necks as fast as a cook cracks eggs, a fiddler cannot turn his pin so soon, as he would turn a man off the ladder." The same love of vividness leads him to anticipate, not only Defoe, but many of the modern writers of fiction who have sought to find in dialect an unexhausted unartificialized field whence to gather telling and direct expressions. Certainly there are few writers of adventures of a later date who might not justly covet Nash his description, in the *Lenten Stuffe*, of the hardships undergone by sea-faring adventurers. "Some of these for their haughty climbing come home with wooden legs, and some with none, but leave body and all behind; those that escape to bring news tell of nothing but eating tallow and young blackamoors, of five and five to a rat in every mess and the ship-boy to the tail, of stopping their noses when they drunk stinking water that came out of the pump of the ship, and cutting a greasy buff jerkin in tripes and broiling it for their dinners."

To come to Defoe, with whom Nash has inevitably been compared, the parallelisms in the works of the two men are many and striking. As Sir Philip Sidney was the precursor of Richardson, so Nash is the direct forerunner of Defoe. Yet, while it is certain that Richardson had read the *Arcadia*, there is no ground, unless a ground be made of internal evidence, for thinking that Defoe had so much as seen any work of Nash's. The passage in the *Unfortunate Traveller* that describes the desolate condition of Rome during the plague, and another in *Christ's Teares*, where a picture is drawn of a bright-arrayed angel with a naked sword who had stopped the plague in former times, might give rise to doubt. But the probability is that both men, in their realistic pictures, were plagiarists from a common source—the general experience and knowledge of mankind. This much is certain, that as Nash was the first in the field with a realistic novel, so also he remained, for a good deal more than a century, the last : he had no disciples, no one improved on or even imitated this way of writing, he abandoned it himself, and fiction developed on other lines. Thus the *Unfortunate Traveller* stands alone among the productions of a many-sided, vigorous, and brilliant age, and among the novels of that age must certainly be counted the most vigorous and brilliant. It would be a still higher compliment to its author if Defoe, by merely going back to nature, should ever be made suspect of going back to Nash.

CHAPTER IV.

THE end of the reign of Elizabeth marks at once the zenith of the English drama and the end of the first period of the English novel. A few desultory novels or pamphlets, modelled on one or other of the three original masters, appeared during the reign of James I., but these are either feeble imitations or reversions to the earlier and unfailingly popular type of "jests." Thus Lady Mary Wroth's *Urania* (1621) is written strictly after the style of Sidney, whose niece she was. Thomas Dekker's prose works contain more than one pamphlet which owes something to Nash, but, invaluable as the *Gull's Horne-booke* and other of its author's works are for their descriptions of the life of the age, they cannot be said to have carried on the development of the structure of the novel. Rather Dekker fell back on satiric and descriptive pamphleteering, and although, in one or two of his pamphlets, notably in the *Raven's Almanack* (1609), he tells a series of stories in good set terms, for the most part his stories are mere anecdotes, sometimes illustrative of the matter in hand, sometimes utterly irrelevant to it, and told for their proper wit. A more elaborate attempt than any of Dekker's is to be found in the vivid little tract called *Westward for Smelts* (1620), where a collection of stories is set in a realistic narrative framework,—whereas Dekker adheres uniformly to the rhetorical or didactic framework. But even here, while the enveloping story, which narrates how five fishwives beguile the voyage from Queenhithe to Kingston by telling each a tale, is of some antiquarian interest, and while the portraits of the fishwives themselves are strongly and minutely drawn after the Dutch manner, the tales told by the way are merely adapted versions of stories at least as old as Boccaccio.

It is no matter for wonder that the novel found it difficult permanently to rise above the artistic level of the *Hundred Merry Tales*. All constructive literary work was apt to seek expression in the drama, and Dekker himself when he had a more intricate story to tell, although he was by no means " our best plotter," told it on the stage, with greater profit and applause than a mere pamphleteer could expect. And so, in point of fact, the novel was swallowed up by the drama, and in due time, after the death of the two last dramatists of the Elizabethan school, Ben Jonson and Dekker, the drama itself, in its frivolous and shapeless old age, was swallowed up by the rising tide of political troubles. From the year 1642, when Parliament decreed the cessation of stage-playing, until a year or two before the Restoration, few plays were acted in England. Moreover the statute of 1648, enjoining the destruction of play-houses, the whipping of actors, and the infliction of fines on play-goers, broke the continuity of dramatic tradition by scattering the companies, and made sure that the drama should not rise again in its old likeness. Other branches of literature suffered only less. The strongest and most active minds of the time were engaged on political problems; and the nation passed, with Milton, from poems to treatises.

Yet in this time of political turmoil and preoccupation, when even love-songs were set to the notes of the trumpet rather than the flute, one species of fiction, as if to vindicate its absolute unconcern with life and its remoteness from living human interests, gained a footing and maintained an elegant existence in England. For it was during the Commonwealth, while Milton was calling Salmasius bad names in good Latin, that translation after translation of the French heroic romances, or *romans à longue haleine*, was offered to an eager public.

The vogue of the later artificial romances of chivalry had never wholly ceased in England. In spite of the blind hostility of the classicists to all mediæval themes, Amadis and Palmerin, whose mediævalism was half theatrical, had maintained their hold upon the public and their influence upon later romancers. In the pastoral school of Sidney and d'Urfé that influence shines in conspicuous fashion; it may also be detected in such works as the forgotten novels of Emanuel Ford, enormously popular in their own day. *Parismus, the Renowned Prince of Bohemia* (1598), and *Ornatus and Artesia*, by the same author, doubtless attained their many editions precisely because they were chary of following the new realistic or witty fashions, but conducted their heroes through the approved exercises of chivalry with old-fashioned ceremony and wealth of episode. Nothing is harder to kill than a school of romance; driven from the high places of literature, it will maintain, in all kinds of inaccessible nooks and crevices of society, a life that demands neither the air of criticism nor the soil of thought. Early in the seventeenth century the English bookseller knew, if the English author did not, that the romance of chivalry was not dead. And there was certainly a public ready for the French heroic romances when they were imported into England from the Hôtel de Rambouillet, the hot-house where the finest of them had been raised.

These romances must be regarded as yet another step in the decadence of the romance of chivalry. They carry to a more extravagant excess the faults inherited or developed by the pastoral romance. The absolute predominance of love as a motive in war and politics, the immense complexity of intrigue, the long soliloquies and sentimental analyses on perfectly conventional lines, the superhuman valour of lovers, and the number of continents that witness their exploits, the excitement of the satire, suspected or intended, on contemporary kingdoms and courts,—all these, familiar already in the pastoral romance, are reintroduced in the heroic, and exaggerated to the point of distraction. Two other traits are added to these—first, the introduction of the historical interest, if it may be so called, by the interweaving of well-known classical or oriental characters, such as Mark Anthony, Cleopatra, Artaxerxes, Mithridates, in the mesh of the intrigue; and, secondly, the peculiar structure of the main plot. For the story which begins on the first page is often simple enough in itself, were it not that every character introduced has also a story of his own to unfold, which story again may contain characters equally interesting and equally desirous of relating the whole of their romantic adventures. Thus the introduction of a new character is a thing the reader learns to fear; it will probably delay the main action for a book or two. And when he finds himself plunged deep into the adventures of one who has no existence even among the characters of the main story, but leads a parasitic life, the shadow of a shade, in the narration of one of these, his patience is apt to fail. The stories are arranged one within another, as if they had swallowed one another in succession, and it is not until they are successively disgorged that the reader can get back to the enveloping story, which after all may disappoint him by proving itself to be the merest covering, with no particular structure or object of its own.

The earliest of the "long-winded romances" proper, *Polexandre*, by the Sieur de Gomberville, was published in 1632 in four volumes quarto, and became the precursor, and to some extent the model, of the later and even more voluminous romances of La Calprenède and Mademoiselle de Scudéry. It was translated into English by W. Browne in 1647, and from this date onward the French heroic romances all found translators and an English folio dress. The most popular of them, *Cassandre*, *Le Grand Cyrus*, and *Clélie*, enjoyed an immense vogue in England, and exercised a literary influence

that for a time carried all before it in the heroic
play. Their popularity, unlike that of the heroic plays,
outlasted the century, and so late as 1752 gave occasion
to the clever, though somewhat fine-drawn, satire of
The Female Quixote, a novel wherein Mrs. Charlotte
Lennox sets forth the perils that environ a young lady
who goes through life applying the ideas and standards
of the heroic romances, and expecting from the Tom
Joneses or Lovelaces of the eighteenth century the
deportment and conversation of the grand Cyrus, or of
Ibrahim, that illustrious Pasha. But it was the generation
to which Mrs. Samuel Pepys and Dorothy Osborne belonged that was trained to appreciate the heroic play,
and to spend long days in the perusal of the heroic
romance ; the clear sense and critical humour of the age
of the *Spectator* were not favourable to their continued
popularity. When the novel arose once more with
Richardson, they soon passed into entire oblivion, be-
queathing their following of trained and patient readers
to the long-winded heroines of *Clarissa Harlowe* or *Sir
Charles Grandison.*

To sketch the story of one only of the French heroic
romances would prove too long a task. Modern critics
are agreed that they are unreadable, and their general
characteristics may be studied with more profit by the
English reader in the original works that were written
by English imitators. For La Calprenède and Scudéry
found imitators in England as well as translators. Roger
Boyle, Earl of Orrery, John Crowne the dramatist, George
Mackenzie a young advocate in Scotland, afterwards Sir
George Mackenzie the king's counsel and " the persecutor

of the saints of God," all produced romances that serve at least to show how powerful a sway the heroics of the French school exercised over literary imagination and production in England. An examination of these works will give some insight into the tastes of polite society at the time when Bunyan was meditating his *Pilgrim's Progress*, and Mr. Thomas Rymer was criticizing Milton's *Paradise Lost*, "which some," as he indignantly remarks, "are pleased to call a poem." By reading these original romances we learn what it was that the ladies and wits of the court of King Charles II. were pleased to call heroic.

The earliest and longest of the original works in this kind, *Parthenissa* (1654), by Roger Boyle, Earl of Orrery, might well intimidate the most omnivorous of antiquarians. Boyle, after spending some of his earlier years and forming his taste in France and Italy, returned to England to take an active part in the Civil Wars, fighting at first on the Royalist side, and later lending his assistance to Cromwell in the pacification of Ireland. The fruit of his leisure, *Parthenissa*, illustrates all the worst faults of the heroic style. It opens with a description of "a stranger richly armed, and proportionably blest with all the gifts of nature and education," arriving at the temple of Venus, at Hierapolis in Syria, to consult the Oracle. While his servant seeks for lodgings in the neighbourhood, the stranger attracts a large concourse of interested spectators by the melancholy of his demeanour and the languor of his gait. Among these, Callimachus, "the Prince of that holy Society," is at last emboldened to invite him to relate his life. This unwarranted piece of folly on the part of Callimachus, is destined to delay the main narrative for several hundred pages, for the stranger at once begins : " My name is Artabanes, I was born in the reign of Orodes, the present King of Parthia, who is also called Arsaces, I had my education with Orodes' son, the Prince Pacorus. . . . My father, whose name is Moneses, was uncle to Tigranes, and only brother to Tiridates his father "—but it would require the exact memory, the leisure, and the taste for genealogy of a " person of honour " of the seventeenth century to go further with this or with any of the similar preambles that introduce the plentiful biographies of *Parthenissa.* It is Parthenissa herself, the daughter of Miraxtorses, a Parthian general, that Artabanes is in love with ; the crosses that inter rupted the smooth course of love are inflicted partly by fate, partly by the ponderous introductions given to themselves by new characters on their entrance into the story. The affairs of Artabanes indeed move smoothly enough at the outset ; he meets and defeats at a tournament one Ambixules, an Arabian prince who travels the country attended by twenty-four negro pages, well-mounted, and each carrying, pendant at the tip of an ebony wand, a portrait of some excellent beauty. These are the portraits of the ladies whose champions Ambixules had overcome in the lists, fighting on behalf of the superior charms of Mizalinza, his own deceased beauty, whose death, and inability when living to tolerate her lover, had united to fan his flame to this heroic pitch. Artabanes, however, makes short work of his pretensions, by slaying him and presenting his collection of pictures to Parthenissa. More formal wooing ensues. The lady cannot be induced to express herself with any clearness; she writes a letter to her lover which causes him to ejaculate, " Unfortunate Artabanes, here is not enough kindness to make thee live, nor cruelty to make thee die!" While he is in this dilemma, compelled to live an unchartered life or die an unchartered death, the lady herself visits him, and relaxes her indifference. Their nuptials would have been celebrated and Artabanes' relation ended, had not a war broken out between Arsaces and the King of Armenia. Artabanes offers his services, and after performing prodigies of valour, takes prisoner a general of the other side, one Artavasdes, who rewards him for sparing his life by relating the particulars of it, at a length exceeding thirty folio pages. If after this the jaded reader should be able to drag on with Artabanes' resumed narration, he will find himself, at page six hundred and thirteen, back at Hierapolis in Syria, with Callimachus' story yet to begin. But never to finish, for the noble author tired of his story, and left it incomplete. Indeed, the world itself would hardly contain a romance completed on this scale, where eight hundred pages slip by, and leave the two principal characters on the spot where they found them, still engaged in the formal preliminaries of an introduction to each other. In the course of one or other of the incidental stories, Mithridates, Hannibal, Spartacus, and others play their parts, and all for love. For it was the love affairs above all else that attracted readers to these huge romances. Here could be learnt the art of paying delicate compliments, of balancing the obligations of contending passions, of writing letters, not very intelligible, perhaps, but bearing on them the stamp of high breeding and fine feeling. "'Tis handsome language," writes Dorothy Osborne of *Parthenissa*, "you would know it to be writ by a person of good quality, though you were not told it." The interminable conversations and correspondence of so many pairs of noble lovers could not fail to serve as a guide to right feeling and polite expression. Mlle. de Scudéry actually prepared a handbook of conversations upon several subjects, as "Of speaking too much or too little," "Of the Difference between Civil Complaisance and Flattery," "Of Raillery," and the like, which work was done into English in 1683, by Mr. Ferrand Spence, the translator of Lucian. It is the least tiresome of her works, and undoubtedly the heroic romances are not without felicities of expression and subtleties of distinction that would serve a minor poet of the fantastic order.

Better conceived and better wrought than *Parthenissa* is Sir George Mackenzie's juvenile romance, *Aretina* (1661), prefaced by a poem to King Charles II. on his happy return, and dedicated, from Edinburgh, "to all the Ladies of this Nation." Riding as it does on the very crest of the wave of French influence, *Aretina* shows the extravagancies of the heroic school at their height. Yet Mackenzie was conscious of where the strength of that school lay—not in the stirring recitation of events, but rather in the subtle dialectic treatment of problems of morality and emotion. In the apology for romances with which he introduces his story, he confesses, "Albeit Essays be the choicest pearls in the

Jewel house of Moral Philosophy, yet I ever thought that they were set off to the best advantage, and appeared with the greatest lustre, when they were laced upon a Romance." And many are the essays which are "laced upon" *Aretina.* An elaborate parable dealing with the political relations of England and Scotland, under the names of Lacedæmon and Athens, occupies the whole of the third book, and was perhaps suggested by Harrington's similar treatment of contemporary affairs in the *Oceana.* The progress of the story is frequently arrested for the discussion of moral paradoxes like those which are maintained by the author of the *Fable of the Bees ;* thus Philarites, the hero of the story and lover of Aretina, maintains at length that vanity is the parent of the virtues, that extravagance is profitable to a nation, and that gaudiness of dress argues modesty. For the rest, the story is comparatively simple, and brings the fortunes of two pairs of noble lovers within sight of a happy conclusion.

In his search for high-flown diction, Mackenzie borrows from all the models known to him. Defending the utility of romances, he echoes Lyly, remarking that " these kernels are best where the shells are hardest, and these metals are noblest which are mudded over with most earth." The father of Aretina was one " who lived rather to study than studied how to live," and certain it is that this would have been his characteristic had he flourished in Sidney's pages. But the affectations that he borrowed are the smallest part of the author's stock ; he is full of original conceits. The heroine and her companion spend the night in a robbers' cave "lying on

the ground, a bed never made since the creation." Two
friends are spoken of as "but one soul bilocated;" in
a storm "Heaven's bottles empty themselves, willing to
cause the earth drink healths to the bon-voyage" of
certain travellers. The art of courtly speech, the chief
attraction, it may be presumed, of the heroic romances,
may here be learnt. This is how a knight may compliment ladies who disclaim skill in the arts—" Accomplishments were very imprudent if they choosed not to lodge
in such rare bodies as yours are, for I am confident they
may travel the world over, before they find any such other
receptacles." To a hermit apologizing for the poverty
of his cell it is polite to reply, "There is nothing worthy
of your choice which is not worthy of our observation."
And although in the exclamation of the Chancellor of
Egypt, when he witnesses the rescue of two fair ladies
from the hands of brigands, the pedantry of the Scottish
moral philosopher and lawyer shines through the language
of the Court of Egypt—" To no purpose," he cries, "is
the admirative faculty bestowed upon man if it be not
exercised in such cases as this,"—yet the sententiousness,
the ingenuity, and the wit of many passages in the book
must have fascinated those readers who were seeking
a pattern of exalted behaviour and indirect high-bred
speech.

Sir George Mackenzie was a friend of Dryden's, and
it was to him that Dryden, as he confesses in the Essay
on Satire, owed the suggestion that he should model
his poetic style on the verses of Denham and Waller.
Prose style was destined, within a very few years of the
date of the publication of *Aretina*, to undergo a similar

remodelling, and the heroics of the French school, with their tortuous sentences and strained figures, were soon to pass out of fashion. So that *Aretina* remains perhaps the best original example in English of the heroic romance, the most valorous, and on the whole the happiest, attempt to naturalize that romance in Britain.

It might be expected that the chief inherent fault of these romances, their hopeless looseness of construction, would be remedied or mitigated in the hands of a dramatist. The solitary romance of John Crowne the dramatist, *Pandion and Amphigenia* (1665), disappoints that expectation. It is no better, in some respects it is worse, than the work of the idlest of titled amateurs. The first hundred pages neither begin the main story nor prepare the way for it; they offer sundry minor stories to the reader while he is waiting. To employ a figure consonant with the theme, these pages are the *hors d'œuvre* of a miserly entertainer; they kill the appetite. When the story begins it is carried on in a halting intermittent fashion, and it never finishes ; that is to say, the characters of the tale are put through the usual drill, and are left ranged in order in precisely their original posture. This paralysis of the story is so common a disease of the heroic romance as almost to serve for definition. Perhaps Crowne's youth may be held to excuse him, for he conceived the story, he says, before he was twenty. In a preface to the reader he is careful to condemn all the faults in romance-writing which he subsequently exemplifies in his tale. A writer should not " bolster up a crooked invention with fungous words," nor make of fiction " an hospital of lame conceits." After this wholesome warning the reader of

Pandion and Amphigenia is at times almost tempted to believe that he is reading a parody, the fungous words and lame conceits throng so fast upon him. To the historical student of literature the book is interesting as another illustration of the powerful and abiding influence of Sidney on the English romance. Never for a moment, until realism began in the eighteenth century, did the writers of prose fiction in England shake off the fantasies of that opiate. The book, written on stray sheets of paper, collected by the author's sister and published against his expressed command, became for a century the training school of the English romancer. In the coarse and clumsy comedy of Anus and Daphnis, introduced as an episode in *Pandion*, Crowne follows the hapless example of the weakest part of the *Arcadia*. Ever and again he appropriates shamelessly in his descriptions, without improvement. "The streets so intermixed with shady trees seemed as if the woods had left their melancholy retiredness, and grown sociable, meant to inhabit the town ; or as if the town had left its cheerful sociableness, and grown to a kind of civil wildness, meant to inhabit the woods" —are we in Thessaly sharing the pursuit of the "coy lady," or is not this pure Arcadia? And even Pamela's prayer, the employmen*e* of which by King Charles brought Sidney under Milton's censure, finds its counterpart here in the prayer of Glycera, who thus addresses the gods while she is drowning, "Since it is your will to drench and pickle up my soul in briny sorrows, to preserve it pure and untainted, and that the stormy gusts of adverse fortune must drive me through a sea of tears, ere I can arrive at the haven that shall put an end to the turmoiling

navigation of this life; Oh then, let this also be your
will——" And the self-possessed lady pours out the
aspirations of her pickled soul.

Sidney is not the only author that Crowne borrows
from. In the poem that occurs incidentally in *Pandion
and Amphigenia* the following stanza will show how the
heroic school could improve on George Herbert :—

> "Sweet day, so calm, so cool, so bright,
>   Thou hast expelled the dusky night,
>   And Sol begins to mount on high,
>   And marry Tellus to the sky."

This single verse sufficiently indicates what interes
Crowne is like to pay on his heavy debts to Sidney.

Towards the close of the century a greater dramatist
than Crowne followed Crowne's example, by preluding
his dramatic work with a novel. In 1692 William Congreve, a young man then unknown to fame, produced a
brief novel called *Incognita*. A novel he called it, for he
is careful to distinguish it from the current school of
romances, which bear the same relation to novels, he
maintains, that tragedy bears to comedy. "Romances,"
he holds, and the description contains some good criticism, "are generally composed of the constant loves
and invincible courages of Heroes, Heroines, Kings and
Queens, mortals of the first rank, and so forth ; where
lofty language, miraculous contingencies, and impossible
performances elevate and surprise the reader into a
giddy delight, which leaves him flat upon the ground
whenever he leaves off."

It is with no pretensions of this kind that Congreve, under the assumed name of "Cleophil," lays his

first-born, a naked and shivering foundling, at the feet of Mrs. Katherine Leveson, and implores her "that if it should want merit to challenge protection, yet, as an object of charity, it may move compassion." After explaining, with the fashionable indifference that moved the scorn of Voltaire, that this piece of literature is the product of "the idle hours of a fortnight's time," Congreve claims for his novel that it is the first that observes dramatic laws. The action is comprised in three days, the scene is laid at Florence, the main design is the marrying of "two couple so oddly engaged in an intricate amour."

To any one sated with the masterpieces of the Grand Cyrus school, this little pamphlet must have come as a refreshment indeed, for here at last is a dramatist, and, what is more, a humourist, at work upon prose fiction. In the description of how Fabritio had "vowed revenge upon Lorenzo if he survived, or, in case of his death, upon his next of kin, and so to descend lineally, like an English estate, to all the heirs males of his family," there is a foretaste of the quality of Fielding. The development of the story, which deals with the fortunes of two friends who attend a masked ball at Florence, each taking the name of the other, and there fall in love, is pure drama, rapid and spirited. The picture of the two lovelorn youths, returned to their lodging, and sighing in company, each imagining that the other sighs out of complaisance, is pure humour. And Congreve displays something of the wit that was to make his name, both in the conversation, or polite "raillery," that he reports as taking place at the ball, and in the occasional introduction

of himself to the reader,—the discussion, so dear to
Fielding, of his own handling of the puppets of his story.
Thus the author refuses to describe the dress of his
heroine, lest he should err "in some material pin or
other in the sticking of which maybe the whole grace of
the drapery depended." But at the description of her
beauty he will "have a fling," although he has "prefaced
it with an impossibility," by the too liberal use of lauda-
tory epithets,—and he writes half a page of delicate mock-
heroic. There is great promise in this early work, and
the history of Congreve's later literary production is only
one more instance of how hardly the novel can maintain
itself in a period of dramatic activity. Successful drama
has generally offered higher rewards to the author, and
has taken the bread out of the mouth of the novelist, by
stealing the material of his stories. The heroic romances
found their public in England during the failure of the
drama, and availed themselves skilfully of the opportunity to foster a new taste in the reading public, a taste
that the drama could never satisfy save imperfectly; a
delight, namely, born of the fashionable leisure of a self-
conscious society, in minute introspection and the
analysis and portraiture of emotional states. In this
particular development of fiction, which has since reached
so high a pitch of perfection in England and France,
the heroic romances are thus an important link.

The "heroic" temper reached its most signal achievement in the heroic romance, but it pervades the greater
part of seventeenth-century literature, and took many
forms during the century. While English poetry was
receiving the final classic stamp at the hands of Milton,

this extravagant ultra-romanticism flourished apace, and attempted to conquer also the domain of verse. Some of the longer narrative poems of the century, as, for instance, Davenant's *Gondibert* and Chamberlayne's *Pharonnida*, are simply heroic romances told in verse ; and the heroic creed, so to call it, is held and expressed by literary critics as notable as Davenant and Dryden. This creed finds expression in that passage of Dryden's *Essay of Dramatic Poesy*, where he says that a serious play "is indeed the representation of nature, but 'tis nature wrought up to a higher pitch. The plot, the characters, the wit, the passions, the descriptions, are all exalted above the level of common converse, as high as the imagination of the poet can carry them, with proportion to verisimility." This utterance may, of course, be taken in a sense in which it is as sound as the soundest of Dryden's criticisms, but it is to be feared that what he had in his mind was nature "wrought up to a higher pitch" by a very palpable process of hoisting, the language and sentiments of Maximin in *Tyrannic Love*, or of Almanzor in the *Conquest of Granada*. For Dryden's practice shows clearly enough that his earlier critical creed was modelled on the teaching of his friend and predecessor, the inventor of the heroic play, the best exponent of heroic doctrine, Sir William Davenant. And Davenant has left on record a very much clearer statement of what his doctrine was in his apologetic preface to *Gondibert*, where he disclaims all intention to level heroic poesy to the reach of common men, and declares that in love and ambition, the two distempered passions to which great souls are especially liable, the

best theme of an exalted poetry is to be found.   It is in
courts and camps, the schools of lofty feeling, that these
two passions burn brightest ; every lover accordingly, it is
found, must be a warrior and a courtier, and Gondibert's
warriors were all lovers, as one of them points out to his
chief on the point of engaging a more numerous enemy :—

> "Victors through number never gained applause,
>   If they exceed our compt in arms and men
>   It is not just to think that odds, because
>   One lover equals any other ten."

Love and ambition as the mainsprings of life, the only
things that the magnanimous man finds life worth living
or death worth dying for, these are the very essentials
of the heroic romance.   It is Sir Philip Sidney's formula
—"For the love of honour and the honour of love," but
with a difference not unlike the difference between the
court of King Arthur and the court of Louis XIV.   The
spirit of the romances of chivalry as well as their form
has suffered a fatty degeneration.   Love has become
fantastic gallantry, honour is passed into a pedantic
courtly etiquette.   And although in the heroic plays of
Dryden and the heroic poem of Davenant even the
extravagance of these sentiments at times receives the
impress of genuine poetry, prose fiction could not be
supported long on so unsubstantial a diet.   The monotony inherent in the practice of making every hero, like
every other hero, a model of courtly manners, was fatal
to the heroic romance, character-drawing in any real
sense was blankly impossible under such a convention.
    Thus the heroic literature of the seventeenth century,
so unreal, so tedious, so patiently wrought, was never

thoroughly naturalized in England; it remained a literature of the polite coteries. With the death of Ben
Jonson and the beginning of the civil troubles the
great literary society that had met at the Mermaid and
Devil Taverns was dissolved, and London saw no real
literary society again until the time of Pope and Swift.
The societies most in vogue were all sects and parties,
uncongenial to the artist. A desire to escape from the
unceasing political turmoil of the time led to the formation of little artificial groups, of literary or scientific
tastes. The nucleus of the Royal Society was formed
at Oxford by men who could not agree upon politics,
and so banished the subject from their meetings. At
Great Tew, near Oxford, Lucius Cary, Lord Falkland,
gathered about him for a few short years before his
death the *convivium theologicum* that included many of
the best philosophical thinkers of the day. In something the same way, in the shallows or backwaters of the
political torrent, were gathered together sundry groups
of literary exquisites who, besides reading and translating the heroic romances, carried out their doctrine by
adopting assumed names and playing at heroic sentiment. Of this kind were the societies that gathered
around Mrs. Katherine Philips " the matchless Orinda,"
and Margaret, Duchess of Newcastle. The Hôtel de
Rambouillet, which presided at the birth of the heroic
romance, was thus exactly imitated in England by the
societies that welcomed it from France. Neither of the
literary ladies who dominated these circles has left anything written in this kind—Orinda remained faithful to
poetry, and the Duchess of Newcastle was probably

incapable of so sustained an effort, for the nine folio volumes of her works are often brilliant but always desultory, and her plays have no other plot, as she wittily and truly confesses, but that of passing away the time that hung heavy on the hands of their writer. But it was in courtly circles such as these that the romance of the day found its public; like the Elizabethan novel, its chief function was to supply an innocent and fanciful pastime for the very prolonged and unrelieved leisure of high-born ladies, who read the romances aloud, and drew from them laws and precedents for their own small courts of love.

There were other women, too, from the time of the later Stuarts onward, who wrote professionally, and not merely to add a grace to ennui. The first of these is one of those numerous writers whom Pope, with careless malevolence, has clamped firmly in the stocks of a single couplet, and left sitting until later students shall take the trouble to make their acquaintance and redeem them. Posterity is content to know that Astræa trod the stage loosely, and so she gets no credit for the merits of her novels. Yet these merits are real, for Mrs. Aphra Behn had passed her childhood in Surinam, where her father was governor; for some years after the Restoration she had lived at Antwerp as a Government agent; and it was on sundry experiences in these two places that she based her two best-known novels, published in 1698, after her death,—*Oroonoko* and *The Fair Jilt.* For making use of incidents of real life in the service of fiction at a time when the heroic romance was at the height of its vogue, she deserves all credit.

And yet it was no literary reform that she effected. Miranda, the heroine of *The Fair Jilt*, whose original, says Mrs. Behn's anonymous biographer, she had met at Antwerp, is a beautiful, accomplished, and very wicked woman, who in a brief career plans the murder of her sister, and gets three men severally condemned to death for crimes of which she has falsely accused them or to which she had instigated them. Yet through all this she retains the affection and admiration of some at least of her victims, and passes her later days in tranquil retirement, thanking Heaven for the afflictions that had "reclaimed her and brought her to as perfect a state of happiness as this troublesome world can afford." The character may well have been real, but the reality and interest fade out of it under the conventional literary treatment. For Miranda's language resembles that of the most high-souled of the heroic ladies, and the jargon about flames, darts, wounds, tortures, and cruel charmers obscures the sombre merits of the original theme. In this novel, as in *Oroonoko*, Mrs. Behn travels to new regions for her stories, but she takes with her the conventional diction and apparel. The story of Oroonoko, the love-lorn and magnanimous negro, of "very little religion" but "admirable morals," who meets a tragic death, belongs to a class of romance that flourished almost a century later, when Rousseau had given popularity to the philosophical ideas that underlie it. In this novel Mrs. Behn is one of the early precursors of the romantic revival, and finds her logical place in that movement. But her bold conduct of a simple story and her popularity with her contemporaries entitle

her also to claim a share in the attempt, faint and ineffective, that the later seventeenth century witnessed, to
bring romance into closer relation with contemporary
life.   The attempt failed for the time, and when at last
achievement came, and the rise of the great schools of
English novelists with Richardson and Fielding at their
head was rendered possible, it was not wrought by the professed writers of romance, but by the essayists and party
writers of the reign of Anne, by Addison and Steele, by
Swift and Defoe, who formed their style under influences
remote enough from the high-flown impossibilities of the
heroic romance.

Thus, just as the sixteenth century saw the decline
of the older romances of chivalry, so the seventeenth
saw the rise, decline, and fall of this later and less
robust romantic development; the heroic romance died
and left no issue.   And the influence that the century
exercised on the growth of prose fiction, the foundations it laid for the coming novel, are to be sought,
not in the writers of romance, but in the followers of
other branches of literature, often remote enough from
fiction, in satirists and allegorists, newspaper scribes
and biographers, writers of travel and adventure, and
fashionable comic playwrights.   For the novel least of
all forms of literature can boast a pure extraction; it
is of mixed and often disreputable ancestry; and the
novelist derives his inspiration, as well as his material,
not chiefly from the pages of his predecessors in the art,
but from the life of his time and the literature that
springs directly from that life, whether it be a broadside
or a blue-book.

CHAPTER V.

THE BEGINNINGS OF THE MODERN NOVEL.

THE story of Antæus, who gained fresh strength from each fall to the earth that he suffered, might well be taken to typify the history of prose fiction. Flat on the ground, after the soaring flights of the heroic romance, gaining fresh vigour from the intimate realistic study of daily life and ordinary character, the novel began its career anew, and with the fairest prospect of success. For the seventeenth century, so poor in original prose fiction, had done much to prepare the way for it when it should arise. Literary activity had displayed itself in many new forms; the newspaper and political and religious controversy had trained up a reading public numbering scores of thousands; above all, an instrument had been prepared for the novelist in the shape of a new prose, invented and first practised for purposes of criticism, homiletic, and science, but easily available for vivid narration or realistic description unencumbered by the metaphorical apparatus of earlier prose-writing. The conditions, material and formal, for the success of the novel, were there by the beginning of the eighteenth century, and awaited only the artist who should perceive them and avail himself of them. The immense and immediate popularity of the novels of Defoe, Richardson, and Fielding, each of whom stumbled, as it were by accident, into the writing of prose fiction, serves to show how ready the public was to welcome and appreciate the new venture. The literary tendencies and developments of the previous century made it certain that that venture should be realistic, dealing with average contemporary life, and no new resuscitation of the thrice-worn themes of old romance ; the eighteenth-century school of fiction, that is, was inevitably a school of novelists.

For after the great school of imaginative writers of the golden age of English literature had passed away, the literary tendencies of the seventeenth century were all in favour of the novel. One or two lonely men of genius built the lofty rhyme or wove the brilliant tangles of the old poetic prose, but the general character of a century is to be estimated most truly from its lesser writers, and not from the visions of a Milton, or the fantasies of a Browne. The works of the lesser writers of the seventeenth century show the rise of a new spirit, foreign to the times of Shakespeare,—a spirit of observation, of attention to detail, of stress laid upon matter of fact, of bold analysis of feelings and free argument upon institutions ; the microscope of the men of the Restoration, as it were, laying bare the details of daily objects, and superseding the telescope of the Elizabethans that brought the heavens nearer earth. No one word will finally describe it : in its relation to knowledge it is the spirit

of science, to literature it is the spirit of criticism; and science and criticism in England are the creations of the seventeenth century. The positive temper, as opposed to the mystic, is everywhere in the ascendant, in spite of the imaginative aberrations of the more extravagant religious and political theorists. In literature illustrations are many; thus satire, which in the age of Elizabeth was the pastime of very young men, who "railed on Lady Fortune in good terms," became deadly earnest after the Civil Wars, in the hands of men like Cleveland, Oldham, Marvell, Butler, and Dryden, who left Nature and Fortune with their withers unwrung, and aimed at the joints in the harness of their enemies. Thus imaginative works, the good, as well as the bad, were exposed to a running fire of burlesque and parody, and reputations were made on travesties of Homer and Virgil. Thus, too, the drama turned away from the broad treatment of human nature and the search for new emotional situations carried so far by Webster and Ford, to the humbler task of social portraiture and the mimicking of individual foibles. A comparison of two great comedies, one written at the beginning, the other at the end of the century, will illustrate the change of which this is only one aspect. How far a cry is it from Ben Jonson's *Volpone* to Congreve's *Way of the World*,—from the heroic villainies proper to no age and clime, drawn by the great master of scorn and humour, to the delicate finesses of social fraud portrayed by the witty man of fashion! And, turning away for a moment from purely artistic literature, it is not hard to find marks of the change, of the new taste for fact and detail, in the historical labours of Fuller, Dugdale, Rymer, and Rushworth, or in the manifold productions of those lesser scribes who bore, as Cleveland scornfully remarks, the same relation to an historian that the maker of mouse-traps bears to an engineer, the diurnal-makers and writers of *Mercuries*. The new generation of readers were all for fact, they wished chiefly to inform themselves and take a side : even the court circles of the Restoration, which yielded for a time to the fascinations of Dryden's heroics, were at least as ready to applaud the *Rehearsal* and the champion of " prose and sense."

One class of literary production, almost proper to the seventeenth century, may rank as an ancestor of the novel in the direct line. The *Character*, a brief descriptive essay on a contemporary type, whether an " Upstart Knight," an " Old College Butler," a " Tobacco-seller," a " Pot-Poet " or a " Pretender to Learning," enjoyed so great a popularity that Dr. Bliss stated that he had made a list of more than two hundred seventeenth-century collections of *Characters* in his copy of one of the most famous of these works, Earle's *Micro-cosmography* (1628). Among the better known of the writers of *Characters* are numbered Bishop Hall, the ill-fated Sir Thomas Overbury, John Cleveland, and Samuel Butler, the satirist. Nor was public interest limited to these characters of types, drawn for the most part satirically ; biography and autobiography also flourished, and men regaled the world with the account of a life that, but for that account, the world would never have heard of. Not only did Lord Herbert of Cherbury, William Lilly the astrologer, and Margaret Duchess of Newcastle write their own lives, but highwaymen and keepers of ale-houses followed in their train. George Fox kept his memorable *Journal*, Pepys immortalized himself in his *Diary*, Evelyn made for himself a securer title to fame than all his scientific labours could have procured, Bunyan wrote what was virtually an autobiography in the account of his religious experiences, and James Howell popularized the habit of publishing familiar letters, valuable rather for their contents than for the rank or notability of their author or recipient. Material for the study of the life of the time —letters, diaries, and biography—begins to abound, and for the scanty Elizabethan documents, such as the few letters, "witty and familiar," that passed between Spenser and Master Gabriel Harvey, preserved by the egotism of the latter worthy, the student finds a library of similar material belonging to the time of the Restoration, when man had begun, often in the most desolate and remote places, the serious, affectionate, and minute study of himself.

The realistic writing of Defoe and the realistic novel in England were the offspring of these ancestors, the children of a taste for fact. Realistic fiction in this country was first written by way of the direct imitation of truthful record, and not, as in France, by way of burlesque on the high-flown romance. The heroic romance in France found parodists in Scarron and Furetière, whose *Roman Comique* (1651) and *Roman Bourgeois* (1666) brought fiction back to scenes of average town and provincial life, and transformed the romance at a blow into the novel. The process in England was longer and slower, but its spirit was the same, and is exactly described by Furetière in his address to the reader prefixed to the *Roman Bourgeois.* In this he claims a moral purpose for his novel, and excuses himself for passing over the crimes of wicked men to censure the petty faults to which all the world is liable. " To this end it is necessary that the nature of the stories and the characters of the persons should be so closely modelled on our own manners that we should seem to recognize in them the people that we meet every day." And for evidence of his success as a preceptor, Furetière relates how the perusal of the story of a certain Lucretia, contained in his novel, had actually cured a fair *bourgeoise* of her infatuated passion for a marquis.

But satire is perhaps more effective to destroy an old school of romance than to create a new. It is certain that the new was not created in England chiefly by way of satire ; even Fielding, whose original intention no doubt was simply to satirize the high-toned *Pamela,* soon forgot Pamela and her creator in the zest of depicting Parson Adams. *Don Quixote,* very early translated into English, bore fruit in the seventeenth century in such works as Beaumont and Fletcher's *Knight of the Burning Pestle* (1611) or Butler's *Hudibras* (1663–1678). Scarron was translated and imitated, but the burlesque method, so admirably applied to the heroic play, left the heroic romance unscathed, and no new fiction sprang out of the ashes of the old.

But in the general literature of the time there are to be found in plenty hints, premonitions, tentative approaches to what was afterwards to be the novel. The work of John Bunyan hardly finds its proper place in a history

of prose fiction; he regarded it as anything but fictitious.
Moreover, in form and outline it bears something the
same relation to the novel proper that the "Morality"
bears to the drama proper. Yet how rich are his works,
not only the *Pilgrim's Progress* (1678), but the *Holy
War* (1682), and the *Life and Death of Mr. Badman*
(1680), in literary, as well as practical and moral lessons,
in demonstrations whereby the novelists might profit to
learn character-painting, admirable narrative, and the
attainment of the illusion of reality. Where was the
professed writer of fiction in the seventeenth century
who could enthral the reader's imagination by his two
opening sentences, and hold him spellbound to the end?
This is how the *Pilgrim's Progress* begins:—

"As I walked through the wilderness of this world
I lighted on a certain place where there was a den,
and I laid me down in that place to sleep, and as I slept
I dreamed a dream. I dreamed, and behold I saw a
man, a man clothed in rags, standing with his face from
his own home, with a book in his hand, and a great
burden upon his back."

This is more than pathetic allegory, it is perfect
narrative and vivid picture; that one descriptive phrase,
of masterly restraint, "standing with his face from his
own home," which contains Bunyan's thought upon two
worlds, at once stirs the hearts of those who read
beneath it, and secures the eager interest of children
in the expectance of coming adventures.

It was well for literature that Bunyan learnt his style
from the English Bible, and not from Mlle. de Scudéry.
His abstractions are more living than the portraits of

other writers. The bathos that was reached by the
heroic romance when it laboured under the additional
weight of allegory may be well seen in the *Bentivolio and
Urania* (1660) of Nathaniel Ingelo, D.D., wherein the
heroic model was employed to set forth the pursuit by
Bentivolio, or Good Will, of his mistress Urania or
Heavenly Wisdom. In the fourth edition of this romance
(1682), "the obscure words throughout the book are
interpreted in the margin, which makes this much more
delightful to read than the former editions." Some one,
therefore, must have read it, let it pass for a book; it
marks for the historian of literature the lowest depth to
which English romance-writing sank. Its unillumined
profundity swarms with low forms of life; polysyllabic
abstractions crowd its pages, and deposit their explana-
tory spawn upon its margin; "the very deep did rot."

The abstractions of Bunyan, on the other hand, are
hardly abstractions; they breathe and move in the
atmosphere and light of his imagination. Giant Pope
and Giant Pagan, Pliable and Mr. Worldly Wiseman,
Faithful and Christian himself are additions to the
portrait gallery of English fiction. In the *Life and
Death of Mr. Badman* the author gives a singularly
minute and realistic biography of a tradesman in a
provincial English town, who leads a sordid and successful life, and dies "like a chrisom child, quietly and
without fear." The grim and awful reality of the whole
sketch is enhanced by numberless matter-of-fact touches,
and by the writer's simplicity and freedom from all
extravagance. Here is no double-dyed villainy, but a
perfectly consistent hard and ugly life, such as Bunyan

had more than once observed, perhaps in Bedford, only projected by him, by implication rather than by direct contrast, against the white background of eternity.

The readers of the *Pilgrim's Progress* doubtless had no literary affectations to unlearn ; for them, Bunyan's style was the style to which they were already best accustomed. But Margaret, Duchess of Newcastle, wrote for the circles that left the *Pilgrim's Progress* severely alone, and in her works there are interesting contributions to the raw material of fiction. In her "*CCXI Sociable Letters*" (1664) she anticipates Richardson in the discovery that letters, to be interesting, need not be really exchanged by living correspondents, and aims at making of them "rather scenes than letters, for I have endeavoured under cover of letters to express the humours of mankind." In the close of her *Nature's Pictures drawn by Fancie's Pencil* (1656) she records her birth and character in statements that had only to be false to ring with the very tones of Defoe : "Neither did I intend this piece for to delight, but to divulge, not to please the fancy, but to tell the truth, lest after ages should mistake in not knowing I was the daughter to one Master *Lucas* of *St. John's*, near *Colchester* in *Essex*, and second wife to the Lord Marquis of *Newcastle ;* for my lord having had two wives, I might easily have been mistaken, especially if I should die and my lord marry again." This anxiety that the reader should be in no way misinformed, this protest and circumstance of veracity, forcibly recalls the style that Defoe adopted for his greatest fiction, after he had made the discovery that biography loses none of its interest when the life it records has never been lived. With Defoe the art of fiction came to be the art of grave imperturbable lying, in which art the best instructor is the truth. And it was to no reputed masters of romance, but to recorders of fact, biographers, writers of voyages and travels, historians and annalists, that Defoe served his apprenticeship.

The change that came over English prose style about the time of the Restoration perfected the instrument of the new fiction. This change is commonly attributed to Dryden, but in this, as in other things, Dryden was the exponent of a movement beyond his control. To the sermons of Tillotson Dryden owned his obligations ; and another writer, famous in his own time, Thomas Sprat, afterwards Bishop of Rochester, gives in his *History of the Royal Society* (1667) an instructive account of one of the influences that made for the new prose. Sprat regards the "luxury and redundance of speech" as one of the chief and most inveterate of the evils which the Society has to combat. "Who can behold," he exclaims, "without indignation, how many mists and uncertainties these specious tropes and figures have brought on our knowledge ?" The "beautiful deceit," from use and education, has come to be esteemed, and a drastic remedy is needed. The Royal Society, therefore, "have exacted from all their members" (Dryden was one) " a close, naked, natural way of speaking ; positive expressions, clear senses, a native easiness, bringing all things as near the mathematical plainness as they can ; and preferring the language of artisans, countrymen, and merchants before that of wits or scholars."

The remedy which is here prescribed for style was needed also by fiction in the time of Sprat, and, before the next century was many years old, fiction, too, had bowed under the yoke, had accepted the dictatorship of fact, and adopted the language of humble life.

It is no straining of language to speak of the *Tatler* (1709–1711) and *Spectator* (1711–1712) of Steele and Addison as brilliant examples of prose fiction. Here, for the first time, are the methods and subjects of the modern novel; all that is wanting is a greater unity and continuity of scheme to make of the "Coverley Papers" in the *Spectator* a serial novel of a very high order. Such continuity as there is in the grouping of incidents round the same characters is due to the idea of a Club, consisting of friends of the author, who assist him in editing the paper, and whose humours and adventures he records. This idea had been long popular before it attained its final development in the *Spectator*. Its original is perhaps to be found in the "Athenian Society" formed by the bookseller, John Dunton, for the production of the *Athenian Gazette* (1690–1696), the first non-political journal established in England. This society really existed, and included among its few members Samuel Wesley, father of the divine. When Defoe started his *Review*, in 1704, he adapted the notion of a society in the "Scandal Club," a fictitious association for the free discussion of those problems of morals, literature, and society which had been treated in the *Athenian Gazette* by way of direct question and oracular response. In a late number of the *Tatler* (No. 132) the reader is introduced to the members of Mr. Bickerstaff's

Club, and a series of character-sketches is given, but little use is made of them subsequently. Indeed the author himself alleges that the particular use he finds for this "set of heavy honest men, with whom I have passed many hours with much indolence, though not with great pleasure," is to lull the thinking faculties, and induce a gentle sleep. And he describes Sir Jeoffrey Notch, the decayed gentleman of ancient family "who calls every thriving man a pitiful upstart;" Major Matchlock, who nightly recounts the battle of Naseby; "honest old Dick Reptile," and the young bencher who "has about ten distichs of *Hudibras* without book." It was doubtless at the hands of Addison that this society, "too little and too lately known" in the *Tatler*, received promotion to a place in the forefront of the scheme of the *Spectator*. The six "gentlemen who are concerned with me in this work" are six types of contemporary society, Sir Roger de Coverley, the bachelor of the Inner Temple, Sir Andrew Freeport, Captain Sentry, Will Honeycomb, and the philosophic clergyman; all of them are introduced in the second number of the *Spectator*. Their later appearances, especially those of Sir Roger and Will Honeycomb, give occasion to fragments of prose fiction inferior to none in the eighteenth century. The dreary "Character" of the seventeenth century, which would have rendered Sir Roger as "An Old Country Knight," and Will Honeycomb as "A Mere Town Gallant," has received its death-blow in these sketches, drawn by men who loved the individual better than the type, and delighted in precisely those touches of character, eccentricities and surprises, that give life to a literary portrait. The keen undiscriminating satire of the generic description has given way to the gentle atmosphere of humour that envelopes and illumines the character of Sir Roger, disarming the dogmatist by showing him that this man's very faults were loveable, and that his virtues may be smiled at as well as praised. A century before the date of the *Spectator* Sir Thomas Overbury had set himself to describe the "character" of a country gentleman. "He is a thing," says Overbury, "out of whose corruption the generation of a justice of peace is produced. He speaks statutes and husbandry well enough to make his neighbours think him a wise man. . . . His travel is seldom farther than the next market town, and his inquisition is about the price of corn : when he travelleth, he will go ten mile out of the way to a cousin's house of his to save charges ; and rewards the servants by taking them by the hand when he departs." After a scornful sketch of the absurdity of his behaviour when he comes to London, Overbury concludes, "But this is not his element, he must home again, being like a dor, that ends his flight in a dunghill."

Had the *Spectator* been content with the essay, moral or satirical, after this kind, the inimitable papers on the life and character of Sir Roger might have been condensed into a single valueless bundle of characteristics, epigrammatically expressed and opprobriously intended, somehow thus :—

"An Old Country Squire is a thing that was a fine gentleman three reigns ago, and is now a mere Justice of the Peace. He is of opinion that none but men of

fine parts deserve to be hanged; yet he will pretend to
wisdom in his own shire, where he can explain the game
laws, and determine a knotty point in the law, after
grave deliberation, with the opinion '*that there is much
might be said on both sides of the question.*'   At the Assize
Courts, to keep up his credit in the county, he will
whisper in the judge's ear, ' *That he is glad his lordship
has met with so much good weather in his circuit.*'   He
is much given to sport, but loves his neighbour's game
better than his own; he will go three miles to spare his
own partridges, and when the farmers' sons open the
gates for him a-hunting he requites them with a nod and
an inquiry after their fathers and uncles.   In church he
is landlord to the whole congregation, and will suffer
nobody to sleep in it besides himself.   In town all his
talk is of how he killed eight fat hogs at Christmas, and
has sent a string of hogs' puddings with a pack of cards
to every poor family in the parish.   When he dies he
leaves for mourning, to every man in the parish a great
frieze coat, and to every woman a black riding-hood,
because it was a cold day when he made his will."

These traits are selected from the *Spectator*, and,
being so selected, cannot even thus be robbed of all
their merit.   They serve at least to show that the
country gentleman was very much the same being in the
days of Overbury and of Addison, that the same model
sat to both artists.   But the invention of the art of
portrait-painting had been made meanwhile, and, in place
of the coarse and grotesque outlines of the early carica-
ture, the Coverley Papers furnish a living likeness of the
man, and endear him to their readers to such a point

that his death has at last to be announced (*Spectator*, No. 517) with all the circumstance of an overpowering affliction. "I question not," says Addison, "but my readers themselves will be troubled at the hearing of it." In that sentence he makes a claim for his own workmanship higher than any that could justly be advanced by all the prose novelists who had preceded him.

It is impossible, therefore, to omit all mention of the *Tatler* and *Spectator* in an account of the rise of the modern English novel. The leaflets composing the *Tatler* and *Spectator* are written from the standpoint of a great novelist, and abound in material which might well have been wrought into a great novel. For the great novelist must be essentially a humourist, just as the great romancer must be essentially a poet. And Addison and Steele, party men though they were, are born observers rather than born fighters; even irony, the most formidable of a humourist's weapons, becomes in their hands a pruning-hook rather than a sword. The temper of the *Spectator* is well defined in that paper (*Spectator*, No. 10) where the author recommends his writings especially to two classes of persons, to women, and to those who "have no other business with the rest of mankind, but to look upon them; . . . in short, every-one that considers the world as a theatre, and desires to form a right judgment of those who are the actors on it." The detached scenes, merry and pathetic, that are chosen from this theatre to furnish entertainment for "the fraternity of spectators" are so numerous and so exquisitely wrought as almost to suggest some regret that no novel dealing with the manners of the times of the later Stuarts and William of Orange has been or could be left by the creators of Sir Roger de Coverley. Many of the descriptions and reminiscences to be found in the *Spectator* serve to show what a wealth of material Addison could have brought to such a work, and what fine use he could have made of it. Some of his most delicate miniatures are drawn from reminiscences that he had doubtless heard in conversation. Of this kind is the account given in the *Spectator* (No. 57), of the call paid in former days by the author and Will Honeycomb on a lady who was an admirer of Dr. Titus Oates, and had the portrait of the Whig idol graven on her snuff-box lid, stamped on her handkerchiefs, painted on the sticks of her fan, and plentifully hung about the room. Another instance is to be found in the description of the young gentleman who wished to stand for a scholarship at one of the colleges of Oxford or Cambridge—for Addison does not specify—during the protectorate of Cromwell, and went to interview the head of the college, "a famous independent minister" of those times,—not improbably Goodwin of Magdalen, Oxford. Nothing could be better painted than this brief scene, where the youth, after having been ushered in by a gloomy servant and kept waiting in a long gallery, darkened at noonday, with a single candle burning in it, is at length led into a chamber hung with black, and confronted by the head of the college, "with half a dozen night caps upon his head, and religious horror in his countenance." The poor boy, who had expected to be tested in Latin and Greek, was so alarmed by these proceedings and by his subsequent examination, culminating in the dreadful interrogatory, " *Whether he were prepared for death?* " that, once safely emerged, he determined wholly to forego an academic education. No one can read this, or the multitude of scenes in the *Spectator* as vividly conceived and described, without perceiving what a novelist English literature would have had in Addison had the times been ripe for the novel. But the reading public had still to be educated, and the *Spectator*, with its circulation rising in comparatively few months from three thousand to thirty thousand copies, and with the host of imitators that it brought into being, not only trained the taste of its public in the direction of the novel, but increased the numbers of that public, until a man of letters could find money as well as fame in successful writing.

Such a man of letters was Daniel Defoe. His first great work of fiction, entitled *The Life and Strange Surprising Adventures of Robinson Crusoe, of York, Mariner* (1719), was written by him at the age of fifty-eight, and is stated, in the preface to the third part, to be an allegoric version of his own history—" of one whole scene of real life of eight and twenty years, spent in the most wandering, desolate, and afflicting circumstances that ever a man went through ; and in which I have lived so long a life of wonders, in continual storms ; fought with the worst kind of savages and man-eaters, by unaccountable surprising incidents ; fed by miracles greater than that of ravens ; suffered all manner of violences and oppressions, injuries, reproaches, contempt of men, attacks of devils, corrections from heaven, and oppositions on earth." No one reads *Robinson Crusoe* for the allegory, but a brief examination of the career of Defoe will not only lay bare the hidden meaning here claimed for the book, but also serve to demonstrate the way in which it came to be written. For Defoe was above all an occasional writer, by no means "long choosing and beginning late," but pouring from the press a profusion of satires, political pamphlets, verses, and moral treatises, to the number of more than two hundred, inspired by the moment and writing under a pressure that sometimes contorts his syntax.

Daniel Defoe, the son of James Foe citizen and butcher, was born in London in the year 1660 or 1661. After giving up the idea of becoming a Nonconformist minister, for which profession he had been educated, he was apprenticed to a hose-factor, and was very early drawn into the troublous politics of the time. He served under Monmouth, issued pamphlets on the principal questions that agitated the reign of James II., and welcomed William of Orange. During the reign of William he enjoyed some Government favour, and, although he was constantly in monetary troubles, was able to set up brick-kiln works at Tilbury, where he employed over a hundred workmen. It was during the High Church reaction after the death of William that Defoe wrote the pamphlet called *The Shortest Way with the Dissenters* (1702), which proved the turning-point of his literary career. In this pamphlet, purporting to be written by a Churchman, Defoe recommends that Dissenting preachers be hanged and their congregations banished, and argues that this is, in the end, the least cruel method of dealing with them, for "the poison of their nature makes it a charity to our neighbours to destroy those creatures . . . that are noxious."

It has become almost a habit with biographers of Defoe, while maintaining that the sentiments of the High Church party were not unjustly represented in this work, at the same time to declaim against the " obtuseness " of the men of both parties who took it for a genuine and serious composition, and missed the " exquisite irony " that it displays. But these positions are mutually destructive. Doubtless the High Churchmen had used strong language, and Sacheverell, in a sermon preached before the University of Oxford only a few months before, had said that every man that wished the welfare of the Church " ought to hang out the bloody flag and banner of defiance " against her enemies. But the real fact is, that Defoe's irony, if it can claim the title at all, is not the irony of a wit. Acting on his own expressed principle that " Lies are not worth a farthing if they are not calculated for the effectual deceiving of the people they are designed to deceive," Defoe produced a very realistic imitation of the High Church argument, faintly touched, perhaps, with exaggeration at places. It has never been made quite clear that his purpose was ironical at all ; he may well have meant to give an expression so clear and emphatic to the views of the extremists of the party as to alienate all moderate men from them, and so strengthen the cause of the Dissenters.

If this were so, he failed ; the authorship of his work was discovered, and the rage of his dupes, of both parties, broke upon him. He was condemned to stand in the pillory three times, to pay a fine of two hundred marks, and to be imprisoned during the Queen's pleasure. He was actually imprisoned for more than a year, during which time his business at Tilbury went to pieces, and his wife and six children were brought face to face with starvation.

From this time onward Defoe had to look mainly to his pen for support, and he played upon a public that had shown itself so ready to be deceived. The " obtuseness" that mistook *The Shortest Way* for a sincere utterance had ruined his fortunes, but it taught him where his strength as a writer lay. Those who had been the dupes of simulated argument could be made the more remunerative dupes of fictitious narration. And in the *True Relation of the Apparition of one Mrs. Veal, the next day after her death, to one Mrs. Bargrave at Canterbury, the 8th of September 1705, which Apparition recommends the perusal of Drelincourt's Book of Consolations against the Fear of Death* (1705), Defoe at last found his cue, and inaugurated that series of realistic fictions which was to close only with his death. Tradition has it that this preface to Drelincourt's book was written for a publisher who found himself with many unsaleable copies of the translation of the book on hand; certainly the ponderous original quarto, which inspired Tallemant des Réaux with more terror than the prospect of death itself, stood sadly in need of some such expert recommendation.

Sir Walter Scott, in his admirable analysis of the devices employed in this story to recommend it to the belief of readers, has pointed out the essentials of Defoe's plausible realism. The first of these is that the author himself, on whose veracity the whole structure depends,

K

should remain out of sight. Accordingly the account given is attributed to "a gentleman, a justice of the peace at Maidstone," and attested by "a very sober and understanding gentlewoman," who lives within a few doors of Mrs. Bargrave, and had the relation from her own lips. Defoe thus invents one character to attest the facts, and another to believe the first incapable of a lie. Further, he invents "a person with the reputation of a notorious liar" to say that Mrs. Bargrave's tale is all a cheat, but he is careful to add that Mrs. Bargrave had no possible interest in telling the story, for she has undergone on account of it much trouble and fatigue, without the gain of a single farthing. It would have required a reader with a hawk's eye and a detective's knowledge of human nature to be suspicious after this of the apparently innocent remark that "*Drelincourt's Book of Death* is, since this happened, brought up strangely." The ordinary reader becomes so interested in the opinion that Defoe's characters have of one another's veracity that he forgets to ask whether they exist.

The impartiality of the narrator is another characteristic of the piece. He gives all the circumstantial evidence corroborative of the story, but does not fail to point out flaws in its absolute cogency. The most important piece of evidence, however, is admittedly flawless. Mrs. Veal made her appearance only one day after her death, looking very well, and dressed in a silk gown, which, in the confidences of a two hours' interview, she admitted to be a scoured silk. When Mrs. Bargrave, in telling the story to one Mrs. Watson, came to this point, " You have seen her, indeed," cried Mrs. Watson, "for none knew but Mrs. Veal and myself that the gown was scoured; for," said she, "I helped her to make it up."

Yet another characteristic of the story would have been regarded, in the present day, as strong evidence of its credibility. The ghost is an uninteresting ghost, a dull, trivial ghost, a lob of spirits, that would have flatly disappointed the expectation of the Duchess of Malfy :—

> "O, that it were possible we might
> But hold some two days' conference with the dead!
> From them I should learn somewhat, I am sure,
> I never shall know here."

Mrs. Veal, when she has discharged her real mission by the remark that "Drelincourt had the clearest notions of death, and of the future state, of any who had handled that subject," and when she has added a few perfectly gratuitous advertisements of Mr. Norris's Poem on Friendship, Dr. Sherlock's book, and one or two others, has completely exhausted her inspiration. She thinks "Elysium" a curious name for heaven, but makes no new suggestion; she almost forgets that she is disembodied and must not drink tea; and, for the rest, her conversation is of her own appearance, the trinkets she had left at Dover, and the ten-pound annuity she enjoyed—which things, as Defoe is careful to remark, were so trifling, "and nothing of justice aimed at in their disposal," that Mrs. Bargrave can hardly have invented them. Defoe is thus seen to have appreciated the argument for the reality of a ghost from the folly and triviality of its behaviour.

He certainly appreciated the value of artlessness in

conciliating belief. His language is the language of an uneducated but honest witness in a court of justice who is asked to tell his story in his own way, and the very irrelevancies, repetitions, omissions made up later, and the like, subserve the main purpose—the engaging of belief. Had the thing been a product of art, the critic is apt to say, the writer would surely have spent a little trouble on obtaining some measure of artistic unity. But Defoe's narratives all aim at exhibiting the processes of memory, untouched by the shaping imagination. And unambitious though such an aim may be, it was perhaps a necessary exercise for the modern novel in its infancy.

In *Robinson Crusoe*, as Mr. Leslie Stephen remarks, artistic unity was imposed on Defoe by the very nature of his subject, while the greatest scope was given him for the effective introduction of realistic detail. In 1715 Defoe withdrew from political controversy, and *Robinson Crusoe* was the first of that series of tales that occupied his retired leisure at Stoke Newington. The extreme simplicity of the framework of this story was all in favour of Defoe's method. The problem of the story has some-times been stated thus—Given a man and a remote and desolate island to make an enthralling romance. But this is really an under-statement of the limitations of the story. For besides the limitations imposed by the subject, there were others not less stringent imposed by the hard, shrewd, practical nature of the man. In *Robinson Crusoe* there are no æsthetic descriptions of scenery, no use is made of the splendours and terrors of the sky and sea as they might affect a man in that overwhelming solitude : to Crusoe the island is his prison and nothing

more, his business is to make it comfortable ; he struggles
with Nature, but spends no unnecessary time or compliment upon his antagonist.   Strangely enough, upon that
tropical isle, where Enoch Arden would have watched—

> " The sunrise broken into scarlet shafts
>   Among the palms and ferns and precipices,"

the chief mental preoccupation of Crusoe is morality.
The tools and the Bible that have been saved from the
wreck represent the two sides of his life, the practical
and the religious, and it is only in the Bible that he finds
God.   Play of the imagination, figurative language, such
as tropical nature extorts from the veriest savages, there
is none.   Robinson Crusoe typifies the spirit of the
Anglo-Saxon race, and illustrates in epitome the part it
has played in India and America.   He keeps his house
in order, stores the runlets of rum, and converts Friday,
telling him that God is omnipotent, that he " could do
everything for us, give everything to us, take everything
from us."   Poor Friday believed in a Great Spirit, and
held that " All things say O to him "—an unpractical
view that receives no manner of notice from Crusoe,
who nevertheless reports their conversations, and honestly
admits that he was " run down to the last degree " by
some of Friday's theological arguments.

But the very deficiencies in the story of Crusoe, and
the imagination of Defoe, only gave the writer fuller
scope for the exhibition of his particular talent.   On a
blank canvas small splashes are striking, and Defoe
forces the reader to take the deepest interest in the
minutest affairs of the castaway.   It is a testimony to

the practical nature of childhood that the book is so widely regarded as the best boy's book in the world. When the story leaves the magic limits of the island, it must be said the interest flags; and at last, in the *Serious Reflections*, subjoined by an afterthought, it positively stagnates. But the main piece of original narrative is a masterpiece, and marks a new era in the writing of prose fiction.

It is a prevalent literary mania to seek for the " originals" of any great work in the quarry whence the stone was dug. Defoe's "original" is to be found in *A Voyage to the South Seas and round the World* (1712), by Captain Edward Cook. Captain Cook narrates the case of Alexander Selkirk, who was marooned on the island of Juan Fernandez from August 1704 to January 1709, and adds, "To hear of a man's living alone in a desert island seems to some very surprising, and they presently conclude he may afford a very agreeable narration of his life, when in reality it is the most barren subject that nature can afford. . . . We have a downright sailor whose only study was to support himself during his confinement, and all his conversation with goats. It would be no difficult matter to embellish a narrative with many romantic incidents to please the unthinking part of mankind, who swallow everything an artful writer thinks fit to impose upon their credulity, without any regard to truth or probability." Here a romance is suggested, but not the romance that Defoe wrote, for he makes it his rule to embellish nothing, and to avoid giving the reader anything at all to swallow. The actual life of Alexander Selkirk, as related in

Howell's *Life of Selkirk* (1829), has many romantic
incidents that are not to be found in *Robinson Crusoe*,
for Selkirk taught cats to dance, and, after his return to
his native parish of Largo, eloped with a lady. Defoe
limits himself to the simplest facts, and makes the most
barren parts of his subject interesting by the very sense
of expectation that so unprecedented a monotony awakes.

Defoe's later works include samples of the picaresque
romance, as *Moll Flanders* (1721), *Colonel Jack* (1722),
and *Roxana* (1724); of sham history, as the famous
Journal of the Plague Year (1722); and of treatises on
the supernatural, written with all his mathematical detail,
as *The Political History of the Devil* (1726), and the
Essay on the History and Reality of Apparitions (1727).
Of the reality of apparitions he is fully convinced. "I
must tell you, good people," he says, "he that is not
able to see the Devil, in whatever shape he is pleased
to appear in, is not really qualified to live in this world,
no, not in the quality of a common inhabitant." His
position is that of Glanvill, the great seventeenth-century
opponent of "Sadducism" and "Hobbism," who makes
the subtle remark that the enemy of mankind, "in order
to the carrying on the dark and hidden designs he
manageth against our happiness and our souls, cannot
expect to advantage himself more than by insinuating
a belief *that there is no such thing as himself.*" Or, to
put the idea in the statelier form it assumes in an earlier
work, the *Pseudodoxia Epidemica*, the devil "contriveth
many ways to conceal and indubitate his existency.
Wherein, beside that he annihilates the blessed angels
and spirits in the rank of his creation, he begets

a security of himself, and a careless eye unto the last remunerations." To the refutation of this scepticism Defoe again and again returns, but his dissertations upon the world of spirits are untouched by any real sense of mystery. The multitude of evil spirits who tempt mankind are little better than a ragged regiment of invisible spies and rogues, the good angels are only a superior kind of police. Defoe selects, in this as in so many other cases, a subject that Nash had treated before him, but the poetic imagination had fled the earth in the mean time; and the other world, described with statistical minuteness, is so like this one, that the reader finds himself wondering why there should be two.

The close simulation of the truth employed by Defoe to gain credence for the story of *Robinson Crusoe* was imitated by Swift to lend plausibility to the *Travels into Several remote Nations of the World by Lemuel Gulliver* (1726–1727). Imaginary voyages and travels cannot, for the most part, be regarded as pure romances; they have generally some ulterior purpose in view, political or satirical. Thus Sir Thomas More's *Utopia* (1516) pictures an ideal polity; Francis Godwin's *The Man in the Moon*, written before 1603, borrows its inspiration from Lucian; Bacon's fragment called *The New Atlantis* (1635) sets forth a scheme for the advancement of science; the Duchess of Newcastle's *Description of a New World, called the Blazing World* (1666), tells mechanical wonders of a fairy people living at the North Pole; the anonymous *Memoirs of Gaudentio di Lucca* (1737), by Simon Berington, describe an imaginary State conducted on philanthropic principles under a patriarchal government; and Swift's great work, after storming the outposts of human policy and human learning, breaks at last in a torrent of contempt and hatred on the last strong-hold of humanity itself. The strength of Swift's work as a contribution to the art of fiction lies in the portentous gravity and absolute mathematical consistency where-with he developes the consequences of his modest assumptions. In the quality of their realism the voyages to Lilliput and Brobdingnag are much superior to the two later and more violent satires: he was better fitted to ridicule the politics of his time than to attack the "men of Gresham," of whose true aims and methods he knew little or nothing; and the imagination stumbles at many of the details of the last book. But the wealth of illustration whereby he maintains the interest of his original conception of pigmies and giants is eternally surprising and delightful. Defoe could have made of Captain Lemuel Gulliver a living man; he, too, could have recorded with the minutest circumstance of date and place the misadventures and actions of his hero: it may well be doubted whether he could have carried into an unreal world that literalism, accuracy of pro-portion, and imaginative vividness of detail wherewith Swift endows it. The cat in Brobdingnag makes a noise in purring like "a dozen Stocking-weavers at work;" Gulliver is clad in clothes of the thinnest silk, "not much thicker than an English blanket, very cumbersome, till I was accustomed to them;" the sailing-boat wherein he shows his skill in navigation is taken, when he has done, and hung upon a nail to dry. These are the sources of the pleasure that children take in the book:

the astonishing strokes of savage satire that are its chief
attraction for their elders derive most of their force from
the imperturbable innocence and quietude of manner
that disarms suspicion.   Like Iago, Gulliver is a fellow
"of exceeding honesty," and he goes about his deadly
work the better for his bluntness and scrupulous pretence of veracity.   But the design of the book forbids
its classification among works of pure fiction ; it is
enough to remark that in *Gulliver* realism achieved
one of the greatest of its triumphs before its ultimate
conquest of the novel.

The novels produced by lesser writers contemporary
with Defoe and Swift are belated examples of Restoration
literature, and have little infusion of the new spirit.
Two women novelists, Mrs. Manley and Mrs. Haywood,
may be classed as imitators of Mrs. Aphra Behn.   Swift
alludes to both, only to call Mrs. Haywood a "stupid,
infamous, scribbling woman," and to record his impression
that Mrs. Manley kept about two thousand epithets in a
bag, and spilled them at random on her pages.   The
works by which chiefly they gained notoriety are petty
chronicles of scandal, deriving their main interest from
the thinly veiled identity of the characters introduced.
The New Atalantis (1709) of Mrs. Manley, and the
Memoirs of a certain Island adjacent to Utopia (1725) of
Mrs. Haywood, can hardly claim to be considered as
examples of the art of fiction, for the readers they attracted sought in them a record of fact.   Interest in
individuals, that interest so much lacking in the "Character" writings of the seventeenth century, is here, no
doubt, to be found in full measure, but unillumined by

any semblance of eternity, the gift of art. Mrs. Manley wrote also *The Power of Love, in seven Novels* (1720), and Mrs. Haywood published a whole tribe of short stories, such as *The British Recluse* (1722), *Idalia, or the Unfortunate Mistress* (1723), *Philidore and Placentia* (1727). These short stories are akin to the comedies of the Restoration, but destitute of the glitter and life of the Restoration stage. Mrs. Haywood's best novels, *The History of Miss Betsy Thoughtless* (1751) and *The History of Jemmy and Jenny Jessamy* (1753), were written at a time when the art of the novelist had been new-created by Richardson, Fielding, and Smollett, so that they are separated by more than time from her earlier and briefer efforts. Some faint idea of the magnitude of the revolution that intervened might be gathered from a comparison of Miss Betsy with one of the heroines of the earlier tales, as, for instance, Placentia. Miss Betsy is all of the new world; she is own cousin to Roderick Random, and has been taken for an ancestor of Evelina; Placentia, a quarter of a century older, is a kinswoman of Clelia and Parthenissa, whom she exactly resembles in life, in love, and in epistolary style,—only differing for the better in the brevity and dramatic symmetry of her history. Mrs. Haywood is a good specimen of that third-rate kind of author that multiplies the faint echoes of a literary success, and writes novels, as an oriental tailor makes garments, to a ready-made pattern, with dexterity and despatch. Her pre-Richardsonian work deserves mention, but it could teach nothing at all to the new novel that was so soon to supplant it.

CHAPTER VI.

RICHARDSON AND FIELDING.

In one or other of the various literary forms dealt with in the last chapter, almost all the characteristic features of the modern novel are to be found. Yet the novel was slow to arise. For many years after the appearance of the masterly sketches and tales of the *Tatler* and *Spectator*, writers were content to imitate these more or less exactly in the literary journals of the day, and to seek for no more ambitious development. It was not until years after Madame de la Fayette had created a new era in French fiction by her novel *La Princesse de Clèves* (1678), not until years after Marivaux by his *Vie de Marianne* (1731) had singularly anticipated Richardson in subject and treatment, although, so far as can be ascertained, without influencing him, that the English *Pamela* was born in 1740.*

The reason of the delay is not hard to assign. New literary forms, although they are invented by the genius of authors, have a success strictly conditioned by the taste of the public. It is not likely that any professional

---

* It seems likely that Richardson had read *The Life of Marianne, with continuation by Mad. Riccoboni*, which appeared in three volumes, 12mo, in 1736.

writer will trouble himself to strike out a new path while
the old paths lead to fame and fortune. And the fact
is that it was the decline of the theatre during the earlier
part of the eighteenth century that made way for the
novel. The drama no longer made any pretence of
holding the mirror up to Nature, the audiences had no
claim to be considered representative of the tastes of the
wider literary public. The fashionable ladies of the
time, as Fielding says in one of his farces, would " take a
stage-box, where they let the footman sit the first two
acts, to show his livery, then they come in to show
themselves, spread their fans upon the spikes, make
curtsies to their acquaintance, and then talk and laugh
as loud as they are able." To the upper gallery the
footmen and servants of the great had free access, and
they imitated their masters in regarding a civil attention
to the actors as the last resource of a jaded mind. In
the pit were assembled the only serious critics of the
play, young templars and city merchants, but their tastes
were little likely to redeem the drama from the triviality
to which it had sunk.

Nevertheless authors had learnt to regard theatrical
success as the crown of literary ambition, and they were
slow to unlearn the lesson. Steele and Addison, at the
very time when by their literary criticisms they were
educating the public to distaste the plays that held the
stage, while by their prose sketches of life and manners
they were showing themselves true followers of Shakespeare, though at a distance, could not rest content
without trying their fortunes also on the stage. Addison's
tragedy of *Cato* (1713) was for factitious reasons a

success; Steele, who had an earlier play "damned for its piety," persevered in the drama until in the *Conscious Lovers* (1722) he produced a comedy that succeeded indeed, but left no issue. And Fielding himself, in spite of the competition of pantomime, spectacle, and opera, for almost ten years kept himself alive by dramatic authorship until the Licensing Act of 1737 curbed his satirical energies, and the unexampled success of *Pamela* in 1740 directed them into a new channel.

The particular tastes that the novel was to satisfy were now no longer catered for by the drama. A small part only of the new reading public were in the habit of going to the theatre, while, on the other hand, the standard plays of the older dramatists had never before had so many readers. The habit of reading plays is curiously illustrated in Richardson's *Sir Charles Grandison*, where Miss Byron, writing to Miss Selby, says, " I know, my dear, you love to read plays," and so excuses herself for writing her narrative in dramatic form with the speakers' names recorded in the margin. In his two later novels Richardson gives a list of the *dramatis personæ* in the beginning, under the heading, " Names of the Principal Persons." It is as if the novel were merely a play with its framework of stage directions expanded for the ease of the reader. And in this form the novel was bound to supplant the play with the reading public. To read a play with full intelligence is at all times difficult for an untrained reader, and the law of least possible effort can be as effectively illustrated from literature as from language. A new form of literature that had all the interest of the drama, but imposed only the slenderest

tax on the reader's attention and imagination, was pre-
destined to success.

It was not a professional writer that made the discovery
of such a new form, but a short, stout, prim, pedantic
bookseller and printer, aged fifty-one, whose excursions
into literature had hitherto been of the slightest—a few
prefaces and dedications, contributed at the request of
others.   In these, however, he had displayed some
literary facility, and Messrs. Rivington and Osborne,
two booksellers who were his particular friends, pressed
him to write a little book " of familiar letters on the
useful concerns in common life."   It was in the course
of preparing this that Samuel Richardson bethought
him of a story, told him by a friend, of a young girl, the
daughter of honest and pious parents, who had been
taken into the service of a great family, had had snares
laid for her honour by her employer's son, "a young
gentleman of free principles," but had subdued him by
her noble resistance, so that at last "he thought fit to
make her his wife."   This incident running in Richardson's head suggested to him the inclusion of a few letters
giving cautions "to young folks circumstanced as Pamela
was," and these few letters grew under his hand until
they filled the book and became nothing other than the
first modern novel.

The account Richardson gave to his friend Aaron Hill
of the inception of the book shows that before it was
completed he had become conscious that he was intro-
ducing "a new species of writing."   His hope was, he
says, that it "might possibly turn young people into a
course of reading different from the pomp and parade

of romance writing, and dismissing the improbable and marvellous, with which novels generally abound, might tend to promote the cause of religion and virtue." And so it came about that a book, the original design of which bore about as much relation to literature as the tunes of a piano-organ bear to music, became when completed the ancestor of a literary progeny like the sands of the sea for number.

Richardson's early life had been in some sort a training for the work on which he was to start so late. His father was a joiner, and a friend of Shaftesbury and Monmouth. Probably he was one of the "brisk boys" that ran behind Shaftesbury's coach in London; at any rate, on the failure of Monmouth's attempt on the throne he "was looked on with a jealous eye," and thought proper on the "decollation," as Richardson phrases it, of that unhappy nobleman, "to quit his London business and retire to Derbyshire, though to his great detriment."

In Derbyshire Samuel Richardson was born in 1689, and received a very slight education, learning no language save his own. His schoolfellows, who nicknamed him *Serious* and *Gravity*, used to press him to tell them stories. "One of them particularly, I remember, was for putting me to write a history. . . . I now forget what it was, only that it was of a servant-man preferred by a fine young lady (for his goodness) to a lord, who was a libertine. All my stories carried with them, I am bold to say, an useful moral."

The same highly moral tendency is seen in the fact that before he was eleven years old he assumed a censor's duties by writing a letter to a widow lady of fifty, collecting from the Scripture "texts that made against her," and contrasting her pretensions to religion with her habits of slander and gossip.

His precocity of sentiment was hardly less. "As a bashful and not forward boy," he says, "I was an early favourite with all the young women of taste and reading in the neighbourhood." They would sew while he read aloud to them, and "both mothers and daughters used to be pleased with the observations they put me upon making." When he was only thirteen, three of these young women revealed to him their love secrets, and induced him to write model letters for them to alter as they pleased in copying. "I have been directed to chide, and even repulse, when an offence was either taken or given, at the very time that the heart of the chider or repulser was open before me, overflowing with esteem and affection."

This apprenticeship to the knowledge of the human heart stood Richardson the novelist in good stead. He was intended by his father for the Church, but the necessary education was out of his reach, and in 1706 he was bound apprentice to Mr. John Wilde of Stationers' Hall, whose daughter, after the manner of all good apprentices, he subsequently married. He set up business for himself, at first in Fleet Street, afterwards in Salisbury Court; throve apace, got the printing of the Journals of the House of Commons, and became in 1754 Master of the Stationers' Company. By this time he was a famous man, his novels all were written—for *Clarissa Harlowe* appeared in 1748 and *Sir Charles Grandison* in 1753—and his later years, though troubled by failing

L

health, were spent in the midst of the grateful incense that rose from the circle of admirers with which he surrounded himself. He died in 1761.

The character of Richardson deserves all the praise it has received from his biographer, Mrs. Barbauld. His integrity and industry were unfailing, and in material affairs he was generous, but his extreme vanity made him repellent to all but professed devotees, and the pusillanimity with which Johnson charged him, "the perpetual study to ward off petty inconveniences and to procure petty pleasures," is to be seen in his works in that attention to the infinitely little which is their weakness and their strength. He was formal, passionless, and unsympathetic. When he was young his seniors confided in him, but in his later years his stiffness alienated his juniors; "my girls," he said, "are shy little fools." The famous council that criticized and applauded the drafts of his later novels consisted almost entirely of women, and included Miss Mulso, afterwards Mrs. Chapone, and the sisters of Henry Fielding. At North End, Hammersmith, he lived in "a kind of flower-garden of ladies," and so became a singular example of an author whose heroines speak better and more naturally than his heroes. It may be doubted whether he ever fathomed the secrets of the male heart.

Richardson has left a portrait of himself in the description he wrote for Lady Bradshaigh, who worshipped him from afar—

"Short; rather plump than emaciated, notwithstanding his complaints; about five foot five inches; fair wig; lightish cloth coat, all black besides; one hand generally

in his bosom, the other a cane in it, which he leans upon
under the skirts of his coat usually, that it may imper-
ceptibly serve him as a support when attacked by sudden
tremors or startings, and dizziness which too frequently
attack him, but, thank God, not so often as formerly;
looking directly foreright, as passers-by would imagine,
but observing all that stirs on either hand of him without
moving his short neck; hardly ever turning back; of
a light-brown complexion; teeth not yet failing him;
smoothish-faced and ruddy-cheeked; at some times looking to be about sixty-five, at other times much younger;
a regular even pace, stealing away ground, rather than
seeming to rid it; a grey eye, too often overclouded by
mistinesses from the head: by chance lively, very lively
it will be, if he have hope of seeing a lady whom he loves
and honours; his eye always on the ladies; if they have
very large hoops he looks down and supercilious, and as
if he would be thought wise, but perhaps the sillier for
that; as he approaches a lady his eye is never fixed first
upon her face, but upon her feet, and thence he raises it
up, pretty quickly for a dull eye; and one would think
(if we thought him at all worthy of observation) that
from her air and (the last beheld) her face, he sets her
down in his mind as *so* or *so*, and then passes on to the
next object he meets."

It is necessary, in passing from the man to his novels,
to say something first about the method of telling a story
by way of letters—a method that Richardson hit upon
almost by accident, but which he continued in his later
novels from choice.   Of the three ways most in vogue
for telling a story, it has been perhaps the least popular,

but it is not hard to see that it suited Richardson's matter and style the best.

The first and most usual way is that the author should tell the story directly. He is invisible and omniscient, a sort of *diable boiteux*, who is able to unroof all houses and unlock all hearts, and who can never be questioned as to how he came to a knowledge of the events he narrates. There are stories that can be told in no other way than this; the favourite way of Fielding, Scott, Dickens, and Thackeray. At a slight sacrifice of dramatic force the events of the story are supplied with a chorus, and at any time that suits him the author can cast off his invisible cloak and show himself fingering the "helpless pieces of the game he plays."

The second method, the chosen expedient of Marivaux, Goldsmith, and Prévost, is to put the whole story in the mouth of the principal character. The realism of Swift and Defoe adopted this method, which gives at once a dramatic centre and a certain unity to the events narrated, from their bearing on the fortunes of one person. For the intense presentment of the main character, as in Charlotte Brontë's *Jane Eyre* or *Villette*, this way remains perhaps the best. Yet it has its difficulties and its pitfalls; every incident of the story must be brought within the knowledge of the narrator; and although the single point of view is valuable to evoke sympathy, it takes from the novelist the privilege of killing his hero, who may be condemned to death without awakening in the reader the slightest anxiety as to his safety in the event. Moreover, if the story extend over a number of years, a detailed account of its earlier

parts can only be given by sacrificing the sense of vivid
and present reality that attends the hearing of a personal
story told by a living voice; the sense of perspective
and contrast is lost, the near becomes far and the far
near, the narrator is forgotten in the actor.   Coleridge,
in his *Ancient Mariner*, gives perhaps the most consummate illustration of the artistic value of present circumstances as a frame for past events; Defoe, in the
intricate maze of his story, is apt to forget the actual
speaker.

In employing a third way, and telling his story by a
series of letters, Richardson endeavours to combine the
advantages of both these methods, to retain the vividness
of personal narration by an eye-witness without sacrificing
the freedom and omniscience of the impersonal author.
For sentimental analysis, in which he excelled, his device
served him well; the microscopic minuteness which he
loved seems less unnatural in a letter written an hour
after the events described than in a story told perhaps
some forty years after.   But he takes little advantage of
the scope that is afforded by his method for variety of
characters and styles, and he does not succeed in evading
the difficulty caused by the fact that the whole of life
does not naturally find its way into letters.   In order to
supply some one to whom the heroine of each of his
novels shall communicate her most intimate feelings, he
is obliged to revive an old stage device, and Tilburina,
in white satin, is attended by her "confidant" in white
linen.   The worthy Pamela, it is true, writes only to
her parents, who take singularly little interest in her
misfortunes, but Clarissa has the invaluable and lively

Miss Howe, and Harriet Byron exercises her absurdly exact memory on the long-suffering Miss Selby, writing, according to the computation of Mr. Leslie Stephen, in the space of three days as much as would fill one hundred and forty-four pages of octavo print. And dramatic propriety stands aghast at the confidences that pass between Mr. Robert Lovelace and his friend Mr. John Belford.

And yet these are hardly defects in Richardson, for they are the very foundation of his art. To spend hours in narrating her most trifling experiences, and recording her most casual conversations, may well be said to make a lady appear small-minded, but how shall those who have followed her story with unflagging interest be the first to make the accusation? Richardson has had not a few readers who smiled, perhaps contemptuously, but continued to read. His power of analysis lies chiefly in this, that no detail is beneath his attention. It is the exact function of the microscope; the commonplace becomes interesting, not by its setting, not by the glamour lent to it by the imagination of a poet, but merely because it is magnified and made novel by detail previously unperceived. Nor are there wanting subtle touches, rapid and minute, that lay bare the very hearts of his characters. Thus Pamela, when she has escaped from her master, receives a humble letter from him asking her to come back. For a moment she is inclined to consent, but remembering his repeated perfidies and cruelties, she ponders her impulse and argues against it : "Therefore will I not acquit thee yet, O credulous, fluttering, throbbing mischief! that art so ready to believe what thou wishest; and I charge thee to keep better

guard than thou hast lately done, and tempt me not to
follow too implicitly thy flattering impulses! Thus
foolishly dialogued I with my heart, and yet all the time,
that heart was Pamela."

By his power in sentimental analysis it was that
Richardson earned the famous eulogy of Diderot, who
gives him a place in his esteem beside Moses, Homer,
and Euripides. And the main interest of Richardson's
persons has never been better expressed than in Diderot's
words, "Ils sont communs, dites-vous (ces personnages);
c'est ce qu'on voit tous les jours? Vous vous trompez,
c'est ce qui se passe tous les jours sous vos yeux et que
vous ne voyez jamais." And Johnson laid stress on the
same quality when he said that there was more knowledge of the human heart in one letter of Richardson's
than in all *Tom Jones.*

More dissection of the human heart, a fuller display of
its processes, there certainly is. But Fielding set before
himself models of epic breadth, while Richardson shows
the defects of his qualities in the extreme slowness of his
dramatic development. The events recorded in the eight
volumes of *Clarissa* occupy eleven months. In *Sir
Charles Grandison* the story is arrested while the characters are displayed, contrasting their thoughts, plans,
and sentiments. And there is an incessant doubling
back on what has gone before; first a letter is written
describing what "has passed," this letter is communicated
by its recipient to a third character, who comments on it,
while the story waits. This constant repercussion of a
theme or event between one or more pairs of correspondents produces a structure of story very like *The*

House that Jack Built. Each writer is narrating not events alone, but his or her reflections on previous narrations of the same events. And so, on the next-to-nothing that happened there is superimposed the young lady that wrote to her friend describing it, the friend that approved her for the decorum of the manner in which she described it, the admirable baronet that chanced to find the letter approving the decorum of the young lady, the punctilio of honour that prevented the admirable baronet from reading the letter he found, and so on. It is very lifelike, but life can become at times a slow affair, and one of the privileges of the novel-writer is to quicken it. This privilege Richardson foregoes. Any one reading *Sir Charles Grandison* at a leisurely pace (it cannot be read fast) must be particularly happy in having no history if he has not lived through more events than he has read through by the time he comes to the end of it. As Johnson again said, " If you were to read Richardson for the story, your impatience would be so much fretted that you would hang yourself. But you must read him for the sentiment, and consider the story only as giving occasion to the sentiment."

There remains to be considered the feature of Richardson's work on which he most valued himself, and which attracted the enthusiastic applause of his contemporaries —its morality. He looked on himself as a moral reformer, and in the preface to *Pamela* he sets forth a portentous list of the " desirable ends " that are " attained within these sheets." By Johnson once more his especial praise is thus summarized : " He has enlarged the knowledge of human nature, and taught the passions to move at the command of virtue."

How his microscope enlarged the knowledge of human
nature has already been shown, but what shall be said
of his success in this loftier exploit? He did not himself think it difficult. In speaking of the lady Clementina, in *Sir Charles Grandison*, a lady who had conceived
a passion for that monster of perfection, whom her
religion forbade her to marry, Richardson excuses himself for implying, towards the close of the novel, that
she marries some one else by saying to one of his correspondents, "I want to have young people think that
there is no such mighty business as they are apt to
suppose in conquering a first love." The passions are
not really very formidable, it seems ; virtue has only to
pipe to them, and they dance the most decorous of con-
certed jigs. And yet the reader, who had expected to
see the lion-tamer go into the den and subdue the raging
animals with a glance, is somehow disappointed when
it is shown to be so easy, and begins to entertain
suspicions that the beasts are stuffed. And the virtue
that subdues them is of no heroic mould. At its worst
and crudest Richardson's conception of virtue is merely
"tickling commodity," an injunction to buy in the
cheapest and sell in the dearest market ; at its best, in
Clarissa, it is far too negative in quality, a sort of show-
man leading his perfectly tamed passions from place to
place. Of a virtue that should inflame the higher, rather
than allay the lower, passions, he had little or no idea.

In *Pamela or Virtue Rewarded* the prudential doctrine
appears in its earliest and most disgusting form. The
main plot has already been indicated ; Pamela's virtue is
rewarded by the success of her scheme to marry the

man who has heaped on her every indignity that sub-humanity could suggest. But he is wealthy and has position, and the original story, in two volumes, closes with a scene of benediction, Pamela's pious parents thanking Heaven that their daughter has laid to heart their early precepts. Two more volumes were after-wards added by Richardson to assuage the fears of those who were not quite easy about the fate of the heroine. In these Pamela "reforms" her husband, and shows herself a model matron in high life.

In *Sir Charles Grandison* there is described Richard-son's beau-ideal of manly virtue. He was moved to write the book by the complaints of those who urged on him that "Mr. B.," Pamela's persecutor, and Lovelace, the chief male characters of the two earlier novels, were both villains, and that it was his duty to give to the world the picture of a true hero, for its admiration and imita-tion. The vanity of Richardson fell into the trap, and in Sir Charles Grandison he designed a man of large fortune, high birth, and perfect breeding, who unites in himself all possible accomplishments, and all the virtues hitherto invented. Sir Charles Grandison's ready bene-volence undertakes the most diverse tasks,—setting up a poor family in life, rescuing a distressed lady from a man of title who is carrying her off by force, making considerate alterations in the structure of his own paternal mansion, and finding a wife for his gouty old uncle. In his youth he is sent abroad to travel on the Continent, and meantime his father dies. He hurries home to console his sisters, and appears,—"a graceful youth of seventeen with fine curling auburn locks waving on his shoulders, delicate in complexion, intelligence sparkling in his fine free eyes, and good-humour sweetening his lively features." This is the sort of language he holds,—"'What I think to do, cousin,' said Sir Charles, 'is to inter the venerable remains (I must always speak in this dialect, sir), with those of my mother. This I know was his desire. I will have an elegant, but not sumptuous monument erected to the memory of both, with a modest inscription that shall rather be a matter of instruction to the living than a panegyric on the departed. The difference in the expense shall be privately applied to relieve or assist distressed house-keepers, or some of my father's poor tenants who have large families, and have not been wanting in their honest endeavours to maintain them. My sisters, I hope, will not think themselves neglected if I spare them the pain of conferring with them on a subject that must afflict them.'"

He keeps his word; throughout the book he speaks in this dialect and maintains this insufferable bearing. He is never subjected to the trials of Job, or of the Vicar of Wakefield. Wealthy, accomplished, universally beloved, with the smoke of devotion and flattery ascending to him from scores of grateful and adoring hearts, he passes through life, bestowing pleasure with a smile, causing pain and remorse with a sigh, improving the occasion at all times, until the reader is seized with a blind desire to enact the part of the adversary, to tear him from place and power and set him to earn his living.

He is more than once challenged to a duel. He

disapproves of duelling, but so skilled is he with the rapier that he can disarm any adversary by a turn of the wrist and let him depart unharmed.

The tribe of women who surround him with adulation attribute his hesitation to marry to his delicate consideration for the hearts that would thus be desolated and deprived of their hope. " He called me *his* Emily," says his ward, Miss Jervois, " but all the world is his Emily, I think." " He is in all instances," says Miss Harriet Byron, who is also at his feet, " an imitator of the Almighty, an humbler of the impenitent and encourager of those who repent." In recounting his good deeds Miss Byron says, " Here I laid down my pen and wept for joy, I think it was for joy that there is such a young man in the world, for what else could it be? And now, with a watery eye, twinkle, twinkle, do I resume it."

Sir Charles's matrimonial affairs form the main interest of the story. It is hardly necessary to say that he does no wooing, but he debates with himself for long to which of two ladies he is the better justified, on moral considerations, in throwing the handkerchief. At last he is safely married to Miss Harriet Byron, who has long been receiving letters of condolence from her connection on the hopeless passion for him that, to her own great horror, she both cherishes and divulges, and there follow two more books of dresses and fêtes.

In the effort to construct an ideally perfect character no man can build better than he knows ; his own conceptions of honour and virtue are inevitably laid bare. Sir Charles meets with no very terrible temptations, but

his conduct is open more than once to the severest
criticisms.   When he is interviewing the Signora Clementina on the matter of the religious difficulties that attend
their suggested marriage, her father and mother, the
Marquis and Marchioness della Porretta, conceal themselves in a cupboard hard by and overhear the conversation.   This would hardly have commended itself as an
honourable course of action to the workmen in Richardson's back-shop,—but since in this book Richardson
classifies his characters as "men, women, and Italians,"
let it be regarded as an eccentricity of Italians, and
excused.   The interview ended, the marchioness con-
gratulates Sir Charles on the perfectly honourable way
in which he has acquitted himself.   He feels no indignation, and when he is again to see Clementina, himself
suggests to the marchioness that she had better get back
into the cupboard.   This she does, and the interview
takes place, Sir Charles being aware that all that they
say is overheard, while the lady is unaware.   It would
be edifying to have the opinion of Tom Jones on this
particular line of conduct.   That sturdy youth would
not be likely to share the sentiments of Cowper's Muse,
who professes that—

> " She cannot reach and would not wrong
>   That subject for an angel's song,
>   The hero and the saint ! "

Nevertheless, as a book, *Sir Charles Grandison* is full
of delight.   It is more elaborately constructed than
either of the other novels, and shows a keen dramatic
sense of situation at times.   The first appearance of Sir
Charles as the deliverer of Miss Byron from the evil Sir

Hargrave Pollexfen, is admirably led up to and contrived. The comedy, which is mainly in the capable hands of Miss Charlotte Grandison, is livelier than might have been expected. And Miss Byron at her best is a charming companion.

Richardson's three novels form a trilogy of a kind, and deal respectively with humble life, with middle-class life, and with high life. In the second of these, *Clarissa Harlowe*, he achieved his masterpiece. There are here none of the unrelated digressions, episodes, and by-plots that are to be found in *Sir Charles;* the story is developed with a leisurely but unrelenting progress from beginning to end. The plot is well known ; how Lovelace, having paid his addresses to Clarissa and having been rejected by her family, induces her to escape from the persecution to which she is subjected at home by casting herself into his hands and trusting to his honourable protection. From this point, early in the story, Richardson is at ease in his theme, and deploys his minute method with really marvellous effect. Clarissa's troubles thicken and darken around her, and through them all, her fortitude and virtue are made to shine brighter and brighter until the end ; Clarissa dies, overwhelmed by her sorrows, and Lovelace falls in a duel with Colonel Morden, the avenger of her death. Nothing in fiction is more impressive than the deliberation with which Richardson carries his story forward to its inevitable end. That end is long foreseen by the reader, but he is not permitted to quicken his step to meet the impending doom. With all the circumspect attention to detail that Clarissa shows in the preparations for her own funeral, without any hurry or any discomposure, the author leads on the story; and in this way chiefly makes his strength and his restraint felt. His restraint is well seen in the description of the death of Lovelace, where inappreciative critics have asked for more horrors, and in his neglect of all appeals to reprieve Clarissa and reform Lovelace. "Virtue Rewarded" he had already treated in *Pamela;* the theme of Clarissa might rather be called "Virtue Triumphant," and in the treatment of this he knew that a happy ending is also a futile ending.

The character of Clarissa, her strength, patience, and gentleness in suffering, is perhaps rather heightened by her weaknesses, her irresolution and want of decision in action. In the earlier part of the story she wails greatly about the "multitude of punctilios and decorums which a young creature must dispense with" in a situation like hers, the inadequacy of her wardrobe oppresses her, and the dread of the indecorous in whatever form prevents her from taking any firm resolve even when she is appealed to by Lovelace,—she weeps and is silent, accepts his protection and calls him a wretch, and so is driven by circumstance from first to last. Her efforts to escape are feeble and seem almost half-hearted. Yet those critics are ill advised who call for the police, asserting that an appeal to the nearest magistrate would have put an end to the heroine's difficulties. Richardson's story and characters would be alike spoilt by the intrusion of probability and realism. He placed himself, says Coleridge, "as it were in a day-dream;" his atmosphere is that of " a sick-room heated by stoves," while Fielding carries

his reader "into an open lawn on a breezy day in May."
Let each be judged after his kind : to break the glass of
Richardson's hothouse and let in the common air would
only be to kill the tropical plants that he has grown
under those fostering limitations ; his characters live in
a sick-room, but they would die in the open air. Any
one who has once learnt to breathe in those confines
must feel the beauty and charm of the sentimental
growths that there luxuriate ; a detached scene from
Clarissa may jar on the critical sense, but read through,
the book carries the reader clear of daily life, creates
its own canons, and compels intent admiration. Lady
Mary Wortley Montagu was one of the severest of
Richardson's critics,—she said rightly that he had no
idea of the manners of high life. She disliked the voluminous candour of his heroines, and could not forgive
him his disrespect for old china,—"which is below
nobody's taste." Yet she fell under the spell of his
sentiment ; "I heartily despise him," she says, "and
eagerly read him, nay, sob over his works, in a most
scandalous manner."

It was by his sentiment that Richardson gained an
immediate and enduring popularity, and became the
founder of a school of novelists. Not in England
alone, where "Sentiment" soon became the badge of
a tribe of writers, but on the Continent, especially in
France, *Pamela* and her sisters exercised a profound
influence, the end of which is not very easily assigned.
The novels were translated into French (one translation
is by the author of *Manon Lescaut*), German, and Dutch ;
Goldoni in Italy wrote two comedies called *Pamela*

Nubile and *Pamela Maritata;* Wieland's tragedy, *Clemen-
tine von Poretta,* and Hermes' novel, *Miss Fanny Wilkes,*
are after the same model, parodied by Musæus in
Grandison der Zweite; and the independent works of
Rousseau (*La Nouvelle Héloise*), Diderot (*La Religieuse*),
Marmontel, and Bernardin de St. Pierre show unmistak-
able marks either in form or in substance of the sentimental sway exercised by Richardson, which continued
in France down to the time when Alfred de Musset
called *Clarissa* "le premier roman du monde." Thus
Richardson is to be regarded not only as the founder
of the modern novel in England, but also as in some
sense the forerunner of all those writers who cultivated
"sensibility," well defined by Mrs. Radcliffe as "a
dangerous quality which is continually extracting the
excess of misery or delight from every surrounding
object,"—the inaugurator of a century and a half of
hyperæsthesia.

A perfect chorus of applause greeted *Pamela* on her
first appearance. "I can send you no news," wrote
Horace Walpole in a juvenile letter; "the late singular
novel is the universal, and only theme—Pamela is like
snow, she covers everything with her whiteness." Yet
there were not lacking a few dissentient voices. The
pretentious morality of the book, lauded by Dr. Sherlock
from his pulpit, and by Pope from his easy-chair, was
of a kind to invite burlesque. As early as 1741, a
burlesque appeared, entitled *An Apology for the Life of
Mrs. Shamela Andrews,* by an anonymous writer. And
by February, 1742, "a lewd and ungenerous engraft-
ment," as Richardson calls it, on the story of the

M

virtuous servant-maid was published under the title
*The History of the Adventures of Joseph Andrews and his
Friend Mr. Abraham Adams.*

This novel, which became the starting-point of a new
school of fiction, was written by Henry Fielding, barrister,
journalist, and playwright, whose early education and
experience of life were little likely to leave him susceptible
to serious impression by the vulgar morality of Richardson. Born in 1707 at Sharpham Park, near Glastonbury,
the seat of his maternal grandfather, descended through
his father, Edmund Fielding, from a younger branch of
the Earls of Denbigh, Henry Fielding had seen much
of men and manners, and was familiar with all classes
of society before he reached the age of thirty-four. He
was prepared for Eton by one Mr. Oliver, who, if he
was indeed the original of Parson Trulliber, "could have
acted the part of Falstaff without stuffing," had a loud
and hoarse voice, and "a stateliness in his gait when he
walked, not unlike that of a goose, only he stalked
slower." About the time of his leaving Eton, while
Richardson was accumulating the stock of morality that
was to be compounded in that specific against elope-
ments, *Clarissa,* Fielding was meditating an elopement
on his own account with a Miss Sarah Andrew, whose
guardian complained that he went in fear of his life
"owing to the behaviour of Henry Fielding and his
attendant or man." Foiled in this project, Fielding
passed over to Leyden to study law with "the learned
Vitriarius," but his remittances from home failing, he
returned to London in 1728, to maintain himself in that
city by his wits. His father, who had married a second

time, did not trouble himself to pay the allowance of
two hundred a year, and Fielding, it would appear,
troubled himself even less. He had already at Leyden
laid the plan of a comedy called *Don Quixote in
England*, and he now turned to the stage for his
livelihood.

Fielding's dramatic labours have been almost eclipsed
by his greater novels; yet he was an industrious and
successful dramatic author from the production of his
first comedy, *Love in Several Masques*, in 1728, down to
his abandonment of the stage and admission to the
Middle Temple after the appearance of his satirical play,
The Historical Register for 1736, and the passing of the
Licensing Act.

In Fielding the stage had found a great humourist and
comic wit, but it failed to keep him, and the reasons are
not far to seek. The dramatic conventions and fashions
of the time gave him too little scope. Vanbrugh and
Congreve, as he remarks in *Tom Jones*, copied Nature,
the comedy writers of his own time only copied them,
and so produced imitations of manners and satires on
foibles that no longer reigned in the fashionable world.
In one of his most successful plays, *The Tragedy of
Tragedies; or, the Life and Death of Tom Thumb the
Great* (1731), Fielding had parodied the extravagances
of Lee, Rowe, Thomson, and Young. But the theme
was soon exhausted, and he sought more scope for the
representation of contemporary life by plunging into
political satire in *Pasquin* (1736), and *The Historical
Register* (1737), in which candidates for Parliament are
introduced bribing away "with right and left," and Sir

Robert Walpole himself is represented under the guise of Quidam, a fiddler, superintending a ballet of Patriots. In the preface to the latter of these two plays, Fielding promised to continue exerting his talents "in ridiculing vice and imposture . . . while the liberty of the press and stage subsists, that is to say, while we have any liberty left among us."

It was not to be long. The same year a bill limiting the number of theatres, and submitting all plays to the approval of the Lord Chamberlain, became law, and Fielding, who was married by this time, turned to the Bar and journalism for his support. He was called to the Bar in 1740, some four or five months only before the appearance of *Pamela* gave him the opportunity for a wider and deeper comedy than could maintain itself on the stage of the time.

In the history of Joseph Andrews, the virtuous serving-man, Fielding probably originally designed no more than a burlesque upon *Pamela*. He gave the illustrious Pamela a brother Joseph, whom he placed in the service of Lady Booby, an aunt by marriage of Richardson's Mr. B., and there subjected him to a series of attacks upon his virtue which Joseph, remembering his sister's lofty conduct, successfully repelled. But either the original butt of Fielding's satire proved too narrow a mark, or, as is perhaps more likely, the subsidiary characters, Parson Adams and Mrs. Slipslop, who are introduced in the third chapter, coming to life in his hands assumed some control of the story ; in any case, the novel soon forgot its original, and from Chapter XI., which deals with " several new matters not expected,"

it becomes a novel of adventure of a type new to
English literature.   So that when Fielding came to
write his preface he found that he too had to defend
and explain a kind of writing hitherto unattempted.
The preface, although it cannot compare with the longer
critical dissertations in *Tom Jones*, yet sets forth very
clearly the aim and character of Fielding's novels.
Joseph Andrews, he says, is a comic epic poem in prose,
admitting light and ridiculous incidents in the action,
and persons of inferior rank and manners among the
characters, both of which are excluded by the serious
epic, the tragedy, or the serious romance.   But burlesque,
as he is careful to observe, although it is admitted in the
diction for the especial delight of the classical reader, is
rigidly excluded from the sentiments and characters,
which are strictly copied from Nature.   It is unnecessary to seek for the monstrous and unnatural when "life
everywhere furnishes an accurate observer with the
ridiculous."   And the preface goes further yet in
pointing out that the only source of the true ridiculous
is affectation, whether it springs from vanity or from
hypocrisy.

The war against shams, against strong hypocrisy or its
feebler descendant insincerity, that Fielding carried on
throughout his life, is here declared.   And yet as an
account of his own comedy and his own humour his
analysis is inadequate.   For his broadest, most delicious
laughter is not a weapon of offence, he seldom shows
his teeth, and for once that he laughs fiercely at human
vanity he will laugh ten times sympathetically, gently,
irresistibly, at human weaknesses and oddities, at the

incongruity of things. Parson Adams, that compound of oddities, is laughed at most by those who love him best, including his creator. All his traits, his absent-mindedness, his impulsiveness, the wisdom that makes him the best of teachers, the childlike simplicity that made him the plaything of knaves, are developed by touches repeated and fearless, which show how little Fielding cared, in painting this inimitable comic figure, to cater for the mirth of those whose laughter is begotten only by some fancied superiority in themselves. There is something almost paradoxical in the succession of ludicrous plights devised for this most loveable and admirable of men, as if Fielding were insisting that the most ridiculous of his characters should also be the least obnoxious to any breath of scorn. When Adams, having failed to induce Towwouse to accept his manuscript sermons in payment of Joseph's bill, leans over the rail of the upper story of the inn, smoking his pipe and pondering some new expedient, with his night-cap drawn over his wig and a short great-coat half covering his cassock, he presented, says Fielding, " a figure likely to attract the eyes of those who were not over given to observation." By the very device of discarding all the stage properties of the virtuous priest, the novelist makes his main character stand forth more conspicuously among the Trullibers, Towwouses, and Slipslops, and gives to the reader profound lessons in wisdom, in understanding, and, it must be added, in humour. " His wit," says Thackeray, " is wonderfully wise and detective ; it flashes upon a rogue and lightens up a rascal like a policeman's lantern." But his work as a novelist is not so entirely subsidiary as some would have it to his work as a magistrate; his treatment even of so very a rogue as Mr. Peter Pounce is not ungentle or unintelligent, and his illuminating humour is not focussed on vice, but shines like the sun on the evil and on the good.

From the date of *Joseph Andrews* to the time of his death in 1754, some twelve years later, Fielding's life was spent in his professional duties and in the unremitting and arduous pursuit of literary excellence. His two later novels, *The History of Tom Jones, a Foundling* (1749), and *Amelia* (1751), appeared after he had, by the influence of his friend Lyttleton, been appointed Justice of the Peace for Middlesex and Westminster, and the later of the two bears marks of the intrusion of his official duties on his leisured thought. The most important of his other writings is to be found in the third volume of the *Miscellanies* that he collected and published in 1743, and is entitled the *History of the Life of the late Mr. Jonathan Wild the Great*. The "fundamental brain-work" necessary for a great work of fiction is not only present but apparent in all Fielding's novels; they can be stripped, as Shakespeare's plays cannot, of their picturesque expression, and something at least of their purport stated in purely intellectual terms. But in *Jonathan Wild* above all Fielding indulges to the full his taste for clearness and unity of intellectual structure. The life of the original of his hero, who died at Tyburn in 1725, is to be found in Johnson's *Lives of Highwaymen* (1734), where it is recorded of Wild that, under sentence of death, he contemplated suicide, being "more especially swayed to such Notions, he pretended, from the Examples of the famous Heroes of Antiquity; who, to avoid dishonourable Treatment, had given themselves a speedy Death." The hint was enough to suggest that Wild's career might be celebrated in epic vein—an idea that would have pleased Swift, who, long before the *Beggars' Opera*, had suggested a "Newgate pastoral." Fielding conducts his narrative under the dominant influence of one prevailing purpose, in the service of which he employs all his irony, never suffering the reader for one moment to forget the main thesis, which is stated at the beginning of the story, restated at the close and illustrated with matchless skill throughout. This thesis is in effect that the elements of "greatness," in the common acceptation of the term, when divorced from that plain goodness of heart which is little likely to foster ambition, are the same in the thief and in men eminent in more reputable professions, as those can testify "who have lived long in cities, courts, gaols, or such places." In sketching the history of Wild, and showing how his career of selfish villainy might have been marred at innumerable points by the slightest liability to humane feeling, Fielding's polished irony achieves a triumph, and presents a picture of almost "perfect diabolism." The humour of the author is at its grimmest in this work, not so much in depicting Wild, the horror of whose character is almost forgotten in its artistic unity, as in sundry subordinate details, such as the conduct of Heartfree's debtors when he is in prosperity, and of his creditors when he is in prison, or that quiet piece of knavery and inhumanity on the part of the keeper of the prison, who keeps Heartfree's reprieve a secret until he

has extracted twenty pounds from Friendly as the price
of a respite for an hour.   The writer whose eyes are
thus open to the possible profundities of human wickedness has earned a right to speak of human virtue, and
by means of the little group of amiable figures—Heartfree, Mrs. Heartfree, the good magistrate, and Friendly
—Fielding relieves the blackness of his picture.   But he
is careful not to confuse his method or depart from the
lines he has marked out for himself; "the low and
pitiful behaviour of Heartfree" in lavishing affection on
his family and reposing trust in his friends, is duly
stigmatized as creating an opinion among those about
him in the prison "that he was one of the silliest fellows
in the universe."   And not only is the interest of the
various adventures well sustained, but the points where
the narrative is retarded or arrested to allow the author
time for the leisurely play of his humour round a single
incident are numerous and striking.   The two chapters,
for instance, which are devoted to Wild's adventures in
the open boat, and describe how, having determined on
suicide, he leaps into the water and thereupon is miracu-
lously saved by climbing into the boat again, are fine
examples of Fielding's characteristic vein.   In this book,
too, as in *Joseph Andrews*, is seen that vivifying power
which brings to life the veriest walking gentlemen and
stage mutes.   The Ordinary in Newgate is a character
merely incidental, and yet with his opinion that any
man who believes in the possible salvation of "a sincere
Turk" is himself incapable of grace, with his taste for
punch and his justification of that taste by default of
Scripture, above all with his sermon, a prophylactic

against the errors of Greek systems of thought, administered to a condemned criminal, he stands distinctly embodied before the reader to whom he has barely been introduced.

In his two later novels Fielding completed that gallery of portraits which transcends for reality and variety the work of all former English narrators, save perhaps Chaucer alone. *Tom Jones*, the work of " some thousands of hours," distributed probably over not a few years, is the Epic of Youth, by a master of comedy. In the prime of his manhood, speaking from a full and ripe experience, but with the zest of youthfulness still easily within the reach of memory and sympathy, Fielding gives in this book his sonorous verdict on human life and human conduct. Whether regarded for its art or for its thought, whether treated as detached scenes of the human comedy, as an example of plot-architecture, or as an attempt at the solution of certain wide problems of life, no truer, saner book has ever been written. Indeed, to borrow the words of the American poet, "this is no book ; who touches this touches a man." Through all the motley scenes of life with which its pages are crowded, the reader finds that keener than his delight in the wealth of scenery and character that is displayed before him is his delight in the strength and excellence of the companionship that guides and befriends him. The very qualities that have been foremost in finding Fielding enemies (if those who waste their time in apologizing for him, allowing him the benefit of the age in which he lived, and pitying him, may be so called) have also found him the warmest friends. His splendid candour, his

magnanimity, his tolerance, spring from no ignorance
or indifference ; he is keenly sensitive to minute traits
of character, and merciless to meanness. Under what
precise set of conditions, and exactly by what persons,
he is to be read, is a question that need trouble no one
long. Books are written to be read by those who can
understand them ; their possible effect on those who
cannot is a matter of medical rather than of literary
interest. Some literary critics, it is true, with a taste for
subdued tones in art, have found some of Fielding's
loudest notes too strident for enfeebled ears, but not to
the great musician can the whole range of the orchestra,
not to the great painter can the strongest contrast of
colours, profitably be denied.

Almost all the great English writers of the eighteenth
century, whether theologians, novelists, or poets, are, in
their essence, moralists, and Fielding is no exception.
To compare his morality with Richardson's is only to
do what his early readers must have done, for the comparison is courted by himself in *Joseph Andrews ;* and
even *Tom Jones* owes some of its features to that rivalry
between these two great novelists of which both were
keenly conscious. Moreover, Fielding's morality has
before now attracted censure. Richardson, never behind-
hand in condemning his rival, says that " the virtues of his
heroes are the vices of a truly good man." Hawkins, the
biographer of Johnson, condemns him as " the inventor
of that cant phrase, goodness of heart, which is every day
used as a substitute for probity, and means little more
than the virtue of a horse or a dog," and thinks that " he
has done more towards corrupting the rising generation

than any writer we know of." And Mr. Edwards of Turrick, Bucks, the author of *The Canons of Criticism*, whose monument in the parish church of Ellesborough records that he departed this life with "decent uncon-cern," displays neither decency nor nonchalance in the eagerness with which he assures Richardson by letter that he has read the *Journal of a Voyage to Lisbon* "with much indignation," and is convinced by the brave humour of that work that "the fellow had no heart." These are early voices, but they have found later echoes.

If terms borrowed from literary criticism could be applied to morals, it might truly be said that Richardson is a classic, and Fielding a romantic moralist. Richard-son lays most stress on code, conformity to the social standard, and judges by the deed done ; Fielding lays most on native impulse, goodness of heart, the individual's conformity to his better self, and uses a novelist's privi-lege in judging his creatures by their motives. The corruption of the classical school in letters springs from a pedantic attention to form and a neglect of inspiration ; so in morals corruption appears as pharisaism, the formal righteousness of a man whose good deeds too often spring from bad motives. The virtues of Sir Charles Grandison might all be comprised under the single head of a rigid attention to good form, with much consequent confusion between trivial and important duties.

Against the pedantry of the formal moralist Fielding delights to hurl his satire. He can clear away in a moment all the "splendid rubbish" that covers up a character, and expose its inherent rottenness or meanness. He never tires of showing how a base-minded man may cover himself with formal righteousness, and how a scapegrace may be good at heart. A good instance of his method occurs early in *Joseph Andrews*, in that scene where Joseph, robbed of his money and stripped of his clothes, is overtaken, groaning in a ditch, by a coach full of passengers. The arguments against taking him into the coach advanced by the lady who " had rather stay in that place to all eternity than ride with a naked man," and by the old gentleman, who fears lest they may be robbed too, are overcome by the contentions of the young lawyer, who advises " to save the poor creature's life for their own sakes," lest they should incur the charge of being accessory to murder. But Joseph will not enter until he is decently clad, and the difficulty would have been insurmountable, for neither the passengers nor the coachman would lend a single garment, " unless the postillion (a lad who hath been since transported for robbing a hen-roost) had voluntarily stripped off a great-coat, his only garment, at the same time swearing a great oath (for which he was rebuked by all the passengers), 'that he would rather ride in his shirt all his life than suffer a fellow-creature to lie in so miserable a condition.' "

By the insertion of the clauses in brackets Fielding here emphasizes his favourite paradox, which became later the main theme of *Tom Jones*. For with all their variety, his novels throughout exhibit in the strongest light the antithesis between the generous or heedless errors of warm-hearted humanity, and the calculating prudence and rigid propriety of persons formally righteous, but without the least tincture of generous feeling.

A desire to make the contrast as striking as possible is no doubt responsible for some of the incidents in *Tom Jones* that have found least favour with the critics. Thackeray protested against Mr. Jones's claim to heroic rank, and an earlier critic, Mrs. Honour, maid to Miss Sophia Western, gave voice to a prevalent opinion when, on being begged to whisper, " for that there was a lady dying in the next room," she exclaimed, " A lady ! Ay, I suppose one of your ladies.—O, Mr. Jones, there are too many of them in the world."

There are certainly none too few, for Fielding is more careful to keep his hero human than to keep him heroic. But perhaps their number would have been overlooked had not the novelist thought proper, after piloting his hero through twelve books of adventure without any indelible stain on his reputation, to rob him of his honour and exhibit him " spunging for a guinea " by the introduction of the Lady Bellaston episode in the thirteenth book. This much-debated incident, however, only lays a strong emphasis on the main theme of the book, and makes its intellectual framework all the clearer. With something of the same paradoxical intent Walt Whitman proclaims—

" I pick out some low person for my dearest friend,
He shall be vulgar, rude, illiterate, he shall be one condemned by
others for deeds done."

And just as Fielding was not satisfied with making the warm-hearted postillion swear, but thought it necessary to transport him for theft, so he is not content to win the sympathy of the reader for Mr. Jones without

giving that sympathy the severest obstacles to surmount
in the shape of "deeds done."

He would have no countenance extended to Tom
Jones on the ground that in spite of all peccadillos he
is at least fairly reputable. And so poor Mr. Jones is
left with little but his warm heart to plead for him. But
if that excused him to Sophia, who else dare refuse him
absolution?

The crew of hypocrites that disport themselves in
Tom Jones, Blifil, Thwackum, Square, and others, are
admirably studied and described. Like Squire Western,
they are of a hardier breed than their modern represen-
tatives, and do not trouble to deceive themselves so
long as they can deceive others. The speech made by
young Master Blifil when he has let loose Miss Sophia's
bird, wherein he claims humanity as the motive of an
action really prompted by spite, is a model of deliberate
and cunning hypocrisy. All Fielding's evil characters,
it may be remarked, are accomplished hypocrites; on
pure vanity or silliness he spends very few of his shafts.
If he had ever drawn up a graduated list of moral
offences, it would doubtless have corresponded very
closely with Dante's, as set forth in the circles of the
Inferno. Sins involving both cruelty and deceit would
have been ranked as heaviest, the sins of the senses as
lightest. Only, the English magistrate, with less austerity
than the Italian seer, would perhaps have been content
to suffer the inhabitants of the higher circles of the
Inferno to remain on earth, or to be saved from the
doom of their actions, while to hypocrites of the darker
sort he is as pitiless as Dante himself. " It is much

easier," he says in the dedication of *Tom Jones*, " to make good men wise than to make bad men good." And therefore he has laboured, not to reform his villains, but to show that indiscretion is responsible for leading virtue and innocence into the snares laid for them. The whole history of Mr. Jones up to the last chapter is a commentary on the evil effects of such indiscretion, the punishment follows close on the heels of the offence, and only those stern censors who would prefer to see the hero hanged can complain when he is happily married.

By the time that he wrote *Amelia*, questions of practical rather than poetic justice had the first place in Fielding's thoughts. The abuses of his time, in connection especially with the administration of the law, the venality of justices and prison officials, the indiscriminate brutality of punishments and their inefficiency in preventing crime, all exercised his mind and energies, and find reflection in the sketches and scenes in *Amelia*. The novel is written in a graver manner, and the introductory chapters, inspired in *Tom Jones* by Fielding's delight in his craft, have no counterpart here. Captain Booth, like the earlier hero, is a man " of consummate good nature," with perhaps a truer and deeper repentance for his faults than the buoyant Mr. Jones ever succeeded in experiencing, and is saved, like his prototype, by the warmth of his feelings and the virtues of his wife. Amelia, like Sophia, is drawn from the life; she is an embodiment of the virtues of Charlotte Fielding, the novelist's first wife, who, after eight years of struggle and privation with him, had died in 1743. The errors of Mr. Booth serve only to heighten the effect of her gentleness and goodness. Tom Jones, "bad as he is," has to serve as hero of the former history, Captain Booth is deposed from that position and reigns only in right of his wife, he exists to be forgiven. But he is forgiven with such grace and delicacy for his faults that it is hard to refuse him forgiveness for his existence. And it may be doubted whether a figure so beautiful and at the same time so perfectly life-like as Amelia has ever been drawn in the whole range of English prose fiction.

To catalogue or appraise Fielding's gallery of portraits would ask for much space. Some of the best of them are still unique in their kind, and have had no copyists. It is more important here, therefore, to set down briefly the advances in the art of novel-writing that he taught to his generation. These were mainly two, the artistic conduct of a complicated plot, and, combined with this, a realism in the characters and events that should be convincing without hampering the freedom of the artist.

Before Fielding's day only short stories had been told well in English prose. Those prose-writers who had chosen to deal with a variety of characters and events in a single narrative, had either jumbled their incidents together in meaningless confusion, or had adopted the simple and monotonous device of Defoe, stringing them on a single thread of consecutive experience without the emphasis that can be obtained from skilful grouping. Congreve, in his single novel, had attempted to intro- duce dramatic conventions ; nobody marked him ; Fielding was happier in finding a large public for works that borrowed their structure, although without any slavish imitation, from the classical epic. The influence

N

of the epic on his work is apparent in his invocations, where his diction becomes poetic, and in mock-heroic scenes, like the battle in the churchyard. But the structure of the story is itself epic, and the relation of the by-plots to the principal theme is everywhere established. Even the digression due to the Man of the Hill is part of the theme of *Tom Jones*, if it is no part of the story. Richardson's handling of his own method is excellent, but he could never become a teacher of method; only his patience and skill could manœuvre those legions of letters and feed them on chopped straw. On the other hand, there could be no better school for a novelist than is afforded by the study of Fielding's plots.

His realism is no less an advance. It is not laborious and minute, but it is sufficient. He does not, like Defoe, "protest too much," for his object is to create an illusion of reality and not a belief in fact. Sophia comes sailing into his story wafted by a poetic invocation, and has not to undergo an inventory of her apparel. Yet for the purposes of a poet she lives and breathes as Moll Flanders never did. Moreover Fielding's acquaintance with life is fully as wide as Defoe's, while his insight is keener and deeper. His last and most heart-felt invocation in the beginning of the thirteenth book of *Tom Jones* is addressed to Experience, conversant " with every kind of character, from the minister at his levee to the bailiff in his spunging-house; from the duchess at her drum to the landlady behind her bar." It was this catholicity that Richardson censured when he made it a reproach to Fielding that "his brawls, his jars, his gaols, his sponging-houses, are all drawn from what he has seen and known." Others before him had seen and known these things, but in Fielding's pages for the first time they are introduced, with no loss of reality, to subserve the ends of fiction ; common life is the material of the story, but it is handled here for the first time with the freedom and imagination of a great artist.

CHAPTER VII.

THE NOVELS OF THE EIGHTEENTH CENTURY.

WITH the greater works of Richardson and Fielding the career of the modern novel may be said to have begun. The early followers of *Pamela* and *Joseph Andrews* were few in number; from 1740 to 1748 the only imitator of any note was Miss Sarah Fielding, whose first novel, entitled *The Adventures of David Simple, containing an Account of his Travels through the Cities of London and Westminster in the Search of a real Friend*, was published in 1744. In spite of the assertion on the title-page that the book was "by a Lady," its authorship was attributed to Fielding, and denied by him for the credit of the 'real and sole author" in the preface that he contributed to the second edition. In a preface to a later work of his sister's he returns to the subject, and reports the saying of a lady of high rank and understanding: "'So far,' said she, 'from doubting *David Simple* to be the performance of a woman, I am well convinced it could not have been written by a man.'" Richardson, whose praises of others were generally emissaries of his vanity, compliments Miss Fielding in 1756 on her knowledge of the human heart: "Well might a critical judge of writing say, as he did to me, that your late brother's knowledge of it was not (fine writer as he was) comparable to yours. His was but as the knowledge of the outside of a clockwork machine, while yours was that of all the finer springs and movements of the inside." The words recall—they were probably meant to recall—an exactly similar comparison made by Johnson between Richardson and Fielding, to the advantage of the former.

The main interest of Miss Fielding's story lies in the sentiment and characters; it is therefore unfortunate that she chose the picaresque romance of incident as the model for the structure of her story. David Simple, an elegant, colourless young man, with a taste for sentimental casuistry, after losing the friendship of his only brother, who attempts to cheat him out of his share of their father's inheritance, goes forth into the world to try to make good the loss. He begins his search on the flags of the exchange, where he is horrified to find the words "good" and "rich" used as perfect synonyms. His subsequent adventures and betrayals furnish occasion for the introduction of many minor characters, some of them not ill-drawn. A certain relief from the languid incident is found in occasional touches of satire that are pure Fielding. Thus, after his first betrayal, the authoress leaves David to his sufferings, "lest it should be thought I am so ignorant of the world as not to know the proper time of forsaking people."

Miss Fielding's slight knowledge of the world disabled her from giving fresh life to the picaresque romance.

The new model in this kind was furnished by Tobias Smollett, whose *Roderick Random* (1748), appearing in the same year as *Clarissa,* and almost exactly a year before *Tom Jones,* became, like them, the founder of a tribe.

Then the floodgates were opened, and the novel rapidly became what Robert Bage, towards the end of the century, calls it, " pretty generally considered as the lowest of all human productions." In his play, called *Polly Honeycombe, a Dramatic Novel,* first acted in 1760, George Colman satirizes the prevalent taste for novels in the person of the daughter of a city merchant, Miss Honeycombe, whose head has been turned, not by the romances that eight years earlier had produced the vagaries of Arabella, the heroine of *The Female Quixote,* but by the small duodecimos of the circulating library. The prologue notes the change :—

> " Cassandra's folios now no longer read,
> See two neat pocket-volumes in their stead."

Further, as warrant for his satire, Colman prefixes a sort of bibliography containing the titles of more than a hundred and eighty novels which, with very few exceptions, had appeared during the decade before the production of his play. In those ten years the novel had once more vanquished the romance.

It is no longer possible, therefore, in the eighteenth century, to deal with the work of the novelists under the authors' names. This legion of novels, which issued from the principal London presses in duodecimo form, at three shillings a volume, can only be treated on some broad principle of classification. Most of them were published anonymously; many of them are destitute of original merit, a few are purely trading ventures attempting to capture success by a dishonest title. Thus the year after the publication of *Tom Jones* there appeared *The History of Tom Jones the Foundling, in his Married State;* the year after the startling success of *Tristram Shandy* an anonymous writer brought out *The Life and Opinions of Miss Sukey Shandy of Bow Street, Gentlewoman* (1760). The classification of this multitude of forgotten novels is, however, neither difficult nor uninstructive. They assimilate themselves to certain well-known types, and serve to show what were the limits of the imaginative empire wielded by the eighteenth-century novelist up to the time of the revival of romance.

The greater names cannot be so summarily treated. Smollett and Sterne were creators of types; Goldsmith's only novel stands by itself, and Johnson's moral apologue called *Rasselas* is an admirably wrought narrative by a master of style. Here and there, too, are to be remarked novels that distinguish themselves by some freshness of scheme or some special merit in execution from the common work of the hack-writers. *Peter Wilkins, The Life of John Buncle, The Fool of Quality,* and some few others, if they cannot be called masterpieces, must at least be distinguished from the simple article of commerce. The rest may very fairly be treated in gross.

The life of Tobias George Smollett serves to point a moral already illustrated by the life of Fielding, for before he turned novelist he had courted success as a playwright. Born in the year 1721 in the parish of

Cardross, Vale of Leven, Smollett was educated to the profession of medicine at the University of Glasgow. The younger son of a younger son, he had little to hope for from his family, and in 1739 came to London to seek his fortune, with *The Regicide*, a drama dealing with the death of James I. of Scotland, in his pocket. His literary ambitions were disappointed, and he found employment as surgeon's mate on a King's ship, at the beginning of the war with Spain.

It was during his five years' service in this capacity that Smollett was enabled to accumulate the stock of experience so necessary for the picaresque romance. He was present at the siege of Carthagena in 1741, he cruised for some time in the West Indies, and by 1744 was back in London, where he set up as a surgeon in Downing Street, West. Like Fielding, he married a lady with a small fortune, and, her property failing to meet either his expectations or his expenses, found himself at no great distance from penury. But his literary capital was now greater than when he had first crossed the Border. The town had refused his tragedy, and had shown very little appreciation of his satires, *Advice* and *The Reproof*, published in the year immediately following the suppression of the rebellion of 1745. But Richardson and Fielding had shown new ways to success in literature, and he had his experience of life, gathered in the most impressionable time of youth, to sell to the public in novel form. This he worked up into two volumes, which were offered to the public, and by them readily accepted, under the title, *The Adventures of Roderick Random*.

Smollett avows frankly in his preface that his book is written in imitation of the *Gil Blas* of Lesage. In the first chapter of a later work, *Ferdinand, Count Fathom*, he gives a fuller list of his originals, enumerating *Guzman d'Alfarache, Don Quixote*, Scarron's *Roman Comique*, and *Gil Blas* as works which delight those very readers who profess disgust at scenes of low life described in the English tongue. The existence of these works certainly gave Smollett some advantage over Nash, who had written his *Jacke Wilton* when only *Lazarillo de Tormes* was available as a model in this kind. Even Defoe had died before the completion of *Gil Blas* in 1735, but Defoe had shown small inclination to borrow from any of them. He knew, as Smollett also knew, that for the realistic novel of humour and adventure, which in the country of its invention has been called picaresque, the purely literary inspiration is hopelessly inadequate. And Smollett fails where he most trusts to it. His later direct imitation of *Don Quixote, The Adventures of Sir Launcelot Greaves* (1762) is poor indeed compared with the full-blooded vitality and jollity of his earliest novel.

"A novel," says Smollett in one of his dedications, "is a large diffused picture, comprehending the characters of life, disposed in different groups and exhibited in various attitudes, for the purposes of an uniform plan." And he gives what is at least a characteristic of his own novels when he adds that "this plan cannot be executed with propriety, probability, or success, without a principal personage to attract the attention, unite the incidents, unwind the clue of the labyrinth, and at last close the scene, by virtue of his own importance." Such

unity of design as his novels may claim is entirely due
to this device of the "principal personage." But his
constructive power is small, and the merits of *Roderick
Random* are more apparent in the parts than in the
whole. It is a very lively panorama, the incidents and
characters of which he borrowed directly from his life
and experience, leaving it to his invention to give them
a certain comic distortion. The known facts of Smollett's
life correspond exactly with what he relates of his hero.
The same birth, the same education, the same naval
adventures lead up to the close of the book in a marriage
very like that which, in 1747, had closed the first chapter
of Smollett's life. So close is the correspondence that
his biographers have felt warranted in eking out the facts
of his life with inferences drawn from this novel.

The success of *Roderick Random* turned Smollett
finally to literature as a profession, and for the next
twenty years the irascible strenuous Scot was a well-
known character in London. Hardly a well-known
figure, for his hot temper and ostentatious independence
made him a difficult friend; "far more disposed to
cultivate the acquaintance of those he could serve,
than of those who could serve him." He came only
into casual contact with Johnson's circle, and was very
far indeed from relishing Johnson's favourite joke. But
he was never a misanthrope like his friend and fellow-
countryman Dr. John Armstrong, of whom Beattie said
that he seemed "to have conceived a rooted aversion
against the whole human race, except a few friends,
which it seems are dead."

Some light is thrown on his methods as a novelist, by

the fact that he travelled to Paris in the company of his friend and disciple, Dr. John Moore, with no ostensible purpose save the acquisition of new literary capital. This was duly employed in the *Adventures of Peregrine Pickle* (1751), a longer and more disjointed work than his first. The autobiographic method did not prove pleasing to Akenside and others, whose characters were burlesqued in this novel; and Smollett could hardly employ the excuse of Dr. John Shebbeare, who says that novelists are like army-tailors, they make suits for all mankind, to be taken and fitted on to their persons by Tom, Dick, and Harry. For Smollett fitted his descriptions to the individual, and took care that they should suit no one else. His method is minute and his satire savage and personal.

One more novel, this time on the model of *Jonathan Wild*, was produced by Smollett before journalism, translation, and history absorbed his time and turned his attention from fiction. *The Adventures of Ferdinand, Count Fathom* (1753), is as inferior to its prototype in conception and execution as Smollett is inferior in mind and art to Fielding. Count Fathom is a feeble knave compared with the great Jonathan, and the ironic conception that is the basis of Fielding's book is here missing. Smollett boasts in his preface that he has attempted "to subject folly to ridicule and vice to indignation," and has at least "adorned virtue with honour and applause." These are really the weaknesses of the book. Indignation is out of place, and the applause bestowed on virtue only helps to confuse and disaffect the reader, who is kept throughout in the company of vice. It is a coarse morality at best that is taught by repulsion from vice, and the plea is often hypocritical. All the more, therefore, is the absence felt of some such intellectual standpoint as Fielding's, to give unity and meaning to the book. Wild, led by his author in triumph to "a death as glorious as his life," and exhibited under the gallows picking the officiating parson's pocket of a " bottle-screw," is a more instructive and a more impressive figure than Fathom, who slinks out of the story to be reformed elsewhere.

Of *Sir Launcelot Greaves*, originally contributed as a serial to *The British Review*, the scheme, as one of the characters remarks, "is somewhat too stale and extravagant." The plot is the merest excuse for variety of scene, and the characters do not live. What he borrowed from Cervantes is as little put to its proper use by Smollett as what he borrowed from Fielding. His work loses its chief merit when he attempts to exchange his own method of reminiscence for a wider imaginative scheme.

His visit to Scotland in the summer of 1766 furnished him with material for his last and best novel, *The Expedition of Humphrey Clinker*, which was completed at Leghorn and published in 1771, the year of his death. The opportunity of treating Scottish scenes and characters, the pleasure of escaping from politics, and perhaps also the influence of a new writer, Sterne, combined to make of this the gentlest and most humorous of his novels.

Smollett was not a great man; he has none of Johnson's massive dignity, or Goldsmith's charm, or Fielding's

generous strength. His combative intensity made it
impossible for him to take the detached view of life that
is characteristic of a great humourist. His expedients
for raising a laugh are seldom intellectual. His stories,
as has been observed by a writer in the *Quarterly Review*
(No. 205), display "such a bustle of coarse life, such
swearing and rioting and squalor, and, above all, such
incessant thumping and fighting and breaking each
others' heads and kicking each others' shins as could
never have taken place in any conceivable community,
or under any system of police, unless the human skeleton
had been of much harder construction than it is at
present." Only those whose bodily vigour is at its
height can derive unfailing pleasure from seeing one
buffoon knock another down. Smollett's own pleasure
in the adventures he relates is obviously akin to the
physical; the accidents that crowd his pages have none
of that intellectual appeal which glorifies the muddiest
misadventures of Parson Adams in Parson Trulliber's
pigsty. But his zest in life is real and infectious, and
his purely external treatment gives a certain refreshing
quality to his pages; over his books at least it is possible
"to unbend the mind."

Of his chief opportunity for the display of character
he does not make full use. The nominal heroes of his
novels are not the most interesting of his characters.
His seafaring men, Tom Bowling, Commodore Trunnion,
Lieutenant Hatchway, and the rest, have generally been
considered his chief contribution to character in fiction.
They are happy and early creations of that burlesque
humour which applies to the whole of life the technical

terms drawn from a single art, profession, or trade. And the death of the Commodore in *Peregrine Pickle* deserves the praise that has been given it. But even the extraordinary wealth of Smollett's nautical vocabulary does not prevent the infliction of a certain fatigue by these gentlemen, who will wrap up the Lord's Prayer or a request for grog with equal ease in a superfluity of far-fetched and monotonous metaphor.

Yet Smollett cannot be robbed of what, after all, is his chief praise; he knew the very spirit of adventure, and gave a long lease of life in England to his revival of the picaresque romance. For his method, less original than Fielding's or Richardson's, was more easily imitated, and the public was long regaled with every conceivable variety of adventures. *The Adventures of Joe Thompson* (1750) were rapidly followed by those of *Dick Hazard* (1754), *Jerry Buck* (1754), *Frank Hammond* (1754), and *Jack Smart* (1756). These are each in one volume; but *The History of Jack Connor* (1752), *The History of Betty Barnes* (1752), *The History of Jasper Banks, commonly called the Handsome Man* (1754), *The History of Will Ramble, a Libertine* (1754), and *The History of Tom Fool* (1760), are each in two volumes. Miss Polly Honeycombe, in Colman's play, modelled her behaviour only on first-rate heroines, Clarissa Harlowe or Sophia Western; but even in her time there was a wilderness of precedent available. Those whose taste for veracious narrative was not cloyed by *The History of Cornelia* (1750), *The History of Charlotte Summers, the fortunate Parish Girl* (1750), and *The History of Pudica, a Lady of Norfolk* (1754), might proceed to *The History of*

Polly Willis, an Orphan (1755), *The History of Miss Sally Sable* (1757), *The History of Amanda* (1758), *The History of Miss Clarinda Cathcart and Miss Fanny Renton* (1765), *The History of Lady Julia Mandeville* (1775), and a hundred others. Fielding, Richardson, and Smollett were the godfathers of all these works. It is worth observing that by far the greater part of the novels of this age could be classified under the three divisions—Histories, Adventures, or Memoirs. A debauch of realism began, and originality was sought in untried subjects rather than in untried methods.

One curious class of novels deserves a passing mention. It has already been remarked that a certain limitation is imposed on the worker in the picaresque form by the necessity of bringing all the events recorded within the cognizance of the hero, who is also, in most cases, the narrator. This particular form, however, was valued by many authors for the opportunity it gave of stringing together detached scenes of scandal and satire without any of the unity imposed by art. But to bring all these scenes under the observation of one hero, even if that hero were a libertine, sometimes proved difficult or impossible. In good time, therefore, a new and looser form was invented, or adapted from Lesage. A guinea or a hymn-book can with perfect propriety be present at scenes to which it would be difficult to introduce a dispassionate human observer. Let the guinea or the hymn-book be endowed with the power of speech, and the last restraint is taken off social and personal satire. An idea of this kind is, of course, as old as fiction and before the rise of the novel it is employed in that paper of the *Spectator* (No. 343) where Will Honeycomb, in the character of a monkey, writes an account of his transmigrations. The novelty of its employment by later writers of fiction consists rather in the scandal and scurrility that they made it excuse. One of the earliest novels in this kind is *The History of Pompey the Little, or the Life and Adventures of a Lap-dog* (1751), wherein clever satirical portraits of certain well-known personages are strung on a slender thread of incident. A fiercer and stronger character was given to the device in Charles Johnstone's satire, *Chrysal, or the Adventures of a Guinea* (1760). The occasions upon which the guinea changes hands are seldom honourable; the gold of which it is composed is first dug up in Peru, then given to a Jesuit by a Peruvian, who was forced to compound in money for beating the priest's dog; it comes to London on a man-of-war, and begins its adventures in fashionable life. One master lost it "on a bet that he could repeat the Lord's Prayer, which he laid on purpose to lose, in order that he might show how entirely he had got rid of the prejudices of education." The contemporary interest of this, as of so many other novels of the time, lay in the fact that real persons were throughout intro-duced under a penetrable disguise. Later instances of the same form in fiction are *The Adventures of a Black Coat* (1760), *The Adventures of a Bank-note* (1770), *The Life and Adventures of a Cat* (1781), *The Adventures of a Rupee* (1782), *Memoirs of a Flea* (1785); and there are many others, for the form remained popular, and has received new developments in modern times.

Thus personal satire and scandal ran their course, and did much to degrade the fine literary forms of Fielding and Smollett. The personal intention, when it is allowed to predominate, is the death of art in fiction. To compare the method of some of these minor writers to the photographic art would be to compliment it unduly, for the camera is used by them in the service, not of art, but of the police. The imaginative structure is the most careless and insignificant part of their work; it is no palace of Romance, no guildhall of Comedy, that they seek to erect, but a hasty, low earthwork, behind which they may lie on their bellies and shoot at their enemies.

To the indulgence of personal animosities under the guise of fiction Smollett had given the countenance of his name and practice. In this respect, however, he was not followed by his biographer and admirer, Dr. John Moore, whose *Zeluco* (1786), owing to the praise bestowed on it by Mrs. Barbauld, has been far too generally accepted as one of the most notable of eighteenth-century novels. Zeluco, the Byronic villain, and Laura, his amiable and suffering wife, are highly conventional types of evil and of good. The two Scots, Buchanan and Targe, the one Lowlander and Whig, the other Highlander and Jacobite, are introduced that they may fight a duel over the reputation of the deceased queen, Mary of Scotland. But long before the date of Moore's novel the Scotsman, like the Welshman and Irishman, had become, partly by Smollett's example, a stock comic character of the novel.

The subtle intellectual humour that Smollett so

completely lacks is the all-pervading atmosphere of the
works of Laurence Sterne.   Yet, if tradition is to be
trusted, the ever-memorable *Tristram Shandy* was begun
by its author, when he was not far short of fifty years of
age, in order that he might defend his own character and
attack a certain physician called Burton, now and for ever
known as Dr. Slop.   But if this were his original intent,
it was soon overgrown and transformed by the marvellous
products of his fancy, and *Tristram Shandy* became one
of the monuments of English humour.

Born at Clonmel in 1713, the son of a poor lieutenant,
Sterne was some years older than Smollett.   The travels
and vicissitudes of his early youth, spent in York, Dublin,
Liverpool, and Plymouth, among other places, and the
vivid memory he retained of his kindly and easy-going
father, were not without their share in enabling him later
to describe the character and fortunes of "my Uncle
Toby." After graduating at Cambridge, Sterne took
priest's orders, and, by the patronage of his uncle, Dr.
Jaques Sterne, obtained the country rectory of Sutton,
Yorkshire.   Here he spent his time for some twenty
years, mainly in reading, fiddling, painting, and shooting,
enjoying the company of his old college friend, John
Hall Stevenson, and distinguishing himself as a member
of the club of " Demoniacs." This course of life was
broken in upon by the electric success of the first two
books of *The Life and Opinions of Tristram Shandy, Gent*
(1759); Sterne visited London, and became the idol of
fashionable society.   The new-sprung generation of novel-
readers, already suffering from a certain monotony of diet,
welcomed a fresh departure in fiction with the gusto of

literary epicures.   But the excitement of London and
of fame overtaxed Sterne's feeble health, and his few
remaining years of decline were spent largely in travel.
He completed nine books of *Tristram Shandy* by 1766,
as well as *A Sentimental Journey through France and Italy*
(1765), and died on a visit to London, in lodgings at "the
silk-bag shop in Old Bond Street," in 1768.

There is a singular blend of two qualities in Sterne's
writing, as in his character.   Humour and pathos are
never in their nature far apart ; in Sterne they are almost
inextricably combined.   His laughter and his tears are
both so facile, and their springs lie so near together,
that the one almost infallibly provokes the other ; he
will laugh at sorrow and find matter of sentiment in a
comical mishap.   It is his keenest pleasure to juggle
with these two effects ; a solemn occasion is to him an
irresistible provocative to burlesque, and his pathetic
sensibility responds to a touch so light that to a less
highly strung nature his tears will seem affected.   Yet
herein lies the delicacy of his writing, and of those exquisite effects, the despair of many a more robust artist,
which are as hard to describe as an odour is to remember.
His reader must be incessantly on the alert for surprises ;
it is only prudent, at a funeral where Parson Sterne
officiates, for the guest to attend with a harlequin's suit
beneath his decent garb of black, prepared for either
event.

The same perpetual faculty of surprise is seen in his
whimsical digressive style ; the same sensitive delicacy
makes itself felt in his subtle analytic treatment of gesture, expression, intonation, all the evanescent details

that together make up character. " The circumstances
with which everything in this world is begirt, give everything in this world its size and shape:" none knew it
better than Sterne, and he makes it an excuse for ex-
patiating at length upon the circumstances, and omitting
the thing itself. The humorous description of gesture
that he learned from Rabelais is applied by him to the
minute delineation of character, in and for itself. The
story he has to tell, if it can be supposed to exist, is
nothing but a starting-point for digressions, an occasion
for defining all that is not his story, but—to use the
favourite figure of Mr. Walter Shandy—might, could,
would, or should have some possible, probable, or conceivable bearing on what would be, or ought to be, his
story. Tristram Shandy himself, whose life and opinions
the author promises to record, just succeeds in being
born, and little more. Thus a critical treatment of
Sterne must inevitably divide itself under the three
headings of Character, Sentiment, and Humour, for these
are held in a state of suspension rather than solution in
a perfectly transparent medium.

The illustration of character by humorous contrast
and grotesque detail is the finest part of Sterne's art.
Walter Shandy, the father of the hero, dialectician and
theorist, is the central figure of the book. With him
are contrasted on the one hand his brother Toby, on the
other his prosaic wife, Mrs. Shandy. And Captain Toby
Shandy's character acquires further relief from the juxta-
position of his faithful attendant, Corporal Trim. In
spite of his extravagance, Sterne records some conversations among these characters that are as life-like

as any in literature.   No one of them, it might almost
be said, understands a single word uttered by any other,
yet the colloquies proceed in composure, for no one of
them suspects the fact.   Only Mr. Shandy is sometimes
annoyed because others do not understand him.   Master,
as he complains, of one of the finest chains of reasoning
in the world, he is unable for the soul of him to get a
single link of it into the head of his wife.

"It was a consuming vexation to my father, that my
mother never asked the meaning of a thing she did not
understand.

" —That she is not a woman of science, my father would
say, is her misfortune ;—but she might ask a question.—

" My mother never did.—In short, she went out of the
world, at last, without knowing whether it *turned round*
or *stood still*.—My father had officiously told her above a
thousand times which way it was ;—but she always forgot."

On the other hand, Captain Toby Shandy, the least
introspective of mortals, is no whit annoyed when his
artless sayings are taken in a wrong sense.   He falls com-
placently to whistling " Lillibullero."

In the much agitated question concerning the debts
of Sterne to previous writers, sufficient stress has always
been laid on his obligation to Cervantes, whose main
conception, borrowed and altered, is the soul of his work.
On the other hand, perhaps too little has been made of
the similarity of his central character to Cornelius, the
father of the hero in Arbuthnot's posthumous *Memoirs of
Martinus Scriblerus* (1741).   The harangues which
Cornelius delivers to his wife before their child is born,
wherein he insists that the child shall not be swaddled lest

the flexibility of his ears be lost, and that he shall be a great traveller, are met precisely as Mrs. Shandy would have met them—" My dear . . . we have but one child, and cannot afford to throw him away upon experiments." Arbuthnot, no doubt, borrowed much from Rabelais, but what he borrowed he handed on to Sterne enriched by his own additions, which reappear in *Tristram Shandy*.

Sterne's sentiment and pathos are as subtle and real as his humour, of which indeed they are truly a part. His failures in pathos are few, and arise, as his latest biographer, Mr. Traill, has well pointed out, from the inartistic intrusion of himself and his own feelings on a scene that might be pathetic enough if it were not marred by his self-consciousness. To see the professor of sentiment at his work extracting pathos from the material submitted to him is disconcerting to the reader. But the severe strictures of Thackeray on the pathos of Sterne, whom he treats as a mountebank, are utterly extravagant. Further, they are the views of a professional rival; both writers have a command of true pathos, both are liable to slips when they become self-conscious or vain of their art. Here is the true pathos from *Vanity Fair* :—

"No more firing was heard at Brussels, the pursuit rolled miles away. Darkness came down on the field and city, and Amelia was praying for George, who was lying on his face, dead, with a bullet through his heart."

Yet the writer of this is responsible also for that highly artificial picture of the death of Miss Crawley, where he introduces himself, as it were thumping out his lessons upon the coverlet :—

"Picture to yourself, O fair young reader, a worldly, selfish, graceless, thankless, religionless old woman, writhing in pain and fear, and without her wig. Picture her to yourself, and ere you be old, learn to love and pray."

There is nothing in Sterne more artificial than this nothing more strained in effect than that phrase "without her wig" introduced as preface to the exhortation. But it would not be fair to say of the great novelist, as he said of Sterne, that he has laid down his carpet (or his coverlet) and has tumbled on it. Rather he has fallen, as the most expertly poised of performers is liable to fall.

It is true that Sterne sometimes tries to obtain an effect of pathos from perilously fragile material, but his successes are triumphs. To leave on one side the famous death scene of Le Fevre, marred only at the end by the appearance of the stage-manager before the curtain, two admirable instances are to be found in the scene with the ass at Lyons in the seventh book of *Tristram Shandy*, and the author's interview with the monk at the beginning of the *Sentimental Journey*. For filigree work in sentiment there is nothing like these in English.

Sterne's humour defies analysis, eternal surprise is of its essence. "If I thought you was able," he says to the reader, "to form the least judgment, or probable conjecture to yourself of what was to come in the next page,—I would tear it out of my book." Order, propriety, fitness, whether artistic or moral, are valued by him chiefly as rules which may be effectively broken. It is easy to believe that he valued the pulpit as a piquant setting for some of his secular witticisms.   The gravity of a divine, however, is not expected in a novelist, and Sterne is forced to caper the more abundantly to produce an equal sense of incongruity.   The spirit of eccentricity soon exhausts itself, and he has won a surer fame by his creation of characters than by all his antic smiles or less engaging leers.

Most of the authors whom Sterne pillaged for his book lent him only trickery and properties, which he often uses with enhanced effect.   Rabelais, Cervantes, and Arbuthnot, on the other hand, furnish the scheme and essentials of his book.   And, of these, Cervantes is the deepest influence.   Only by the eighteenth century did his great romance really capture the English imagination.   Fielding, Smollett, and Mrs. Lennox wrote direct imitations of it, already enumerated, and Richard Graves added another to their number in *The Spiritual Quixote* (1772), a work wherein the Methodists are satirized by the exhibition of the adventures of Mr. Geoffry Wildgoose, a young Oxford gentleman who adopts the new religion and travels the country with Jeremiah Tugwell, a village cobbler, for squire.   But it is rather in the greater independent works that the infection of *Don Quixote* is best seen—in *Tom Jones*, in *Roderick Random*, and, above all, in *Tristram Shandy*.   To learn from a master is no plagiarism, and questions of petty theft sink into insignificance beside the fact that Cervantes, if any one, taught Sterne how to create that wonderful and original character, "my Uncle Toby."

The imitators of Sterne had no such success.   His rarest quality, his humour, is strictly unique and

inimitable.   " He offered the ass at Lyons," it has been
well said, " not a bundle of hay or a thistle, but a maca-
roon.   He offers the reading public something it never
tasted before or since."   Hence his imitators, unable even
to counterfeit his humour, were driven to content themselves with cultivating his lachrymose sensibility.

Chief among these is the Scottish writer, Henry
Mackenzie, novelist, playwright, and essayist, who sprang
into fame at the age of twenty-six by the publication of
The Man of Feeling (1771).   Mackenzie was long a
distinguished figure in the literary society that welcomed
Burns to Edinburgh towards the close of the eighteenth
century.   His serial papers, *The Mirror* and *The
Lounger,* his authority as a critic, and the versatility of
his literary talent have all contributed to procure for him
a higher fame than his novels considered by themselves
would warrant.   Scott, the most generous of critics,
writing while Mackenzie was yet alive, calls him " the
Northern Addison," and claims for him as a novelist
a place beside Sterne.   With Sterne at his weakest
Mackenzie at his strongest may fairly be ranked.   " The
illustration of the nicer and finer sensibilities of the
human breast," his single theme, is entirely unrelieved
by any touch of humour or satire, and the Man of
Feeling—all feeling and nothing but feeling, becomes
merely maudlin.   The two lines in the prologue to *The
Prince of Tunis* (1773), his earliest play, wherein Mackenzie recommends it to his audience, might fitly be
inscribed as preface to all three of his novels :—

> " With you his cause I leave, his story hear,
>   And if applause it merit ;—shed a tear "

And even this, the only applause that he sought, is not easily obtained from later generations, trained by whole tribes of sentimental impostors to refuse tears to careless or confident beggars.

The direct influence of Sterne on Mackenzie is best seen in *The Man of Feeling*, where the looseness of construction in the story, a mere succession of scenes designed to awake tender or compassionate sensibilities, and the abrupt turn of the phrases are obviously borrowed from the author of the *Sentimental Journey*. In his later novels, *The Man of the World* (1773), and *Julia de Roubigné* (1777), Mackenzie treats variants of the same theme, and his plots, though more ambitious, are scarcely more successful. The last of the three especially, which is similar in plot to *Othello*, is a story poorly qualified to exhibit the merits of Mackenzie's method. The real skill and subtlety he shows in painting small delicacies of feeling and etiquette are ill suited with a tragic catastrophe involving strong passions. And the device of telling the story by means of letters, with its apparatus of confidants and witnesses, lays a heavy burden of improbability upon a feeble tragedy.

The school of novelists that cultivated sentiment for its own sake became rapidly merged late in the century, and especially after the French Revolution, in the theoretic school that cultivated sentiment in order to show how superior are the impulses of the heart to the artificial canons of society. Thus the history of the sentimental school from Richardson onwards, through the French writers that he influenced, loses itself later in the history of the Romantic revival, of which it really

forms a part. For Rousseau, the great precursor of the
Romantic movement, enlisted sentiment in the service of
theory, and from his time onward they are seldom found
apart. So that the influence of Sterne cannot fairly be
traced far in the history of the novel. The sentiment
he taught was developed by his successors for purposes
unknown to him; the man of feeling became an apostle,
and posed as the regenerator of society.

The contributions of Johnson and Goldsmith to prose
fiction are examples of pure eighteenth-century work.
It was in the year 1759, some months before the publication of the earliest instalment of *Tristram Shandy*,
that the great Cham descended into the arena of the
novelists with his moral apologue called *The History of
Rasselas, Prince of Abissinia*. His immediate object in
writing it was, as the printer told Boswell, "that with
the profits he might defray the expense of his mother's
funeral and pay some little debts that she had left."
There could be no doubt that a novel by the great
lexicographer would be eagerly bought by the public,
and, in seeking for a framework for his story, it is possible
that Johnson was directed to Abyssinia by the memory
of his labours, twenty-five years earlier, on the translation of Father Lobo's *Voyage to Abyssinia*. However
this may be, the theme of the story was all his own.
The natural gloom of his temperament, deepened by
the sadness of the occasion, finds fuller and stronger
expression in *Rasselas* than in the poem that treats the
same subject, *The Vanity of Human Wishes*.

It has been doubted whether *Rasselas* may justly be
considered as a novel at all. The conversations held

between the characters, it has been pointed out, are to be criticized, not in relation to circumstance and verisimilitude, but after the manner of an essay, in relation to truth. And certainly the strong moral and didactic purpose cannot be gainsaid. But the youth of the modern novel was a season of experiment, no rules of form had been determined, and a moral directly inculcated had never been disallowed. Far later in the century a noted literary critic, out of compliment to Richardson, refused to his works the title of novels, preferring to class them as excursions in "imaginative ethics." The sermon has played its part, as well as the drama, the epic, and the narrative poem, in shaping the form of the novel.

Sermon or novel, *Rasselas* was written at a time when Johnson had first attained his full command of literary expression. In the essays of *The Rambler*, begun some nine years earlier, his inversions, abstractions, monotonous sentences, and long words seem almost to exhibit, if the thought be not heresy, an imperfectly educated person struggling to acquire a polite diction. They certainly make his style as unsuitable for narrative as for the light ridicule of social foibles. *The Rambler* is not easy to read; or rather, to speak as the case demands, the otiose prolongation of the periods and the superabundance of polysyllabic vocables render the task of the intrepid adventurer who shall endeavour to peruse the earlier performances of this writer an undertaking of no inconsiderable magnitude. On the other hand, the later highly finished and effective style of the *Lives of the Poets* has an epigrammatic quality, a studied

balance of phrase and a dogmatic ring, like the stroke of
a hammer, that would infallibly interrupt the flow of
imaginative narrative. In *Rasselas* the merits of both
manners are combined to produce that ease of narration
and those memorable and weighty turns of phrase which
give it its principal distinction.

The main theme is never forgotten. The prince,
educated in the happy valley, and taken with his sister
into the world, is acquainted with human aims and
human enjoyments, only that their futility and insuffi-
ciency may be demonstrated, and the verdict again and
again recorded with merciless severity. The "choice of
life" is indeed difficult. The pastoral life is marred by
ignorance, discontent, and stupid malevolence. Prosperity means disquiet and danger. Is happiness to be
found in solitude? "The life of a solitary man will be
certainly miserable, but not certainly devout." Is
marriage to be preferred? "I know not whether marriage be more than one of the innumerable modes of
human misery." Will varied pleasures serve to wile
away the time? "Pleasures never can be so multiplied
and continued as not to leave much of life unemployed."
May the true solution be found in the pursuit of virtue?
"All that virtue can afford is quietness of conscience, a
steady prospect of a happier state; this may enable us
to endure calamity with patience; but remember that
patience must suppose pain."

All the sterner traits of Johnson's character, his uncompromising rectitude, his steadiness of outlook on
unrelieved gloom, his hatred of sentimental and unthinking optimism, have left their mark on *Rasselas*. What

was perhaps less to be expected, the structure of the
plot is masterly, the events are arranged in a skilful
climax, culminating in the story of the mad astronomer,
whose delusions supply the picture with a shade darker
than death itself. "Few can attain this man's knowledge," says Imlac, "and few practise his virtues, but
all may suffer his calamities. Of the uncertainties of
our present state the most dreadful and alarming is the
uncertain continuance of reason." And a note of
personal sadness is struck towards the close in the
declaration of the virtuous sage, who confesses that
praise has become to him an empty sound. "I have
neither mother to be delighted with the reputation of
her son, nor wife to partake the honours of her husband."
The words recall a similar phrase in the famous letter
to Lord Chesterfield, but the defiant strain that they
there introduce is exchanged for a subdued and deepened
melancholy. Taken as a whole, *Rasselas* is one of the
most powerful of moral fables to be found in any literature, and the lighter and wittier passages, such as those
on the functions of a poet and on the definition of a life
"according to nature," relieve its inspissated tenebrosity
with something like an air of comedy.

Its admirable comedy is perhaps the highest merit
of Goldsmith's only novel, *The Vicar of Wakefield* (1766).
The story of its discovery by Johnson, as told in Boswell,
is one of the best known and most characteristic passages
of Goldsmith's life. The picture of Goldsmith arrested
for debt, changing the guinea sent him by his friend for a
bottle of Madeira, helpless and angry, while a completed
novel which sold at the first offer for sixty pounds lay

written in his desk, has often been employed to illustrate the improvidence of authors. It might be better used to illustrate the providence of an author who was an improvident man. No one ever drew a firmer line between the works he wrote to last and the compilations that his necessities extorted from him than was consistently drawn throughout his life by Oliver Goldsmith. It did not occur to him to expect fame from his histories, political or natural. His whole aim, he remarks of his *History of England,* was "to make up a book of decent size that, as Squire Richard says, would do no harm to nobody." As little did it occur to him to treat his carefully wrought original works as so much merchandise, or a sop for the bailiffs. And perhaps Johnson's kindly offices prevented *The Vicar of Wakefield* from receiving its full share of the correction and polish that Goldsmith bestowed on all his best work.

"There are an hundred faults in this thing," says the author in his preface. Later critics have been unable to discover more than one. The plot is loosely constructed, and hastily huddled up at the close. His delight in exhibiting a good man unmoved by adversity led Goldsmith to multiply misfortunes upon the head of the ill-starred Vicar, until, when he came to the end, he found he had raised more troubles than he could lay. So that the restoration of the entire family to happiness is conducted in the same summary and ineffective fashion as in the tag to the Book of Job. Goldsmith drops a daughter or two in his haste, and asks the reader's imaginative co-operation in settling the rest of the family satisfactorily. It is more the reader's business, after all, than his own, for he makes it clear from the first that the happy ending is no part of the scheme of the book. The heading to chapter xxviii. shows as much. "Happiness and Misery," it runs, "rather the result of Prudence than of Virtue in this life; temporal evils or felicities being regarded by Heaven as things merely in themselves trifling, and unworthy its care in the distribution." This lofty lesson, which shows Goldsmith also high among the moralists of the century, receives additional enforcement in the author's manifest carelessness as to the temporal destiny of his characters.

Thus *The Vicar of Wakefield* is remarkable for its single characters, remarkable for its incidents of pathos and humour, but has no sustained development of plot. The tangential property of Goldsmith's mind, the happy Irish inconsequence, that led him in his *Animated Nature* to include among the varieties of the human race dwarfs and giants, mummies and waxworks, because he had seen some of these in a show at Chelsea, made him averse to all rigid or reasoned structure in his novel. He is the gayest and wisest of companions on the road, all the more because he is unaccustomed to a destination. The studied alternate preaching of *Rasselas* is as striking a contrast as could be found to the many unsought felicities in the easy conversation of *The Vicar of Wakefield*. It is a part of Goldsmith's charm that all he writes seems to come by chance; his events happen, as in life. Once or twice there is an appearance of greater study, as in that fine example of classical irony in the description of the elopement of Olivia,—where the Vicar is

in the act of congratulating himself and his wife on
the stainless virtue of their children and honour of
their name—at the moment when Dick comes running
in to announce Olivia's flight.   But a similar evidence of
design can hardly be traced throughout the book.   The
character of the Vicar is Goldsmith's chief care, and his
portrait must take rank very near Parson Adams and
My Uncle Toby, both of whom he resembles in his
simplicity and innocent vanity.   Like Adams, too, he
rises to heights of grave dignity in his vindication of
virtue, witness the fine speech he makes in reply to
Mr. Thornhill's surprising invitation.

Goldsmith's living characters are few in number, and
are most of them to be found repeated in his various works.
In *The Citizen of the World* (1762), a series of essays
reprinted from *The Public Ledger*, he gives some of his
brilliant character-sketches in their earlier form.   The
devices of his gentle and irresistible humour are also
comparatively few, but they bear repetition, and they
are all his own.   The swindler's method of proving
to the Vicar his acquaintance with Solomon Flamborough is a good example of the drollery that Goldsmith loves.   "Honest Solomon and I have been
acquainted for many years together.   I remember I
always beat him at three jumps; but he could hop on
one leg further than I."   Convinced by this touching
reminiscence, the Vicar accepts a draft on his neighbour
Flamborough in payment for his horse.

No praise is too high for Goldsmith's style.   *" Nullum
quod tetigit non ornavit,"* or, to give it in Johnson's earlier
conversational version, he has the art " of saying anything

P

he has to say in a pleasing manner." His plenary belief in the importance of the art of literature, in style and wit, led him to undertake tasks for which he was poorly equipped. " The labours of these men," he says, speaking of the zoologists who are his butt in *The Citizen of the World* (No. 89), " do not amuse the public." So he occupied their ground, and gave the world, as Johnson said he would, " a very fine book upon the subject," a text-book of science which, in spite of the author's belief that the cow sheds her horns every two years, and that the tiger inhabits the backwoods of Canada, has managed to hold its own as literature.

He has the gentlest of laughs—an excellent thing in a humourist,—and is untouched by the fiercer satirical spirit that runs riot in many of the novels of the time. Rather than have nothing to laugh at, he would feign stupidity or conceit and laugh at himself—a habit that persons of pure Saxon descent sometimes fail to comprehend. Hence the talk about his petulance and childish self-importance. But that " he was a very great man" was recognized after his death by the European continent, where his novel speedily established itself as a masterpiece and model.

With Goldsmith's work the great period of the eighteenth-century novel may be said to close. There was no diminution in the number of novels that left the press, but the greater part of these were imitations. Richard Cumberland, in his *Arundel* (1789), *Henry* (1795), and *John de Lancaster*, shows himself an imitator of Fielding. Robert Bage, in his productions, from *Mount Henneth* (1781) to *Hermsprong, or Man as He Is Not* (1796), comes nearest of all imitators to Richardson, and surpasses Richardson in drawing the characters of women like Miss Anna Howe or Miss Charlotte Grandison. But new schools had arisen; new influences were at work, some of them visible enough in Bage's later novels; and these were not the chief novelists of their time. The Romantic revival had begun. So that a summary of the characteristics of the school of the eighteenth century must limit itself to the great original masters and the writers of their time.

Never was there a body of writers of whom it might more truly be said that their work is a criticism of life. The phrase expresses their limitations as well as their highest merits. Since the time when Pope had begun his poetical career by the publication of an *Essay on Criticism*—a strange inversion—the spirit of criticism had dominated creation. Humour and morality—critical in their essence and application—have been seen to be the great qualities of the eighteenth-century novelists. And even these qualities tend, in the bulk of writers, to assume highly practical stereotyped forms. Sterne's humour is not satirical, Goldsmith's morality is not utilitarian, but these are exceptions. Lesser writers than these afford a better index to the spirit of the times. The theme of the eighteenth-century novel is the history of persons, regarded as moral beings, and treated in relation to each other and to society. A wide enough subject, perhaps, but not the whole of life. In how practical a spirit it was treated might be curiously illustrated by a detailed examination of the plots of the period. There are not many among them that dare to

let vice go unpunished by the magistrate, or that refuse
substantial damages to injured innocence. Even Goldsmith conquers his strong romantic tendency, and
hustles his Vicar back into his benefice. Frances
Sheridan, the wife of Dr. Johnson's preternaturally
dull friend, and the mother of the dramatist, made
herself a name by her *Memoirs of Miss Sydney Bid-
dulph, extracted from her own Journal* (1761), chiefly
by withholding from her heroine all compensation for
the severe afflictions heaped upon her head. Charles
James Fox thought the book the best novel of the age;
the praise Johnson gave it has an undertone of dissatis-
faction. "I know not, madam," he said to the authoress,
"that you have a right, upon moral principles, to make
your readers suffer so much." But the right was sparingly assumed by the novelists of the time, and such a
plot as the story of Romeo and Juliet, or of the Bride of
Lammermoor, where the darker shades of woe are something more than a mere setting for Christian long-suffering, was unknown to the century that delighted in
Hogarth's exhibition of the fortunes of the virtuous
apprentice.

The lesser writers, whose work exhibits small tincture
of art, show the satirical, didactic, practical tendencies
of the time in exaggerated decadent forms. Fielding
in his treatment of legal abuses, Smollett in his attack
on the Methodists, and his social and political satires,
had given way to these tendencies, so soon to carry all
before them. In weaker hands the novel became a mere
handbook of etiquette, a pamphlet on some political or
social abuse, an attack on a Government, a class, or a

person. The practice of anonymity was well-nigh universal; the finely fashioned vessels of art were debased and made to serve, as at a Scythian drinking-bout, for missiles or truncheons. Let the title of one novel, published in 1768, indicate the nature of many, *The Life and Adventures of Sir Bartholomew Sapskull, Baronet, nearly allied to most of the great men of the Three Kingdoms. By Somebody*. Or a better instance could perhaps be found in the famous novel of Henry Brooke, called *The Fool of Quality* (1766–1770). This work, it is true, does more than buffet the noble Sapskulls of the time; 't sets up, in the history of Henry, Earl of Moreland, a pattern of natural education and simple virtue. But the author has so many interests, such width of mind, so keen a desire to further a vast variety of political and social reforms, that his story is completely overlaid by moral digressions; he is so occupied in works of public benevolence that he starves his child. The definition of a gentleman, the honour due to commerce, the British constitution, the position of women, imprisonment for debt, and the statutes at large receive his careful attention in philosophic essays, often brilliant. For this reason John Wesley and, later, Charles Kingsley praised and republished the book. Its great merits would ask for recognition were it not that they are also its greatest faults, if it be considered as a novel. Artistically it is a chaos, and such unity as it has is due chiefly to the binder.

All these preoccupations, social, political, satirical, the marks of a fashionable town literature, served to heighten the prevalent indifference to scenery, and the neglect of wild nature as a background for man in imaginative literature.   James Howell, in the seventeenth century, said he had rather go fifty miles to hear a wise man than five to see a fine city.   He might have added that he would have gone further still to avoid seeing a high mountain, for he calls the Alps " uncouth huge monstrous excrescences of Nature," compared with which the Welsh mountains are mere " pimples."   Dr. Johnson took up the attitude of his century when he reproved Mr. Thrale for his interest in the dispositions of wood and water, hill and valley, during a journey through France.   "A blade of grass is always a blade of grass," said the sage, "whether in one country or another ; . . . men and women are my subjects of inquiry ; let us see how these differ from those we have left behind."   The renewed employment of wild scenery as an effect in fiction, the exhibition once more of man " crawling between heaven and earth," was linked, at the time of the Romantic revival, with the movement for stripping man of his social and conventional lendings, for reducing human nature to its simplest terms, freed from all the tyrannies of custom.   Woods and hills were found to furnish the most effective background for a naked man.

To say that the eighteenth-century novel has its limitations is therefore true, but it would be absurd to make of these limitations grave defects.   A saner, finer body of literature than the best of the fiction from Richardson to Goldsmith is not often to be met with in a nation's history. Its energy and variety are wonderful.   While the couplet of Pope held poetical literature hidebound, while the "twin coursers of ethereal race " that drew the car of

Dryden were urged on by poetasters until constant flogging had reduced them to a very sorry pair of jades,—prose literature, on the other hand, showed, and showed chiefly in the novel, vitality, versatility, experiment. Addison, Swift, Fielding, Johnson, Sterne, Gibbon, Burke —it would be impossible in any other century to name so great a variety of distinguished prose styles. Prose was no longer a beggar for the leavings of poetry, but had imposed on poetry its subjects and its methods. And when the romantic spirit first touched prose literature, its sanity disappeared, and there followed decades of nightmare and fever. So that no English romancer proved himself a worthy peer of the novelists until Scott, like Chaucer and Shakespeare, blended once more the opposed elements of comedy and romance.

CHAPTER VIII.

THE REVIVAL OF ROMANCE.

THE reappearance of romantic prose fiction in England, and the inauguration of a school of romance-writers by Horace Walpole's brief tale, *The Castle of Otranto* (1764), suggests all those complex and difficult problems that have gathered round the discussion of the Romantic revival. A complete statement of the causes and nature of that revival is perhaps hardly to be attained, the movement will always appear in different lights to different critics, or to the critics of different countries. Modern French critics have naturally been inclined to lay most stress on the reintroduction of "lyricism," that heightening of the sentiment of self, and that substitution of the impulse of the individual for the judgment of the community, which was heralded by Rousseau. Yet these traits do not show themselves early in the English revival of romance, and when they do show themselves in prose they are largely a product of French influences. A more conspicuous feature of English, as of German, Romanticism in its earlier phases is indicated in the name which has been applied by Mr. Theodore Watts to the whole movement—"the Renaissance of Wonder." No better term could be invented to gather under one treatment a vast variety of forms and methods, and to mark the characteristics that are shared by the *Lyrical Ballads* of Coleridge and Wordsworth with the crude fictions of Walpole and Lewis.

Others of the characteristics of Romanticism are abundantly evident in the English movement; the revived feeling for Nature, the introduction of exotic methods and models, the renewed interest in mediævalism, the increased employment of pictorial effects in literature; all these could be exampled very early in the movement. But the works which are commonly taken as the beginning of the movement in England, *The Castle of Otranto*, Bishop Percy's *Reliques of Ancient English Poetry* (1765), Macpherson's (1761–1763) and Chatterton's (1770) forgeries, do not display all these. They do display the attempt to reawaken the spirit of wonder, more particularly by resuscitation of the themes and fictions "of a grosser age."

Thus the revival of the supernatural, the most obvious occasion for wonder, is the main part of the English Romantic movement, as exhibited in imaginative prose. Later on, the French movement supplied a confluent to the stream, revolutionary rather than romantic; the "lyrical cry" is heard in the prose romances of Godwin and of Shelley as the scream of the individual, "born free, but everywhere in chains," struggling to disengage himself from the fetters of society, education and religion. And although the two streams blended in one, it is still possible roughly to classify the writers of romantic prose fiction during the period that joins the centuries as belonging to two schools—the School of Terror, with Mrs. Radcliffe, "Monk" Lewis, Maturin, and others, for its principal exponents; and the School of Theory, numbering many writers, with Godwin at their head.

Throughout the eighteenth century writers of tales and novels had frequently had recourse to the supernatural, but never with the aim of awakening the spirit of wonder. Swift's *Gulliver*, like the later "adventure" novels, introduces supernatural conditions purely by way of postulate, in order to satirize existing society. It was but thinking, as Dr. Johnson remarked, of big people and little people, and carrying out the idea with mathematical consistency; always magnifying the pores of the skin to the point of disgust, and minimizing the intellectual and political interests of nations to the point of ridicule. *Gulliver* is a grotesque fable, and the Oriental apologues so common in the pages of *The Spectator*, *The Adventurer*, and other periodicals of the time, are fables too, where the supernatural is introduced, not for the emotions it may itself awaken, but as a new and serviceable platform for the preacher or the jester. Thus Dr. Hawkesworth's tale of *Almoran and Hamet* (1761) has a supernatural basis: the elder of two kingly brothers is endowed by a genius with the power of exchanging forms with whomsoever he pleases, and thus is enabled to carry on a plot against his brother, and to attempt to supplant him in the affections of the beautiful Almeida. But the object of the tale is to show how powerless are fate and metaphysical aid to crush virtue, and how little magical power can add to the happiness of a vicious possessor. The author was the biographer of Swift and the admirer of Johnson; his tale is the offspring of *Gulliver* and *Rasselas*.

The Life and Adventures of Peter Wilkins (1751), by Robert Paltock, stands alone in the age. It has no ulterior purpose, moral or satirical, the supernatural winged beings who inhabit the country of Graundevolet are the playthings of the author's fancy. But his fancy, graceful though it is, is mechanical and mathematical in essence; there is nothing in it of the shaping spirit of imagination. Leigh Hunt, who expresses an enthusiastic admiration for the book, gives utterance to this defect when he complains that the author has not made his flying women light and airy enough. Speaking of the admirable and lovely Youwarkee, he adds, " At best the woman would have been wilder, more elvish, capricious, and unaccountable. She would have ruffled her whale-bones when angry; been horribly intimate, perhaps, with bird's nests and fights with eagles; and frightened Wilkins out of his wits with dashing betwixt rocks and pulling the noses of seals and gulls." The fact is that it is mechanical exactitude and mechanical consistency that Paltock is aiming at in the description of his supernatural beings, and not the higher artistic consistency that finds a basis and a justification for the supernatural in the awakened hopes and fears of mankind. He is treading in the track of Defoe, and some of his realistic devices are tedious in their prolonged and arbitrary detail. The artificial language that he invents for his islanders is a good example of the realism that hinders the imagination; it may be expedient to call flying men and flying women *glumms* and *gawrys*, for there are no single words for them in English, but the reader is only impeded by having to learn that *roppin* means "marmalade," and "marriage" is a pleasanter word than *hunkum*. Many persons have learnt Spanish in order to read *Don Quixote* in the original, fewer will be found willing to master some hundred new and useless terms in order to penetrate the disguises of a writer who thinks in English.

Thus *Peter Wilkins* would lose little or nothing of its merit if it were robbed of its supernatural equipment; the emotional interest that it excites is distinctively human, and Youwarkee is a model English wife, encased in an embarrassing parachute. All the realistic flummery that surrounds the flying people, their institutions and habits, is very easily conceived, and leaves the reader cold and unmoved. There is no satire, although traces of a reactionary tendency are perhaps to be recognized in the picture of a model people who are vegetarian, who cannot write, and who maintain the custom of slavery. But the book is chiefly a fanciful contribution to Natural Philosophy, an ingenious exercise for the physical speculator; parts of it might almost have been contributed to the Royal Society in its early days, and would doubtless have pleased the mechanical Bishop of Chester, who is said to have been chosen by the author as sponsor for his hero. Of the romantic employment of the supernatural, properly so called, it has no tincture.

The attitude of the age towards the marvellous has been best expressed, as might be expected, by the great exponent of the age, Dr. Samuel Johnson. " To select a singular event," he says, speaking of Gray's poem, *The Bard*, "and swell it to a giant's bulk by fabulous appendages of spectres and predictions has little difficulty; for he that forsakes the probable may always find the marvellous.   And it has little use; we are affected only as we believe; we are improved only as we find something to be imitated or declined.   I do not see that 'The Bard' promotes any truth, moral or political."

"*We are affected only as we believe.*"   The sentence gives a terse and final statement of the chief eighteenth-century heresy.   It is the key to the religious controversies of the century, reaching an abyss of bathos in the apologetics of Paley; it is the key likewise to the dominant methods in the art of fiction.   But the statement is not true, for we are affected also as we imagine. And his recognition of this long-forgotten truth entitles Horace Walpole, who hit upon it in blundering dilettante fashion, and illustrated it by his *Castle of Otranto*, to a high place among the founders of modern Romanticism.

The Castle of Otranto, a Gothic Story : translated by William Marshal, Gent., from the original Italian of Onuphrio Muralto, Canon of the Church of St. Nicholas at Otranto (1764), is the title of the brief story that founded a school of romance.   After the assured success of the book, Walpole discarded these solemn pretences, and came forward, in his preface to the second edition, with an acknowledgment of authorship and an interesting account of the inspirations and aims of his book. This preface is enough to show that the *Castle of Otranto* was a more serious and deliberate experiment than its prototype of Strawberry Hill ; its author meant it to last longer than the lath and plaster battlements with which he decorated his toy Gothic mansion.

Fifty years before the success of Scott, the attempt was here made "to blend the two kinds of romance, the ancient and the modern," to reintroduce, that is, the greatest possible freedom of invention, and to give full rein to fancy by the admission of the supernatural element of the old romances, at the same time borrowing from the newly developed novel its close adherence to nature and life in the matter of character and conversation. "The old romances" that Walpole had in mind were probably most of them no older than the pastoral and heroic schools, and a precedent that swayed him more is supplied by the later part of the preface, where Shakespeare is proclaimed as the great model for the heightening of the sublime by contrast with the commonplace or the ridiculous. The defence of Shakespeare that Walpole interpolates in his preface is highly significant. A revival of romance in England must have meant a revival of Shakespeare, but here he is definitely and closely associated with the first stirring of the new spirit. He is made responsible for "the deportment of the domestics" in the *Castle of Otranto* years before he taught Mrs. Radcliffe and Maturin, who were both steeped in Shakespeare, their best artistic effects. "I might have pleaded," says Walpole, "that having created a new species of romance, I was at liberty to lay down what rules I thought fit for the conduct of it: but I should be more proud of having imitated, however faintly, weakly, and at a distance, so masterly a pattern, than to enjoy the entire merit of invention, unless I could have marked my work with genius as well as with originality."

Originality the work may safely claim. The mountainous helmet, with its waving sable plumes, which crashes down into the courtyard of the Castle of Otranto at the very beginning of the narrative, unheralded and unexplained, may be taken as a symbol and type of the suddenness with which supernatural terror was re-introduced into English fiction by Horace Walpole. Here, with a decisive hand, was struck the keynote of all those later romances which gave only too much ground for Goethe's pithy maxim, "The classical is health; and the romantic, disease." The very violence and crudity of Walpole's originality proved an invitation to his imitators to better the instruction he gave them. But romantic after the manner of Shakespeare the work is not. For nothing is more characteristic of the great masters of romance than the subtlety and guardedness of their use of the supernatural. Their ghosts do not come uncalled for. Macbeth is startled when the witches speak to him, because what they have to tell him is familiar to his thoughts. The tricks and fantasies of supernaturalism are meaningless and powerless save in alliance with the mysterious powers of human nature, and, failing this, not all the realistic circumstance in the world can give them life or meaning. And where this alliance between the evil within and the unknown powers without is less marked, the care wherewith a great romancer prepares the way for the supernatural, so that it comes as the bodily fulfilment of an unbodied fear, is well seen in the palmary instance of *The Ancient*

Mariner. The skeleton ship, with the spectre-woman and her death-mate, is ushered in by all the silences and wonders of a tropical sea, by loneliness and dreams.

But Walpole was no poet, and the gaiety and inconsequence of his excursions into the supernatural can hardly avoid the suspicion of latent humour. Huge hands and legs clad in armour obtrude themselves at odd moments on the attention of alarmed domestics, whose account of their experiences furnishes the comedy of the book. When Manfred offers marriage to the Lady Isabella, " at that instant the portrait of his grandfather, which hung over the bench where they had been sitting, uttered a deep sigh, and heaved its breast." On another occasion "three drops of blood fell from the nose of Alfonso's statue." And portent follows portent, each more surprising and unintelligible than the last; the surmises of the reader as to the cause and meaning of the whole incongruous dance are like the conjectures offered by the spectators of the descent of the helmet, "as absurd and improbable as the catastrophe itself was unprecedented." Moreover, *The Castle of Otranto,* as a story, is raised on the structural scheme of the modern detective novel; the puzzle which every page complicates finds its solution only in the last few pages. But this particular structure is perfectly unwarrantable and ineffective where the solution itself contains free use of the supernatural. Even in so fine a story as *Dr. Jekyll and Mr. Hyde,* the reader is unjustifiably cheated into attempting a natural solution of apparently inexplicable phenomena. The supernatural solution, when it comes, is no solution; there are a hundred ways of explaining the impossible by the impossible. In its fit artistic place the supernatural explains the natural, and itself needs no explanation. The secret of such an employment of the supernatural is given by Coleridge in his account of the inception of that monument of the Romantic revival in England, the *Lyrical Ballads*. "It was agreed that my endeavours should be directed to persons and characters supernatural, or at least romantic; yet, so as to transfer from our inward nature a human interest and a semblance of truth sufficient to procure for these shadows of imagination that willing suspension of disbelief for the moment, which constitutes poetic faith. Mr. Wordsworth, on the other hand, was to propose to himself, as his object, to give the charm of novelty to things of every day, and to excite a feeling analogous to the supernatural, by awakening the mind's attention from the lethargy of custom, and directing it to the loveliness and the wonder of the world before us."

That these "two sorts" of poems were part of one series and of one scheme gives its chief importance to the poetic confession of faith contained in the *Lyrical Ballads*. For, indeed, the two processes described by Coleridge are mutually indispensable. The man to whom the natural has never seemed supernatural can by no device make the supernatural appear natural. And Wordsworth himself, who was confined to one half of the task, is seen in his finest poems constantly on the verge of passing from the disembodied marvels of the mind to authentic and embodied powers more than human. In such lines as these—

> " There's not a breathing of the common wind
>   That will forget thee ; thou hast great allies ;
>   Thy friends are exultations, agonies,
>   And love, and Man's unconquerable mind,"

he approaches the mythopœic, while he expresses one of the simplest and intensest of human feelings.

But Walpole, writing not only thirty-five years before Coleridge and Wordsworth, but also long before Burns and Cowper, and long before the French Revolution, was both in the eighteenth century and of it. To have awakened the hidden springs of supernatural terror is a sufficiently notable achievement. To transfer to super-natural characters "a human interest and a semblance of truth" from his inward nature was beyond his power, for in that inward nature he recognized nothing akin to the supernatural.

Thus Walpole remains one of those paradoxes with which the history of literature abounds. The inaugurator and, in some sense, the founder of a literary movement that took Europe by storm, his temper and character would have qualified him better to be its critic, or even its parodist. With no intention of criticism or parody, but in mere playfulness, he made a wooden jack-in-the-box. Wooden though it was, it served as a decoy for the multitude of ghosts that squeaked and gibbered in the highways of literature for half a century and more, until, in *Frankenstein* and *Melmoth the Wanderer*, the romantic orgy reached its height.

The violence of the machinery of *The Castle of Otranto* was palpable even to followers and imitators of Walpole. In *The Old English Baron*, originally called *The Champion*

of Virtue, a Gothic Story (1777), Miss Clara Reeve, who
wrote this her first novel at the mature age of fifty-one,
set herself to temper the improbabilities of her original,
and to keep her story within " the utmost *verge* of
probability." Her compromise is inherently weak; she
succeeds in writing a story with nothing in it more
inexplicable than a subterranean groan, at the cost of
most of the interest that the earlier work excites. " It is
so probable," says Horace Walpole, who read the book,
" that any trial for murder at the Old Bailey would make a
more interesting story." The supernatural is best justified
by the methods of poetry; Miss Reeve attempted its
justification by an added prosiness. In her relation to
the romantic movement she thus appears as a reactionary,
and the plea that her ghost is almost credible raises a false
issue in criticism. Some years before she wrote, Bürger
had marked out, in his poem of *Lenore* (1773), the path
that English romanticism was to follow.

But the influence of Germany operated slowly on
English literature, and one of the greatest of the English
Romantic School, Mrs. Radcliffe, never succeeded in
conquering her fear of the supernatural so far as to allow
it a place in her novels. Yet her series of fictions, from
The Castles of Athlin and Dunbayne (1789) to *The Italian*
(1797), exercised so enormous a power on the new
generation, and displayed so many decisive advances on
previous romantic essays, as to earn her a foremost place
among the earlier apostles of Romanticism.

Anne Ward (1764–1823) became Mrs. Radcliffe in
1787 by her marriage with William Radcliffe, barrister
and journalist. Her novels were written in rapid

succession during her early married life, at a time when her husband's proprietorship of the *English Chronicle* kept him employed during the evenings, and left her many solitary hours. She gained fame and fortune by her books, and then relapsed into private life as suddenly as she had emerged, living to see the triumph of many later romantic authors who borrowed and adapted her methods.

Her ignorance of the world at the time when she wrote was complete and many-sided. Human character she knew, not from observation but from dreams. The landscapes for which she is so justly famous are pictures of countries she never saw. There is nothing in her books that she did not create. And it is a testimony to the power of her art that her fancy first conceived a type of character that subsequently passed from art into life. The man that Lord Byron tried to be was the invention of Mrs. Radcliffe.

The plots of her stories have often been censured for their timidity. With an unprecedented control over the secrets of terror, a power of awakening by a touch all the vague associations and suggestions of superstitious awe, she yet shrinks from following Walpole, and never plunges into the frankly supernatural. Further, and here perhaps lies her chief mistake, she does not allow the supernatural even as a possible refuge. The explanations whereby her multiplied mysteries are ultimately dissipated, run on such severely natural lines as to recall the simplicity of Snug the joiner, and the reader is almost ashamed of his terrors when he is confronted with the dull mechanic who has simulated a lion so marvellously.

To historical precision there is no pretence. In *The Mysteries of Udolpho* (1794), a story dealing with events of the year 1584, Parisian fashions, French opera, and French manners, are spoken of as dominating the world. Humour, after the example of Walpole, is relegated to the servants' hall. The stock characters are few, and reappear in each successive novel under altered names. A young, beautiful, and accomplished lady, over whose existence there hangs an unsolved mystery, who is much given to a tender melancholy, and is liable at any moment to be taken with a short fit of rhyming or of fainting, is the Mary-Julia-Adeline-Emily-Elena of the tales. Her lover is frank, generous, impetuous, wild, and romantic. The virtuous among her relatives share her passion for twilight, solitude, the gentler emotions, and the wilder aspects of nature. With or without them, she is commonly imprisoned or detained in a Gothic ruin situated on precipitous rocks or in a dense forest. The villain of the tales may be best introduced by Mrs. Radcliffe's description of Schedoni in *The Italian.*

"There was something terrible in his air, something almost superhuman. His cowl, too, as it threw a shade over the livid paleness of his face, increased its severe character, and gave an effect to his large melancholy eye which approached to horror. . . . There was something in his physiognomy extremely singular, and that cannot easily be defined. It bore the traces of many passions, which seemed to have fixed the features they no longer animated. An habitual gloom and austerity prevailed over the deep lines of his countenance, and his eyes were so piercing that they seemed to penetrate, at a single glance, into the hearts of men, and to read their most secret thoughts."

A few stray lines from *Lara* (1814) will serve to show how Mrs. Radcliffe's villain became Byron's hero :—

> " That brow in furrowed lines had fixed at last,
> And spake of passions, but of passion past ;
> A high demeanour, and a glance that took
> Their thoughts from others by a single look ;
> And some deep feeling it were vain to trace
> At moments lightened o'er his livid face."

The machinery as well as the characters of these novels became the commonplaces of later romancers. The secret corridors, sliding panels, echoing vaults, and hidden trapdoors, the mouldering manuscripts discovered in massive chests and read at night by the light of a flickering candle, are all expedients beloved of Mrs. Radcliffe. The manuscript device, occurring in the works of Walpole and Miss Reeve, became so common a convention as almost to demand classification among the possible modes of telling a story. Mrs. Radcliffe strains it almost to breaking point ; her manuscripts invariably become illegible at the point where some dire secret is about to be revealed. Maturin, in *The Fatal Revenge, or The Family of Montorio* (1807), surpasses her in temerity. Here are the closing words of a document discovered by one of the characters in that work :— " Was that shriek fancy ?—again, again,—impossible ! Hark ! there is a tumult in the castle—lights and voices beneath the turret . . . What is this they tell me ? " The most instantaneous and agitating of experiences, down to the death-gasp, are duly recorded on parchment, and stored away in a vault to await an appropriate discovery.

The absurdities of the renascent romance are many, and are to be found on the surface. The merits of Mrs. Radcliffe are less obvious to a generation for whom her devices are no longer new. Yet with her works the Romantic School sprang at once to maturity. The Romantic movement may be described, in one aspect, as an invasion of the realm of prose by the matter of poetry; and in this regard no bolder inroads are to be chronicled from first to last than those that she planned and executed.

She has a fine command over the world of association and suggestion, distinctively poetic, and " a significant and expressive uncertainty of strokes and colouring." She knows the value of the mere absence of definition, the power of vacuity, darkness, solitude, and silence. And thus, to use a phrase drawn from Burke's treatise *Of the Sublime and Beautiful* (1756), (itself a herald of the Romantic movement), she compels us to "yield to sympathy what we refuse to description." The famous scene in *The Mysteries of Udolpho*, where Emily unveils the awful picture, sufficiently illustrates the method : "She paused again, and then with a timid hand lifted the veil ; but instantly let it fall—perceiving that what it had concealed was no picture, and, before she could leave the chamber, she dropped senseless on the floor."

"*It was no picture*," and the reader exhausts his imagination on terrors before he learns, at the close of the book, that it was, in point of fact, a waxwork.

Another cardinal expedient of Mrs. Radcliffe and the

school at large consists in the isolation of sense impressions commonly associated. Sights without corresponding sounds, sounds without corresponding sights, a touch in the dark—whether of the clammy hand of a dead person, or of "the mealy and carious bones of a skeleton," these things are made to yield a nameless subtle horror. The art of suggestion has been carried further since Mrs. Radcliffe's time; at first by Maturin, and later, in much more delicate fashion, by Nathaniel Hawthorne and Mr. Stevenson. Hawthorne's treatment of the supernatural, whereby he neither affirms nor denies it, but creates its atmosphere, and leaves the reader to please himself, has never been surpassed; and a favourite resource of Mr. Stevenson's for evoking terror, the pursuit, namely, of the hero by an active and malicious blind man, is a fine example of how the superhuman may be suggested by defect.

The remaining contribution made by Mrs. Radcliffe to romantic method is to be found in her employment of scenery. Nowhere but from the poets could she have borrowed this; the tales of Horace Walpole and Clara Reeve are without background, and Charlotte Smith's best known novel, *The Old Manor House* (1793), although it displays a happy subordinate employment of scenery, came too late to influence the greater writer. The essence of Mrs. Radcliffe's scenery is that it is fictitious, lending the richness and fulness of harmony to the thin wavering melody of the plot. In the power which she assigns to flood and fell, sunset and storm, over the moods and passions of her characters, she becomes at times almost Wordsworthian. And her scenery, although artificial, is not glaringly unreal; there are traces of observation of some real atmospheric effects, and her descriptions bear witness to the acuteness of her senses. Sights are not allowed to obscure sounds, and sensations of odour and respiration, all the vague organic impressions that count for so much in the effect of natural surroundings, find their record. But perhaps the most remarkable point in her treatment of nature is the breadth and unity of her pictures. She never forgets the whole in the parts; details are sparingly introduced and generally with telling effect. Her landscapes might be named after the particular emotions they are built to house—terror, regret, security, or melancholy—and they would be in perfect keeping.

Thus, in more than one way, the prose of Mrs. Radcliffe anticipated and guided the poetry of the Romantic revival. Prose like hers could not hope to remain prose long; but technical inaptitude and the precedent set by the novelists prevented her from writing in verse. The narrative poems of the next century owed much to her influence, while the novel proper pursued its course on independent lines. It remains only to chronicle the further history of the School of Terror in its two principal later exponents, Lewis and Maturin.

Matthew Gregory Lewis, who gained notoriety at the age of twenty by the publication of *The Monk* (1795), had been much influenced in his youth by the study of German models. He professed himself greatly stirred by Goethe's *Leiden des jungen Werther* (1774), which speedily spread over civilized Europe. After an introduction to Goethe himself, he wrote to his mother:

"You must not be surprised if I should shoot myself one of these fine mornings." As a matter of fact he was little likely to fall a victim to the sentimental mania, which he ridiculed in a juvenile work called *The Effusions of Sensibility*. His taste was rather for horrors, thick and slab, and it was the perusal of *The Mysteries of Udolpho* that encouraged him to *The Monk*, written, according to his own account, in the space of ten weeks at the Hague. His biographer compares him to Correggio, gazing on the pictures of Michael Angelo and exclaiming, "Anch' io sono pittore!"

Lewis's acquaintance with literature, and especially with the German resuscitations of feudalism, monasticism, ghosts, and hobgoblins, enabled him to fill his museum of atrocities with a large variety of articles of vertu, including the Inquisition, the wandering Jew, and the bleeding nun. But his imagination is gross, boyish, and vulgar, and his horrors rest mainly on a physical basis. He was foolish enough to throw over all the restraints that Mrs. Radcliffe had observed, and to attempt explicit climax. The end of the monk Ambrosio is a good example of his work. The monk renounces his salvation to escape the stake, and a demon carries him clear of his persecutors. The journeyman imagination of Lewis is not content, however, with this approved ending; he follows the two to the remote and desolate precipice whither the monk is carried. There it appears that the demon's promise is now fulfilled; he has saved his client from prison. "'Whither have you brought me?' said the monk at length in a hollow trembling voice: 'Why am I placed in this melancholy scene? Bear me from

it quickly! Carry me to Matilda!'" There ensues an
unnecessary conversation, in which the demon has the
last word, "'Thus I secure my prey!' As he said this,
darting his talons into the monk's shaven crown, he
sprang with him from the rock. The caves and mountains rang with Ambrosio's shrieks. The demon continued to soar aloft, till, reaching a dreadful height, he
released the sufferer."

The *Tales of Wonder* (1801), to which Walter Scott
and John Leyden contributed, contain Lewis's earliest
attempts to revive the old ballad. The Anacreontic
metres frequently selected, give a heightened absurdity
to the rococo horrors of the tales. A stanza in *Alonzo
the Brave*, here reprinted from *The Monk*, thus describes
the posthumous activity of "the false Imogene"—

> " At midnight, four times in each year, does her sprite,
>   When mortals in slumber are bound,
> Arrayed in her bridal apparel of white,
> Appear in the hall with the skeleton knight,
>   And shriek as he whirls her around!"

It is a testimony to the prevalence of the romantic
intoxication that this kind of stuff seduced for a time
the strong and sane imagination of Scott, who produced
a companion picture to it in his *Frederick and Alice.*

But the insolence of coarse horror soon exhausts its
themes; the grave gives up its dead, and has no more
to give to the realistic artist. It was by the subtlety of
his mental analysis and his power of suggestion, wherein
he far excelled Mrs. Radcliffe, rather than by the bold
atrocities of realism, wherein he endeavoured to outbid

Lewis, that Charles Robert Maturin (1782–1824) earned his title to the headship of the School of Terror.

In his first novel, *The Fatal Revenge ; or, The Family of Montorio* (1807), published under the assumed name of Dennis Jasper Murphy, he explains his intent. " I have presumed," he says, " to found the interest of a romance on the passion of supernatural fear, and on that almost alone." Love, he urges, is felt in its purity by comparatively few ; fear, on the other hand, especially the fear arising from objects of invisible terror, is universal and irresistible in its appeal. Objects of terror, by no means always invisible, abound in this spectre-haunted, corpse-ridden story. The question asked by the old servant Michelo, " Is it then possible to know the living from the dead ? " finds a ready answer from the reader : it is quite impossible in the family of Montorio. The plot, like the greater part of those constructed by Maturin, is perplexed in the extreme ; it can barely be disentangled. And in this novel Maturin allows the example of his predecessors to weigh too much with him ; his real strength lay in regions untrodden by Walpole or Lewis.

Of his subsequent romances, from *The Wild Irish Boy* (1808) to *The Albigenses* (1824), universal criticism has pronounced *Melmoth the Wanderer* (1820) to be the masterpiece. The favourite Rosicrucian idea, already borrowed by Godwin for philosophic purposes in *St. Leon* (1799), is here turned to the best imaginative use. The lurid figure of Melmoth, who has gained earthly immortality at a price never to be named or thought on by those who would keep their sanity, the paralyzing glamour of his eyes, the withering smile, wherein malignity

and levity have not extinguished pathos, as he proposes
to his victims the *incommunicable condition* of their release
from the madhouse or the prisons of the Inquisition,
these things besiege the memory like some dream that
confuses itself with waking hours. The story is made
up of a number of ill-strung episodes, far apart in time
and space, united only by the awful sense of that impending approach, as the utmost dangers and terrors of
earth press heavier on the protagonist of each successive
tale. The greatest scenes of *Melmoth*, as, for instance,
the accounts of his midnight wedding with Isidora, of
his subterranean pilotage of Monçada as they escape
from the monastery, of his last awful and rapid trans-
formation to the decrepitude of age, are as fine effects
of subtle terror as were ever devised by a literary
master.

The secret of Maturin's treatment of the supernatural
lies almost wholly in his power of suggestion. Not
only in the broader sort of delineation by single violent
effects, which might be exampled from those lines in
the *Ancient Mariner*—

> " I took the oars : the Pilot's boy,
> *Who now doth crazy go*,
> Laughed loud and long ; "

not only in the aposiopesis of which he is so fond is his
mastery evinced, he excels also in the delicate manipu-
lation of all unreasoning apprehensions and superstitions.
His observation of strange things in nature is singularly
acute. When Monçada is examined by the Inquisition,
he describes one of the judges trembling on his seat,
"while his shadow, magnified by the imperfect light,

pictured the figure of a paralytic giant on the wall opposite to me." That is the clue to Maturin's effects; he sees the shadow before he sees the body, and he chooses the shadow, for it is often many times larger and more terrible than the body. His analytic knowledge of the human mind is excellently employed in the service of terror. Wordsworth's lover was struck with a thrill of fear on seeing the moon set behind the cottage of her he loved; his Margaret, in the intensity of her desire for intercourse with the dead, is strangely moved by the rustling of the grass and the passing of the clouds; it is the highest praise that can be given to Maturin to allege that he oftentimes works with sentiments as subtle as these.

It is impossible rigidly to demarcate the School of Theory in fiction, or to name many authors, or even single works, that belong to it wholly. Towards the end of the eighteenth century theory was rife in England, and speculations on politics, religion, marriage, and education were not slow to find expression in the novel. But a novel that does no more than give vivid, concrete expression to some definite moral or political lesson is either a bad novel, or its merits are irrelevant, if not positively detrimental, to its main theme. A tale "illustrative of the truths of Political Economy" is likely to spoil two good things—political economy, to wit, and the tale as an imaginative product. The world of men and women must be maimed to be fitted accurately to the general laws of the economist, and the laws themselves lose, in the process, the regal security of pure science.

It is therefore more in particular traits and tendencies, common to many of the novels of the time, than in special authors or works that the marks of system and theory are to be sought. The French Revolution communicated a strong impetus to English speculation on the foundations of law and custom. And if a central expression were required for all the influences at work upon those authors who made fiction a vehicle for abstract thought, it would have to be the name of one who, more than any other, was the precursor of the Revolution in all its aspects—Jean Jacques Rousseau.

The characteristic doctrines of Rousseau, expounded in the works which range from the Discourse written for the prize of the Academy of Dijon in 1749, down to the *Nouvelle Héloïse* in 1761, and *Emile* and the *Contrat Social* in 1762, fermented in European literature for the rest of the century. The doctrines themselves might have had a less startling success had they not been bathed in the sentiment and winged with the ardour of the man's extraordinary temperament. Rousseau owed much to English writers, to Locke and to Richardson, for instance. But Locke, the cautious upholder of the constitutional principles of the English Revolution, would have been amazed at his pupil; and the sentiment of *Clarissa*, redolent of the proprieties, had none of the infectious power of the sentiment of Saint Preux, although, considered as a novel, Richardson's work is infinitely finer than the *Nouvelle Héloïse*. The simplest of the materials borrowed by Rousseau were transformed, by the chemistry of his temper, into intoxicants and solvents. His effusion of sentiment is no greater than

Sterne's. "The danger lay," as Mr. John Morley remarks, "in the mischievous intellectual direction which Rousseau imparted to this effusion."

The fundamental conception of Rousseau's work is to be found in his exaltation of "the State of Nature." "The return to Nature," sometimes insisted on as the essence of the Romantic movement in England, may mean almost anything—residence in the country, the unrestrained expression of the emotions, or the violent levelling of all social distinctions. It was largely due to Rousseau that it came to mean all three, and that a love of natural scenery and a highly strung emotional sensibility became inextricably associated with rebellion against political institutions and social canons.

The "natural man" was at once seized on by the novelists to play a leading part in their pages. He was no new invention; Mrs. Behn's best novel *Oroonoko, or The History of the Royal Slave* (1698), contains a full-length portrait of him, and a description of a people who represent "an absolute idea of the first state of innocence, before man knew how to sin: and it is most evident and plain, that simple nature is the most harmless, inoffensive, and virtuous mistress. It is she alone, if she were permitted, that better instructs the world, than all the inventions of man : religion would here but destroy that tranquillity they possess by ignorance; and laws would but teach them to know offence, of which now they have no notion." The conception of a perfectly virtuous primitive people, with no law and no religion, is here fully developed. But it was Rousseau who first pointed it as a powerful weapon of offence against existing civilizations, and gave it the revolutionary shape it assumes in the lines of Burns—

> " Courts for cowards were erected,
> Churches built to please the priest."

How little Oroonoko was appreciated as a revolutionary agent may be inferred from his reappearance, under a changed name, in the pages of Dr. John Shebbeare, a political writer of Johnson's time, on the Tory side. In his single memorable novel *Lydia, or Filial Piety* (1755), written before Rousseau's longer works, he introduces the reader, in the very first chapter, to "patriotism, heroism, fainting, dying, loving, sentiment, and generosity, all amongst Indians in America." Cannassatego, the noble Indian warrior who is brought to Europe as a foil for the vices of the Bounces, Macbrogues, and Muckworms that fill the book, is a counterpart to Mrs. Behn's hero, and gains the love of Yarico, a dove-like Indian maiden. But he has vowed to visit Europe, and when he meditates postponing the performance of his vow, he is thus taunted by his friend Decanessora : " Can it be imagined that violated honour can be received among the *Indians* with applause ? Will not the sachems pronounce that none but *Europeans* are guilty of that meanness ? " Yarico, his betrothed lady, was a very exceptional Indian squaw, for she had "a thousand times exclaimed against that pernicious principle of glory, which delights in war and slaughter. She conceived it the most unnatural idea which can enter into the human heart, that rage and the destruction of mankind should prevail over the softer passions of love and

R

friendship, and fame be obtained by what ought to be the horror of humanity."

Imported from savage lands by Mrs. Behn and Dr. Shebbeare, the "natural man" soon became a naturalized Englishman. Protest was useless, although Johnson uttered a criticism both adequate and final when, on finding the position maintained by Lord Kaimes that virtue is natural to man, he remarked, "This is saying a thing which all mankind know not to be true." As a hero of fiction, nevertheless, the natural man had irresistible attractions for authors of the Revolutionary period. He is the Hermsprong of Robert Bage's best novel. He is the Frank Henley of Thomas Holcroft's *Anna St. Ives* (1792). How his primitive virtues might be regained, was the problem of morals; how they might be retained, unsullied by calculation and convention, was the problem of education. And these problems left their mark, not only on the works of those French writers that felt the influence of Rousseau—Bernardin de St. Pierre, Madame de Genlis, and many others— but also on the innocent schemes devised by the authors of *The Fool of Quality* and *Sandford and Merton*. A new and singular type of hero shared with Mrs. Radcliffe's Byronic creations the admiration of the age. Sentimental and philanthropic, he is also entirely independent of the opinion of his fellows; he neither respects nor understands social distinctions, and stalks through the world superior to all its artificial standards. The good he conciliates by a simplicity that discards all false honour, false modesty, and false pride; the bad he disconcerts by the Socratic paradoxes of the nursery. The description

of Frank Henley put by Holcroft into the mouth of
Coke Clifton, his worldly rival, illustrates these traits :
"Exclusive of his obstinacy, the rude pot-companion
loquacity of the fellow is highly offensive. He has no
sense of inferiority. He stands as erect, and speaks
with as little embarrassment, and as loudly as the best
of us; nay, boldly asserts, that neither riches, rank, nor
birth have any claim. I have offered to buy him a
beard if he would but turn heathen philosopher. . . .
Among the most ridiculous of what he calls first
principles is that of the equality of mankind. . . . He
derives from Adam, what time the world was all 'hail
fellow, well met!' The savage, the wild man of the
woods, is his true liberty-boy; and the ourang-outang,
his first cousin. A lord is a merry-andrew, a duke a
jack-pudding, and a king a tom-fool: his name is man!"

The writers who divulged this conception of man in
English fiction belonged, for the most part, to the same
social circle, and held the same political principles.
Thomas Holcroft (1745–1809), the eldest of them, had
made good use of his mixed experiences of life among
stable-boys and strolling actors in his first novel, *Alwyn;
or the Gentleman Comedian* (1780). But this work,
although it contains much interesting reminiscence and
some vigorous satire, belongs wholly to the older school
of fiction. It was in his later novels, particularly those
produced soon after the Revolution, *Anna St. Ives*
(1792), and *Hugh Trevor* (1794–97), that Holcroft developed his political creed. In these two works, which
are in some sense companion pictures, representing
respectively ideal and real characters, are to be found

almost all the doctrines which received consecutive logical exposition in the *Political Justice* (1793) of William Godwin. As Godwin himself admitted his obligations to Holcroft, it is enough to study the outcome of these doctrines in the works of the younger and more distinguished writer.

William Godwin (1756–1836) had been educated in a creed drawn from the writings of Sandeman, and after passing through most of the primary colours of belief and disbelief, with many intermediate tints, had adopted the theoretic principles of the French Revolution in their most uncompromising form. On these he aspired, almost alone among Englishmen, to build a perfect scheme of Man and Society. The main features of this scheme are well known. "Give to a State liberty enough," he said, "and it is impossible that vice should exist in it." The Throne, the Church, the Army, and the Law, he would fain see gently but rapidly abolished. Man is a readily perfectible being ; and his vices and failings, including avarice, jealousy, and hate, would disappear with the institutions that have produced them. His very virtues, in so far as they are partial and con-cerned with anything less than "the well-being and happiness of every intellectual and sensitive existence," would be superseded. For friendship, gratitude, patriot-ism, and family affection, a regenerated society would find no use.

That the sincere upholder of these doctrines should have been a fine writer of novels is the real marvel ; much as if a blind man should prove a capable painter. Not that his theories do not leave plentiful traces on his fictions. In his earliest novel, *Things as they are; or the Adventures of Caleb Williams* (1794), the passages that betray the politician are many. The gang of thieves that seize upon Williams after he has fled his master's house, consists of men at open war with the wickedness of society, and unwilling to stain the purity of their cause by cruelty, malice, or revenge. The prison in which he is confined is the text of much millennarian discourse. And Collins, the virtuous and amiable steward, is a mouthpiece for Godwin's theory of man. Hatred of evil is unreasonable, said Godwin, for the bad qualities of men are forced on them by circumstance; and the sentiment finds expression, hugely undramatic, in the speech of Collins: "You know my habits of thinking. I regard you as vicious; but I do not consider the vicious as proper objects of indignation and scorn. I consider you as a machine; you are not constituted, I am afraid, to be greatly useful to your fellow men. . . . I am sorry for your ill properties; but I entertain no enmity against you, nothing but benevolence. Considering you in the light in which I at present consider you, I am ready to contribute everything in my power to your real advantage. . . . It is more necessary for me to feel compassion for you, than that I should accumulate your misfortune by my censures."

Yet with all these things the interest of *Caleb Williams* is very real and very well maintained. The character of Falkland, in which all the milder virtues have been overshadowed by the memory of his crime, the sleepless curiosity of Williams in the effort to ascertain his master's secret, the price he pays for success in the persecution that dogs him unremittingly, together make up a story of an interest too powerful to permit it to be enslaved to a frigid scheme of Utopian politics. The moral of the history and fate of Falkland is contained in one of the concluding reflections : "Of what use are talents and sentiments in the corrupt wilderness of human society?" The tale is meant to enforce this reflection, but in point of fact it denies to the reader much opportunity for reflections of any kind, and keeps his sporting instincts excited by the pleasures and hazards of the chase. The professed moral is as irrelevant as a philosopher in the hunting-field.

In his later novels, especially in *St. Leon* (1799) and *Fleetwood* (1805), Godwin shows a greatly increased knowledge of life and character. For this increased knowledge the author of the *Political Justice* apologizes in two highly conscientious prefaces. "The affections and charities of private life" are eulogized in *St. Leon*, and, indeed, the author has come to believe them "not incompatible with a profound and active sense of justice in the mind of him that cherishes them." At any rate they are "inseparable from the nature of man," and may be used as a stepping-stone to general benevolence. And after all, "it is better that man should be a living being than a stock or a stone." Godwin the philosopher stands rebuked by this discovery of Godwin the novelist. In *Fleetwood* further occasion is given to the enemy of progress to blaspheme, for in that work respect is expressed for marriage. This is an institution which, on the occasion of his own marriage some years before, the philosopher had recommended his fellow-men " never to practise, but with the greatest caution." A few years before that again he was for total abolition. And now the jealousy that was not, and the marriage that was not to be, are both, it appears, needed for an old-fashioned melodramatic plot. In attempting to justify his inconsistency, Godwin does not plead, as he well might, that effete institutions and characters, such as the king, the priest, and the wife, may be permitted to survive in fiction. His defence is that great changes must be carried out in concert and gradually; it would be absurd for a solitary individual (such as Fleetwood) to act prematurely in the matter.

The novels ushered in by these delightful solemnities are an interesting pair. The supernatural plot of *St. Leon* is something of a weakness, for of mystery Godwin had no sense. The secret of immortality and wealth is conveyed to St. Leon in the most squalid fashion possible by a stranger whom he secretes in the summer-house of his garden. The protests of his children (" Papa, I wish you would not let a man get into the summer-house, who shuts all the shutters, and locks the door "), reasonable in themselves, do not heighten the feeling of awe. The relations of man to society are Godwin's real theme, and he shows power and subtlety in the chain of disaster that he draws from the necessity of secrecy—the one condition of the magic endowments.

The best of his imaginative work is to be found in *Fleetwood*; not so much in the main story, with its stock villain and maligned wife, as in the early reminiscences of Fleetwood and the episodical autobiography of Ruffigny, where the author displays a sensibility to scenery and a vivid remembrance of the feelings of childhood that would be remarkable even in a less arid mind.

It would be easy to trace the theories and fashions that mark Godwin's novels through many of the works of his contemporaries. One of the best of the tales of Mrs. Opie, *Adeline Mowbray ; or the Mother and Daughter* (1804), is influenced by Godwin's theories, as well as founded in part on his history; and Mrs. Inchbald's two novels, *A Simple Story* (1791) and *Nature and Art* (1796), show the prevalent ideas on education and social convention spoiling the outlines of the work of a real artist. In *Nature and Art* especially, Mrs. Inchbald sets herself to exhibit the fortunes of two cousins, William and Henry, the one brought up in a deanery, where "men were paid to tell him how to think," the other imbibing honour and virtue at their source among the savages of Zocotora Island. Returned to civilization, Henry "would call *compliments, lies—reserve,* he would call *pride — stateliness, affectation —* and for the monosyllable *war,* he constantly substituted the word *massacre.*" The gentle excitement that these and similar habits supplied to the deanery is less easily produced in a reader to whom word-games of this kind are by no means new. But with its continuation the story suddenly rises to almost tragic stature. The scene where William, as a judge, condemns to death the girl he had deceived and deserted is great, not from the boisterous strength of the situation, but from the strength of its telling. That and the character of Miss Milner in *A Simple Story* entitle Mrs. Inchbald to a very high place among the novelists proper of her day.

One large class of stories may, without extravagance, be said to belong, by way of pendant, to the Revolutionary movement. Rousseau had given enormous prominence in his published writings to the question of education, and had maintained that novels, even the novels of his admired Richardson, were no fit diet for the young. Madame de Genlis, whose scheme of education is pure Rousseau, would allow her Adèle to read novels freely until she reaches the age of fourteen, when they must be put away with other childish things. By this means it was believed the taste for them might be broken, just as Sir Thomas More's Utopians guarded against avarice by applying gold to the meanest or most puerile uses. From the general condemnation that Madame de Genlis passes upon novels, the trio of Richardson is alone exempt. In order to supply a more wholesome form of reading for the young, the same lady produced a library of tales ; she seems to regard it as the obvious duty of a mother to write all the stories her daughter reads. In England a host of writers soon arose to supply the new demand. From the date of Thomas Day's *Sandford and Merton* (1783–89) onwards there was never lacking in England abundance of tales for the young, and it is not a little curious to observe how many of them have a strong flavour of the theories of the Revolution. Rank and wealth are almost always denuded, in these stories, of their fair share of the trappings lent by the imagination. " 'Tis only noble to be good,"—a definition of nobility which it is permitted to those of maturer years to supplement by a study of Burke's *Peerage.*

The School of Terror and the School of Theory are by no means exhaustive categories for the prose fiction of the Romantic revival. Of the earlier attempts at historical fiction and the revival of mediævalism it is most convenient to treat in connection with Scott. The Orientalism that is so striking a feature of the later French Romantic movement is exemplified in England by a single work, the *Vathek* (1786) of William Beckford. This romance is infinitely finer than Walpole's Gothic toy, but it is less historically important. Walpole is a direct ancestor of Scott, while *Vathek*, unless Moore's much later *Epicurean* (1827) be affiliated to it, remained without distinguished progeny. Written originally in French, although not, as Beckford in later life pretended, at a single sitting, translated into English, and surreptitiously published by the author's friend Samuel Henley, *Vathek* has maintained its position as the finest Oriental tale written by an Englishman. The breath of the Romantic movement stirs in it, and distinguishes it in kind from the exquisitely witty Oriental tales of Count Anthony Hamilton, on which it was modelled. The grotesque extravagance of Eastern supernaturalism only tickled the fancy of Count Hamilton ; it held the imagination of Beckford. " I tremble whilst relating it," he writes of his story, " and have not a nerve in my frame but vibrates like an aspen." The occidental point of view, whether of humour or scepticism, is in this tale almost abandoned. The author's enjoyment of comic extravagance peeps out, no doubt, in the description of the great Vathek, who "wished to know everything; even sciences that did not exist;" who lost his appetite when overcome with agitation, so that "of the three hundred dishes that were daily placed before him, he could taste of no more than thirty-two;" as well as in the introduction of the ominous stranger, who was "so abominably hideous, that the very guards who arrested him were forced to shut their eyes as they led him along." These touches, and the like throughout the story, are of French origin; but Beckford's own great merit lies rather in the sublime extravagance that follows hard upon them, attaining its highest in the infernal majesty of Eblis, who makes of the hearts of his victims a receptacle for eternal fire. The stamp of incredulity is on the tales of Hamilton and Voltaire; with them the Eastern imagination is a mere laughing-stock for the Western wit; it is Beckford alone who, accepting the new fantastic domain as his own by right, forgets the world of reality, and raises his palace in the shades. In the same attempt Southey was less successful; and a free employment of the grotesque in the service of serious emotion is a disastrous experiment for little artists.

With the two romances of the boyhood of Shelley, *Zastrozzi* (1810) and *St. Irvyne; or, The Rosicrucian* (1811), this account of the revivalists may fitly close. The sovereign transmutation that the dull, hard stuff of Godwin's doctrines suffered in the crucible of Shelley's imagination is known to all readers of the poems. In the *Epipsychidion* the nightingale pours forth a song suggested to her by the croaking of the frog. But in his earlier romances Shelley's imagination is wild and crude, so that they combine more than the violence of Maturin's early work with more than the absurdity of Godwin's complacent dogma. It is a strange mixture, and an odd world. These lovers, who regard legal marriage as an impropriety, and these villains, whose mildest feeling is an ecstasy of malignity, are types drawn from different schools. Romance, in these works, has once more reached the extreme of its tether; the world of adjectives is exhausted, raptures fall back into the ineffable, agonies into the indescribable. So monotonous a protest of the inadequacy of language ceases to work its effect, and instead of heightening the situation, serves only to lower the literary art.

CHAPTER IX.

THE NOVEL OF DOMESTIC SATIRE: MISS BURNEY, MISS AUSTEN, MISS EDGEWORTH.

THE world and life were not wholly conquered for the novel when the last of the great school of eighteenth-century novelists laid down his pen. Since the days of Mrs. Aphra Behn and Mrs. Haywood, women had written novels in plenty, but their novels attempted pictures of life as it is seen through the eyes of men. Even Mrs. Radcliffe, a great inventor in romance, posed her heroines in attitudes engaging or pathetic for appreciation by their lovers and the world at large, making little or no attempt to fashion them from the heart outwards. Not until the greatest of women romancers arose in Charlotte Brontë was passion represented as it could only have been conceived by a woman. But for the portraiture of the world as it might appear to "a very young lady," intensely self-conscious, instinct with the proprieties and the delicacies implanted by careful guardians—for the description of her social embarrassments and discomforts, less power and less daring sufficed. The heart may be laid bare without a blush when it has been prepared and inserted under clerical

supervision. To describe the world as it seems to a
woman utterly pre-occupied with the thought of how she
seems to the world, asked much skill but little courage.
The new departure was taken and the new school
founded, in 1778, by Miss Burney in her justly famous
novel *Evelina.*

The comedy of life, as Fielding conceived of it, made
at all times comparatively little appeal to those for whom
life was entangled with more manifold restrictions and
set within narrower limits. The bluff open-air reality of
Squire Western became hardly real when transferred to
the literary drawing-rooms of the close of the century.
The fact is that the tone of society and manners under-
went a very rapid and complete change during the
eighteenth century, and a reaction against the brutality
and coarseness so common in the days of Defoe and
Swift led to an excess of fantastic refinement ; a wave
of delicacy submerged the nation and carried it far from
its earlier standpoint. The case of the " old lady of
family," mentioned by Sir Walter Scott, who read the
works of Mrs. Aphra Behn in her youth, but in her
old age turned from them in horror to peruse the politer
fictions of Miss Maria Edgeworth, is a fair measure of
the change in taste witnessed by the century. Jane
Austen speaks of the *Spectator* as " a voluminous publication, hardly any part of which would not, either by its
matter or manner, disgust a young person of taste."
Mrs. Brunton, in her excellent novel *Self-Control* (1811),
assigns to one of her characters the heart-felt opinion
that " Tom Jones's warmth of heart and generosity do
not appear to me of that kind which qualify a man for

adorning domestic life." Domestic life, rather than the old wild life of the road, became the standard and the subject of the novelists ; it was adorned with a complete literature of its own by the talents of Miss Burney and Miss Edgeworth and the genius of Jane Austen. The thirty years or so before the appearance of *Waverley*, in 1814, were the years of the triumph of woman, creator and created, in the novel ; they were the years also during which Miss Edgeworth and Lady Morgan struck out those first attempts in the portrayal of national character which may claim the merit of having suggested his most brilliant successes to Sir Walter Scott.

"The romance of the tea-table," which has been suggested as a fitting name for the works produced by Miss Burney, Miss Austen and their school, is not altogether free from an unwarrantable suspicion of disrespect. It indicates justly enough the area of their domain, a party gathered around a tea-table gave verge enough for the best work of these novelists ; it does not indicate the marvellous power deployed upon that humble social surface. Their novels might rather perhaps be called novels of domestic satire ; the satirical motive and craft are always there, but " social satire " is too wide a name for it. Man is stripped of the public trappings on which he prides himself, he is bereft of all wider social relations, and appears simply and solely as a member of a family,—by that let him stand or fall. When they transgress the domestic threshold, and attempt conquests in a larger world, Miss Burney and Miss Edgeworth stray into farce or fashion : Miss Austen, with the sleepless prudence of perfect sovereignty, is never to be tempted beyond the limits of her parlour. A description of a sea-fight or a murder by Miss Austen, a record of the conversation among a party of ladies around the tea-table of a vicarage by Sir Walter Scott, are gems for which the collector of curiosities may search in vain.

Frances Burney (1752–1840) was born at King's Lynn, Norfolk, where her father was organist. She was almost entirely self-educated, and passed her girlhood in London, whither her father moved in 1760, while her two sisters were being educated in France. She began to write almost as soon as she could read, and had completed her first novel, *The History of Caroline Evelyn*, before she was fifteen. But her stepmother was hostile to her literary propensities, and this work was burnt by its author in the presence of her sister Susannah. The writers whose names are enumerated with veneration in the preface to *Evelina*—Rousseau, Johnson, Marivaux, Fielding, Richardson, and Smollett—were doubtless her chief literary instructors; novelists have generally been insatiable novel-readers.

The world of imagination that she had created and inhabited could not be destroyed with the lost work, and Miss Burney pursued in her meditations the further history of the family to which Caroline Evelyn belonged. The result was *Evelina; or, The History of a Young Lady's Entrance into the World* (1778), published anonymously by Lowndes after it had been refused by Dodsley. The story of the sudden rise into fame of the authoress, of the intoxication she found in the approval of Burke and Reynolds and the friendship of Johnson, can be read in the earlier pages of the inimitable *Diary*. Miss Burney had scored the great literary success of her generation.

She thought of turning playwright, but the problem of how "to preserve spirit and salt, and yet keep up delicacy," proved too much for her, and she went to work at once on her second novel, *Cecilia; or, The Memoirs of an Heiress* (1782). Through the intimacy of Mrs. Delany she was next introduced to the court as second keeper of the robes. Apollo serving Admetus was probably more at ease in his work than Miss Burney attiring Queen Charlotte and waiting on Madam Schwellenborg. But the episode yielded some of the best satirical work in her diary. Her two later novels, *Camilla* (1796) and *The Wanderer* (1814), were written for money after her marriage with Monsieur D'Arblay. She survived her friends and relatives, witnessed the whole career of Sir Walter Scott, and became a white-haired shadow in a world where Tennyson and Carlyle were literary celebrities.

Her first and best novel, *Evelina*, gave a new lease of life to the eighteenth-century school by opening up a new realm of possibilities and showing how the method of the masters might be applied to a more delicate material. Caroline Evelyn, the heroine of her youthful work, was a girl of obscure birth who, having been disowned by her husband, a profligate nobleman, died shortly after the birth of her daughter. Evelina is educated by a clergyman, and enters the fashionable world to find herself claimed by her mother's relatives, the elderly Madam Duval, who had been originally "a

S

waiting-girl at a tavern," and the Branghtons, silver-smiths of Holborn. The misadventures and humiliations to which Evelina is subjected by the merciless vulgarity of her relatives during her courtship by Lord Orville form the plot of the story, slight but sufficient. The intensity with which Miss Burney feels these things, and the fidelity with which she represents them, would perhaps have been unattainable by a novelist of a wider range; they are natural and convincing from the pen of Evelina, who confides her mishaps to her clerical guardian by letter. Miss Burney is no less caustic than Miss Austen; the Holborn beau, Mr. Smith, with his "fine varnish of low politeness," and the two giggling Misses Branghton with their innocently gross confidences and grosser reticences, are as vulgar as anything to be found in the pages of her greater successor. But she is less detached and impersonal,—she cannot smile as Miss Austen smiles over the rabbit-warren of human littlenesses; at times she seems on the point of forgetting that there is nothing tragic in offence given to a peer's sense of propriety—so warmly does she espouse Evelina's grievances. Social miseries, in all their intensity and variety—some of them, by an odd repetition, undergone by herself years later at Windsor — surely never had a more enthusiastic recorder. The tortures Evelina suffers have the vividness of a nightmare; they are not exaggerated in representation, but they are so completely isolated, kept so far from the wash of the larger passions and interests of life, that what might have been a dull discomfort becomes a frightful incubus.

The success of her first novel led Miss Burney to

make a much more ambitious and much less successful attempt. The plot of *Cecilia* gives the old pre-eminence to questions of etiquette, social prejudices are exhibited in over-mastering opposition to human feelings, and lose an easy victory only by division among themselves. The love of Mortimer Delvile, a scion of a proud, ancient, and penniless family, for the heiress Cecilia is thwarted by the condition on which she holds her fortune, that the man who marries her must assume her name. Here was a situation fitted for Miss Burney's talents and within her competency. But she embroiders it profusely by the introduction of supernumerary characters and strained tragic or mirthful episodes. Successful comedy of manners is objective in essence, and loses its footing when it outruns experience : the figures of Cecilia's three guardians—the vulgar miser, the dissipated man of fashion, and the haughty aristocrat— carry no conviction of reality and exhibit no credentials, although they are set in action prettily enough. The Vauxhall scene, so extravagantly praised by rightly partial critics, wherein Mr. Harrel escapes from his duns and shoots himself, is spirited melodrama, but nothing more; there is not a breath of genuine terror in it all. And the fops, witlings, and jargonists are mere types, the products of a busy comic wit that has lost its way. Miss Cecilia Beverley, older than Miss Evelina Anville and a little more self-possessed, steers her way through this motley crew with credit and composure, sharing perhaps the feeling of the reader, that she need not disturb herself about them; they are there, playing their tricks, tumbling and shouting, for the amusement

of the public, like mountebanks on a Derby day in the
intervals of the races.

Madame D'Arblay never regained the simplicity of
theme that marked the best work of Miss Burney, and
she lost the simplicity of style that makes of *Cecilia*
a sprightly book. Her later novels suffered from degeneration of manner due to the infection of Dr.
Johnson's stately English. To attempt the Johnsonian
period without a familiar knowledge of the Latin tongue
is to practise diving before learning to swim; thereafter
there is life to be saved at sea. Her reputation must
rest on her two earlier novels, and it would lose little of
its stability if the later of these were removed. Her
brilliant, shrewd satire and close observation were un-
matched in her own time, and she prepared the way for
Miss Austen, who subscribed for *Camilla*, and took the
title of her earliest novel, *Pride and Prejudice*, from the
concluding sentences of *Cecilia*.

There is little to tell about the brief life of Jane
Austen (1775–1817). Born at Steventon, a country
village of North Hampshire, where her father was rector,
she passed the first twenty-five years of her life, and
wrote her first three novels, in the surroundings and
society that she has made classic. *Pride and Prejudice*,
written by the time she was twenty-one, was refused by
Cadell; *Northanger Abbey* was bought for ten pounds by
a publisher in Bath, and by him kept in a drawer for
years until it was redeemed for the same simple sum by
the writer's family. To write three novels consecutively
with never a prospect of publishing one, bespeaks a
calling and zest in the work.

After an interlude of eight years, spent in the wider society of Bath and Southampton, she returned in 1809 to a cottage at Chawton, not far from Steventon; and here, living with her mother and sister (her father had died at Bath), she produced the second trio of her novels, *Emma, Mansfield Park,* and *Persuasion.* Then at last *Sense and Sensibility,* written in 1797–8, was accepted by a publisher and produced in 1811. Three of the others followed during the remaining years of her life; *Northanger Abbey* and *Persuasion* were published after her death. She died in lodgings at Winchester, and was buried in the Cathedral.

The late and partial fame that she enjoyed in her lifetime never seduced her into a misleading ambition. Her own words when the librarian of Carlton House invited her to write "an historical romance illustrative of the august House of Cobourg" deserve record. " I could not sit down to write a serious romance under any other motive than to save my life; and if it were indispensable for me to keep it up, and never relax into laughter at myself or at other people, I am sure I should be hung before I had finished the first chapter. No, I must keep to my own style, and go on in my own way; and though I may never succeed again in that, I am convinced that I should totally fail in any other." It is hard to believe that she did not know the flawless perfection of her own work. She told fairy stories to her nephews and nieces; to the public she gave her version of the human comedy, in six books.

The comparison between Jane Austen and Shakespeare, suggested by Macaulay, is curiously attractive.

Both left scant record of their personal convictions and emotions; indeed the *Sonnets* are a fuller confession than can be gathered from all the letters and remains of the later writer. Enthusiastic students of Miss Austen have ransacked her novels for traces of her affairs of the heart, and of her political and religious opinions, in a manner and with a result that recall the efforts of Shakesperian commentators. There is at least a semblance of likeness in the attitude that each assumed to friends and family, to Stratford and to Steventon; the purchaser of New Place who did not collect and publish his own works may be compared, perhaps mistakenly, with the lady who refused literary society and wrote for her own and her sister's diversion. The stirring events of the times they lived in are as little reflected or recorded in the pages of one as of the other. These may be resemblances merely fanciful. What is not fanciful is the sameness of artistic impersonality, of serene abstraction from life, that characterises both writers equally. Of the two, Shakespeare, eternally susceptible to temptation by a gleam of poetry, exhibits the less majestic calm. He can hardly be content for long with the supremacy of an inferior kingdom. "The hand which drew Miss Bates," says Mr. Goldwin Smith, in his admirable *Life of Jane Austen*, "though it could not have drawn Lady Macbeth, could have drawn Dame Quickly or the nurse in 'Romeo and Juliet.'" The same hand, had it attempted the description of the murder of the little princes in *Richard III.*, would never have slipped into the poetic metaphor that gives to Shakespeare's hired assassins so unreal an air.

The perfection of Miss Austen's workmanship has been seized upon by unfavourable critics and used as a weapon of offence. She is perfect, they allege, only as some are virtuous, because she has no temptation; she lives in an abject world, dead to poetry, visited by no breath of romance, and is placidly contented with her ant-hill, which she describes with great accuracy and insight. It would be unjust to this type of criticism to interpret it merely as a complaint that one who was of unsurpassed power in comedy and satire did not forego her gifts and take up with romance and tragedy. If it has a meaning worth considering, it means that even the comedy of life has in it shades of pathos and passion to which she is constitutionally blind. And this is to mistake her art. The world of pathos and passion is present in her work by implication; her delicious quiet mirth, so quiet as to be inaudible to gross ears, is stirred by the incongruity between the realities of the world as she conceives them, and these realities as they are conceived by her puppets. The kingdom of Lilliput has its meaning only when it is seen through the eyes of Gulliver. A rabbit fondling its own harmless face affords no matter of amusement to another rabbit, and Miss Austen has had many readers who have perused her works without a smile. Sympathy with her characters she frequently has, identity never. Not in the high-spirited Elizabeth Bennet, not in that sturdy young patrician Emma, not even in Anne Elliot of *Persuasion*, is the real Jane Austen to be found. She stands for ever aloof. Those who wish to enjoy her art must stand aloof too, and must not ask to be hurried through her novels on a personally conducted tour, with their admirations and dislikes prepared for them.

What, perhaps, has led hasty or unintelligent critics strangely to misread her is that she never obtrudes the contrast spoken of above; hardly ever, even as narrator, speaks in her own person. By the most delicate of irony she allows the opinions and feelings of her characters to colour her own matter-of-fact narration. "There certainly are not so many men of large fortune in the world as there are pretty women to deserve them," she remarks, on the first page of *Mansfield Park*. Stupid readers, who ought to be in her books instead of outside them and trying to read them, agree with her; good serious critics, on the trail of fine sentiments, exclaim in sorrow that she says a hundred things like this. But she is thinking of the matrimonial prospects of the three Misses Ward, and putting herself at the point of view of the family, with a certain subtle literary politeness that is charm itself. Her own views on the subject of marriage she does not trouble to explain. But the folly of some of her characters implies the existence of wisdom; the selfishness and pettiness of others involve the ideas of disinterestedness and magnanimity, just as a picture painted in cold tints would lose its meaning if there were no blue and red in the scheme of the universe. To ask for all colours, always, within the limits of the frame, is absurd.

She compares her own work to miniature-painting on ivory, "on which I work with so fine a brush as produces little effect after much labour." In loving elaboration of detail she resembles no other writer so much as a special

favourite of hers, Cowper, whose letters display the same
voluminous fearlessness in the treatment of the trivial,
with a like happy result.   To quote her except by pages
at a time would be to do her an injustice.   Here are no
sudden white-heats of exalted imagination or momentary
illuminations of the abysses of human life, but a steady
stream of daylight on familiar objects, a perfect proportion,
and a clearness that seems to the inexpert to be due to
emptiness.   The absolute transparency of her style, the
medium in which her creations live and move, is illusive
in its nature ; her readers can pass from the commonplaces
of life to the actions and speeches of her fictitious characters with so little sense of shock, so faint a realization
that they are passing from life to a convention, that it is
not to be wondered at if her craft has been ignored
or denied.   Art was never applied to average material
with so little ostentation and so wonderful an effect.
Her characters do not grow in her mind as she writes,
but step fully realized from her mind into the book.
In the opening pages of each of her novels there occur
traits of character which can be truly appreciated only
on a second reading.   Her close observation and un-
tiring realism might entitle her books to be used as historical documents—authoritative descriptions of middle-
class life in the English counties during the period of the
Napoleonic war.   Only her satirical effects at times betray
the freedom with which she is handling and shaping the
material supplied by life.

Satire is the element in which she lives.   It would be
difficult to name an English author, except perhaps Swift,
whose works are more intimately pervaded with the spirit

of satire. Their methods and scope are, of course, utterly different: there is not a trace of the savage indignation of Swift to be found in all her writing. And yet her power, wielded by a less gentle and submissive temper, would have furnished a very efficient light-armed auxiliary to the war engaged in by Gulliver. She has the true fighter's instinct for the weak point in the adversary's armour, although she exhibits it only in the tourney of a summer's day. It is amusement, not victory, that she seeks, and her feats are like that feat of Saladin in *The Talisman*, who although he could not cleave an iron mace asunder with a broadsword, could cut a veil of gossamer as it floated in the air.

In Miss Austen's works the analytic novel, with its interest depending almost entirely on the delineation of character, reached its highest polish. It is not the least wonderful thing about this wonderful lady that her work shows scant traces of development; her first novel is as completely modelled and as perfectly life-like as her last. Miss Maria Edgeworth (1767–1849), on the other hand, attained to the novel proper only by degrees, timidly breathing the spirit of life into the dry stuff of copy-books and didactic manuals. In her childhood, spent in Oxfordshire and London, she came under the influence of her father's friend, Thomas Day, and began to reflect on the education of children while she was herself a child. At the age of fifteen she went with her father to Edgeworthstown in Ireland, where the rest of her life was to be passed, and in the same year began to translate the famous collection of letters on education written by Madame de Genlis under the title *Adèle et*

Théodore. If her taste for theory was precocious, she had at least sufficient opportunity of studying education as an applied science, for her father, who married in steady succession most of the women that his friend Day fell in love with, was the patriarchal progenitor of twenty-one children. Under his direction Miss Edgeworth produced her *Parent's Assistant* (1800) in six volumes, and *Early Lessons* (1801); she assisted him also in his work on *Practical Education* (1798). The cares of the household did not monopolise her attention; she studied the life around her, both of the fashionable world and of the Irish peasantry, to good effect, and at the age of twenty had written the novel which appeared many years later as *Patronage* (1814). Her *Moral Tales* (1801) were written to illustrate the principles of her father's educational doctrine, but in *Castle Rackrent* (1800) and *Belinda* (1801) she struck out for herself in the two lines of fiction that she made especially her own. Her later stories, most of them produced before her father's death in 1817, the last, *Helen*, published in 1834, contain nothing better than these.

The Irishman and the Scot, long familiar as comic figures to the novelists of the eighteenth century, who had inherited them from the earlier comedy of manners, had never before Miss Edgeworth's time ventured to claim serious treatment at the hands of writers of fiction. The character of Thady Quirk, the old dependent of the family in *Castle Rackrent*, and the narrator of its history, was thus a genuine new departure. The reader, instead of being introduced to a conventional comic Irishman with his trite brogue and his every word an Irish bull, is here made to view the manners and fortunes of the landed gentry through the eyes of an Irish peasant. The character is seriously, if not very strongly, conceived, and the humour of it is maintained far above the farcical nonsense that had hitherto satisfied English audiences and English readers as an adequate exposition of the Irish nature. Intelligent and sympathetic throughout, the book would have augured well, had it found worthy followers, for the future of the Union. But the *Tales of Fashionable Life*, wherein many incidental Irish characters appear, were its chief immediate successors, and the greatest distinction of Miss Edgeworth's method must be that, if his own generous statement may be taken literally, it inspired Sir Walter Scott. "Without being so presumptuous," he says in the *General Preface* to the Waverley novels (1829), "as to hope to emulate the rich humour, pathetic tenderness, and admirable tact, which pervade the works of my accomplished friend, I felt that something might be attempted for my own country, of the same kind with that which Miss Edgeworth so fortunately achieved for Ireland—something which might introduce her natives to those of the sister kingdom, in a more favourable light than they had been placed hitherto, and tend to procure sympathy for their virtues and indulgence for their foibles." It was this idea more than any other that gave to the Waverley Novels their highest value and prevented them from being a mere repetition in prose of the earlier poetic successes of their author.

All Miss Edgeworth's stories are in effect "Moral Tales," and it is their chief fault that the moral suggests the tale far more frequently than the tale suggests the moral. Her morals are simple, clear, and hard, and the characters that she puts in action are stiffened to fit them. Even the story of *Vivian*, highly praised by Sir Walter Scott, was written to illustrate the dying precept of an excellent and wise mother, "My son, learn early how to say No!" Often the very title— *Ennui, Manœuvring, The Absentee*—paralyzes the story by anticipation. "It has been my daughter's aim," said Richard Lovell Edgeworth in one of his prefaces, "to promote, by all her writings, the progress of education from the cradle to the grave." There is no escape from this, save by an early death. And Miss Edgeworth's world, let it be admitted, is a dull place; for human character, although it repelled, attracted, and at times amused, never puzzled her in the least. Even complexity of badness is disallowed, and the errors, faults, and foibles that she excelled in depicting are distributed parsimoniously, one to each person, for clearness' sake. In the gay world of fashion she shakes off something of her pedantry, and her worldly women are among her best sketches. It is difficult to say what she might have done had she ever succeeded in getting clear of her fetters. The marvel is that so spirited and humorous a series of portraits should have been produced as illustrations to the text of an educational hand-book— for so she conceived of her work.

Of the multitude of women who practised the art of prose fiction at the beginning of the century, comparatively few followed in the steps of Miss Burney, Miss Austen, and Miss Edgeworth. The novel proper, with every-day life for its subject and realism for its method, has this advantage over the romance, that it is harder for the second-rate writer to imitate it with success. Among the more successful disciples of this modest school Mrs. Brunton ought to be named. Her two completed novels, *Self-Control* (1811) and *Discipline* (1814), have suffered eclipse from the work of her fellow-countrywoman, Miss Mary Ferrier, whose first novel, *Marriage*, appeared in 1818. Mrs. Brunton has little indeed of the humour that distinguishes her greater successor ; her purpose is to inculcate and illustrate the power of religious principle, but she endows her purpose with some few living characters, and enlivens it with incident enough to relieve the gentle melancholy of her numerous descriptive passages. Oblivion has a better title to most of its victims.

If the novelists proper of the time were few, the romancers were legion. From the Minerva press in Leadenhall Street romances poured forth in shoals during the years before the appearance of *Waverley*. Of this vast body of worthless literature the single character-istic is imitation, shameless and unintelligent, of the most popular French and English models. Mrs. Radcliffe, Godwin, and "Monk" Lewis, Rousseau, Madame de Staël, and the Baronne de Montolieu (whose best-known novel, *Caroline de Lichtfield*, had been early translated by Thomas Holcroft) furnished the stuff of innumerable silly composites of sentiment and horror. The novel became purely an article of merchandise. Publishers would advertise effective or thrilling titles and find willing journeymen to supply the tales to order.   In this way, if his critic is to be believed, Mr. T. J. Horsley Curties, one of the larger purveyors of shoddy, obligingly contracted to fit a tale to the engaging title, *The Bloody Monk Udolpho*, already advertised by an ingenious caterer for the market.*   Charlotte Dacre, who wrote under the name of "Rosa Matilda," Sarah Wilkinson, Mary Charlton, Agnes Musgrave, and many others found a ready sale for their wares, making wild work of history, ethnology, and grammar in the search for romantic effect.

> "Some force whole regions, in despite
>   O' geography, to change their site ;
>   Make former times shake hands with latter,
>   And that which was before come after."

Literature has no concern with these works, which fulfilled the utmost end of their being when they found a purchaser.   But it is worth noting that the largest and readiest sale was generally found by writers since forgotten, and that at the close of the eighteenth, as at the close of the nineteenth century, the novel of the season, by the very aptitude with which it caught the idle trick of the time, secured for itself a durable oblivion. Where are now the readers of Mrs. A. M. Bennett's first novel, *Anna ; or, The Memoirs of a Welch Heiress, interspersed with Anecdotes of a Nabob* (1785), of which the whole impression sold on the first day of issue?   Who has read *Vicissitudes abroad ; or, The Ghost of my Father* (1806), in six volumes, by the same lady?   Yet two thousand copies of this work were disposed of at thirty

---

* Vide *Romance Readers and Romance Writers*, by S. G. (1810), Preface.

six shillings on the day of publication. And the
numerous romances of Regina Maria Roche, whose
Children of the Abbey (*c.* 1796) is still occasionally to be
found in a village library, have suffered not thinking on,
with the hobby-horse of many a more modern writer.
Here and there, in this desert of forgotten things, a
name or a title rouses memory. *The Wild Irish Girl,
a National Tale* (1806), of Miss Sydney Owenson,
afterwards Lady Morgan, is still remembered, partly for
its spirited sketches of Irish life, but more for the social
celebrity and great personal charm of its author. Not
even the fierce attacks made on her by the early
reviewers of the *Quarterly* and *Blackwood* can now
inspire an interest in her other romances. They have
found what one of her reviewers denied to them, "that
last poor plea in palliation of tediousness—an end."

One humble purpose these weak romances served,
they furnished the novelists with food for laughter.
Wherever they have existed side by side the novel has
been the critic and the satirist of the romance. Not
the least delightful works of Miss Edgeworth and Miss
Austen are those in which they banter the illusions and
follies produced by the romances of their time. In
Angelina; or, L'Amie Inconnue, one of the *Moral Tales,*
Miss Edgeworth tells how Miss Angelina Warwick, after
corresponding in sentimental ecstasies with an unknown
lady called Araminta, is at length induced to leave her
home and seek asylum with her friend in a romantic
bower in South Wales. The mishaps that befall her
on her journey, her disappointment on finding that
the sylvan bower is a comfortless dirty cottage, and

the authoress of "The Sorrows of Araminta" a burly
vulgar slattern whose real name is Rachel Hodges, are
comically described.   But the book cannot bear comparison with the more delicate humour of Jane Austen's
Northanger Abbey.   The rude contrast between illusion
and reality that is the keynote of Miss Edgeworth's
book is far more subtly and humorously rendered by
Miss Austen.   Isabella Thorpe's catalogue of romances,
"all horrid," are proved to be horrid with a fine irrele-
vancy.   "A particular friend of mine, a Miss Andrews,
a sweet girl, has read every one of them.   I wish you
knew Miss Andrews, you would be delighted with her.
She is netting herself the sweetest cloak you can con-
ceive."   And Catherine's experiences at the abbey are
as perfectly probable as they are delightful.   Not even
the temptation of parody can induce Miss Austen to
force a single note.

   That the romances of the day were read, as well as
written, chiefly by women, the plot of these two novels,
wherein the heroine has her head turned by the perusal
of current literature, may be held to witness.   Precisely
the same situation is made use of in two more satirical
novels, *Romance Readers and Romance Writers* (1810),
by S. G., and *The Heroine; or, Adventures of Cherubina*
(1813), by Eaton Stannard Barrett.   In the former of
these Margaret, the daughter of the Rev. Edward Mar-
sham, is led into eccentricity and disaster by her taste
for popular fiction.   Her extravagances are amusing
enough.   She takes Phelim O'Gurney, a day-labourer, for
a duke in disguise, and kisses his shirt as it flutters on
a hedge; but the author alienates sympathy by the

T

portentous gravity of her plot, and the dark designs of
Lady Isabella Emerson, who supplies the heroine with a
packet of carefully selected novels by Rousseau and de
Staël in order that her virtue may be undermined in the
interests of the villain of the piece, are as absurd as any
romantic aberration. Bad novels, if bad they be, should
receive a lighter treatment. On the other hand, *The
Heroine* deserves high praise for its admirable and divert-
ing burlesque. In this work the adventures of Miss
Cherry Wilkinson, who, convinced of her high birth,
assumes the name of Cherubina Willoughby, are narrated, without a dull page, in a spirit of the purest fun.
Taught by the novels of Mrs. Radcliffe, Miss Roche,
and the Baronne de Montolieu, she practises all accomplishments suitable for a romantic heroine. Tripping,
gliding, flitting and tottering, the only proper modes of
motion, she masters : "of these tottering ranks first, as
it is the approved movement of heroic distress." The
scene wherein she disclaims her father, an honest yeo-
man, is excellent : "'Hear me, Wilkinson,' cried the
fair sufferer, rising with dignified tranquillity. . . . 'Is
it possible that I, who was born to be a Heroine, and
who must therefore have sprung from an idle and
illustrious family, should be the daughter of a fat, funny
farmer ? Oh, no sir ; no thank you.'" Her adventures
in the squalid parts of London, and her attempt to
establish herself, with a retinue of feudal attendants, in
a disused castle, are solemnly related by herself, in the
third person, with the happiest mirthful effect. The
simplicity of the new Wordsworthian poetry comes in
for a share of the satire, but on the whole it may be

said that no better winged shaft was ever sped at a flight of romantic daws. Appearing as it did the year before *Waverley*, the book may be taken as a healthful presage of the appearance of the true romance, or at least as a sign that the futilities of the false were in a fair way to be laughed out of existence.

CHAPTER X.

WITH Sir Walter Scott the wheel has come full circle. The threads of this history may well be knit up with the name of one who combined in his novels elements of excellence so diverse and, before his time, so seldom found united. So long as prose fiction adhered to the form of the novel proper, and was ambitious of distinction in character-drawing and realistic incident, it had for formidable rival the drama. In the foregoing pages that rivalry has been chronicled; the victory was won for the novel by the great writers of the eighteenth century. Then came the Romantic revival, and the novel, cherishing new ambitions, found itself confronted with a new antagonist; the themes that had of old been chanted by the minstrel were claimed as his own by the poet. It is no longer a struggle between the drama and the novel, but a renewal of the old battle between verse and prose for the prerogative possession of romantic themes. In this conflict, too, prose was the victor. For the prose romancer could fortify his romance with all the elements that had proved the main strength of the novel, with comedy and realism, reflection and humour, introduced as auxiliaries to the more purely poetical virtue of the main story. The career of Sir Walter Scott illustrates the struggle and the victory. He achieved fame, and "took the bread out of the mouths of the novelists" by his metrical romances, *The Lay of the Last Minstrel* (1805), *Marmion* (1808), *The Lady of the Lake* (1810), in which the historical and romantic interests are at their height; then, turning to prose, he proved that these interests need not be imperilled by the admixture of qualities that are known only to prose. In his works the novel proper and the romance, which had been long coquetting with each other, were at last wedded. Since his time the pair, joined in one, have asserted empire over a wider and wider domain; the novel, like Bottom in the *Midsummer Night's Dream*, who was anxious to play all parts, has assumed the functions of many other literary forms.

Walter Scott (1771-1832) grew up to manhood while the Romantic movement was in the full tide of its influence. He early became "a glutton of books," especially of works of fiction. Early in life, he says, he "nourished the ambitious desire of composing a tale of chivalry, which was to be in the style of the Castle of Otranto, with plenty of Border characters and supernatural incident." He began such a tale, but laid it aside on the success of the ballads which his study of German dramas and romances had moved him to write. The fragment was subsequently published as an appendix to the *General Preface* to the Waverley novels.

His zeal for Scottish legendary lore showed itself in the frequent "Border raids" of the years during which he was "making himself." Again, about the year 1805, he came near to embarking on the novel, writing one-third part of the first volume of *Waverley.* But the opinion of a friend was unfavourable, and Scott was unwilling to risk the loss of his considerable poetical reputation. He turned to verse romance and to editorial and critical work; at last, in 1814, when Byron was threatening, or more than threatening, his popular supremacy in verse, he returned to the old idea, and completed and published *Waverley; or, 'Tis Sixty Years since.*

The poverty and feebleness of his predecessors in the art of weaving a romance on a framework of historical events have caused their number, and even their existence, to be forgotten. Yet Scott was not the modern creator of the historical romance, although he was the first to bring to its composition an adequate knowledge and an artistic instinct. An interest in past history, a desire to revive in fiction the picturesque elements of bygone institutions and customs, were of the essence of the Romantic revival. The practitioners of historical novel-writing, before Scott, were not few in number, although few indeed were qualified for the task. The novels produced by them constitute the silliest, feeblest body of work to be found in the annals of prose fiction. Horace Walpole and Mrs. Radcliffe had aimed at the illusion of antiquity, with fair success; but they avoided explicit historical allusions, and did not attempt to introduce into their stories well-known historical

personages. Some of the authors who followed them cast
aside their diffidence, and, unmindful of the canon that
the principal characters of an historical novel should
not themselves be historical, paid the inevitable penalty
of their ignorance and rashness. In *The Recess, or a
Tale of Other Times* (1783–1786), Miss Sophia Lee
produced one of the earliest of modern historical novels.
The heroine is one of twin sisters, the offspring of a
secret marriage, unknown to history, between Mary
Queen of Scots and the Duke of Norfolk ; the events
of her life are represented, with almost incredible effron-
tery, as interwoven with the lives and fates of Leicester,
Burleigh, Essex, Pembroke, Southampton, James of
Scotland, and others. Queen Elizabeth herself is
brought on the stage, displaying the " coarse virulence
that marks her manners " in the style of an eighteenth-
century dowager. *The Canterbury Tales*, written later
by Harriet and Sophia Lee in collaboration, were praised
and utilized by Lord Byron. This earlier novel is an
outrage on history and no credit to fiction.

Bad as it is, however, it is better than many of the
novels that followed it. The historical novelists who
preceded Scott chose a century as they might have chosen
a partner for a dance, gaily and confidently, without
qualification or equipment beyond a few overworn verbal
archaisms. No Gifford arose to break these writers on
the wheel, although of them, as truly as of the " Della
Cruscans," it might be said that they

> " For *ekes* and *algates* only deign to seek,
> And live upon a *whilome* for a week."

A few of their titles may serve to show the range of

their unchastened historical ambition. *Edwy and Elgiva, an Historical Romance of the Tenth Century* (1811), by John Agg; *Gondez, the Monk, a Romance of the Thirteenth Century* (1805), by S. W. H. Ireland; *The Borderers, an Historical Romance, illustrative of the Manners of the Fourteenth Century* (1812), are types of a class. In these three novels Dunstan, Edward I., and Chaucer, among others, are assaulted. In the last of them the Scottish poet Dunbar is introduced as a contemporary of Chaucer, much as if Wordsworth and Dryden should be spoken of as friends and rivals.

To none of these writers was Scott under any obligation. Miss Jane Porter, it is true, authoress of *Thaddeus of Warsaw* (1803) and *The Scottish Chiefs* (1810), claimed, in the preface to a late edition of the former work (1831), that she was the inventor of the historical romance, and that Scott was her imitator. There is no reason for thinking the second article of the claim any better founded than the first, for Scott was punctiliously careful to acknowledge the smallest debts. In the matter of the imaginative handling of history he does acknowledge one debt. In the year 1808 there was published an historical romance, entitled *Queen-hoo Hall*, which had been left unfinished at his death by the antiquary Joseph Strutt, and was arranged and hastily completed by Scott, whose brief contribution to it includes the fine song—

" Waken, lords and ladies gay ! "

The poor success of the book led Scott to reflect on historical romancing in general, and his own mislaid manuscript in particular. Strutt and Miss Edgeworth

are thus acknowledged as godfather and godmother
respectively to *Waverley*.

Queen-hoo Hall, which was designed to illustrate
English life and manners of the reign of Henry VI., is
taxed by Scott with an overweight of antiquarian knowledge, and an employment of "language too ancient."
The book is absurdly full of allusions to forgotten
customs, but the language put into the mouths of the
characters is pure, and when possible recondite, Elizabethan. The conclusion arrived at by Scott as to the
right use of archaic diction is fully stated in his criticism
on the work of Clara Reeve. "He that would please
the modern world," he says, "yet present the exact impression of a tale of the Middle Ages, will repeatedly
find that he will be obliged, in despite of his utmost
exertions, to sacrifice the last to the first object, and
eternally expose himself to the just censure of the rigid
antiquary, because he must, to interest the readers of the
present time, invest his characters with language and
sentiments unknown to the period assigned to his story ;
and thus his utmost efforts only attain a sort of composition between the true and the fictitious, just as the dress
of Lear, as performed on the stage, is neither that of a
modern sovereign, nor the cerulean painting and bear-
hide with which the Britons, at the time when that
monarch is supposed to have lived, tattooed their persons
and sheltered themselves from cold. All this inconsistency is avoided by adopting the style of our grandfathers
and great-grandfathers, sufficiently antiquated to accord
with the antiquated character of the narrative, yet copious
enough to express all that is necessary to its interest, and

to supply that deficiency of colouring which the more ancient times do not afford."

The practice that he here recommends is the one he himself followed, and handed on to most of the more modern writers of historical novels. His wide and clear knowledge of history made it plain to him that absolute antiquarian and historical accuracy must be foregone. Earlier writers had flattered themselves that they were teaching history in their novels. In the preface to *A Peep at our Ancestors* (1807), a novel dealing with the times of the Norman Conquest, the author, Henrietta Mosse, remarks that " no small portion of *moral* culpability attaches to that writer, who, for the convenience of his own pen, wilfully represents as true what he knows to be false." From the condemnation incurred by this offence the historical novelists before Scott were saved by invincible ignorance. The things they knew to be false were so few. Scott saw the incompatibility of the aims of history and fiction, and satisfied himself with seeking verisimilitude rather than antiquarian accuracy. The difficulty is a real one; to this day it is hard, if not impossible, for a novelist who lays his scene in the fourteenth century to convince or gratify a student who has enjoyed the writings of Chaucer and Froissart. Such a novel can be rescued from triviality only by genius, which knows how to touch lightly on transitory fashions, and to rest the interest of the story on the unchanging fashions of the human heart. *Quod semper et ubique et ab omnibus* is the saving creed of a novelist.

And herein lies the greatness of Scott. It is late in

the day, and it is no part of the purpose of this history,
which reaches its goal with the publication of *Waverley*,
to criticise Sir Walter. Let him be praised in words
taken from Carlyle's unworthy essay, wherein the name
of "greatness" is refused to him because he had no
express message to deliver. "Be this as it may, surely
since Shakespeare's time there has been no great speaker
so unconscious of an aim in speaking as Walter Scott."
He saw life, and told the world what he saw. Has any
writer since his time supplied it with a fuller, fairer vision?
From Ivanhoe to Edie Ochiltree, from Lucy Ashton to
Jeanie Deans, from the knightly achievements of the
crusades to the humours of the Scottish peasantry,—this
is the panorama he reveals, and he casts over it the light
of his generous, gentle, and delicate nature. His very
style, loose and rambling as it is, is a part of the man,
and of the artistic effect he produces. The full vigour
and ease with which his imagination plays on life is
often suggested by his pleonasms and tautologies; the
search for the single final epithet is no part of his
method, for he delights in the telling, and is sorry when
all is told. The asceticism of style belongs to a different
race of artists, the lesser of whom are sadly anæmic.
Sir Walter Scott is the first of the modern race of giants
in fiction; his rapid series of great novels inaugurates a
new era. Let the historian of the novel learn from
Goldsmith's art-critic; of other writers he may observe
that their work would have been better had they taken
more pains, but if he claim the possession of any critical
faculty at all he must praise the works of Sir Walter Scott.

INDEX.

--- ∞ ---

THE END.

THE POETICAL WORKS OF ROBERT BROWNING

Complete Edition—Edited and Annotated by the Rt. Hon. Augustine Birrell, K.C., and Sir Frederic G. Kenyon, K.C.B. With Portraits.

Two Volumes.—*10s. 6d. net each.* Two Volumes.—Printed on India Paper, *24s. net.* One Volume.—Printed on India Paper, *21s. net.*

Pocket Edition.—Eight volumes (size 6¼ by 4⅛ in.), printed on India Paper, with a Portrait in each volume. Bound in cloth, *3s. 6d. net each* ; or, in leather, *5s. net each.* Cloth case to contain the eight volumes, *5s. net.*

SELECTIONS FROM THE POETICAL WORKS OF ROBERT BROWNING Crown 8vo. *6s. net.* And Small Fcap. 8vo. *2s. 6d. net.*

BROWNING : HOW TO KNOW HIM

By W. Lyon Phelps, Professor of English Literature in Yale University. *7s. 6d. net.*

THE BROWNINGS FOR THE YOUNG

A Selection from the Poetry of Robert and Elizabeth Barrett Browning. Edited by Sir Frederic G. Kenyon, K.C.B. *2s. net.*

THE ENGLISH NOVEL

From its Origin to Sir Walter Scott. By Sir Walter Raleigh, M.A., Professor of English Literature in the University of Oxford. Tenth Impression. *4s. 6d. net.*

SHAKESPEARE'S PREDECESSORS IN THE ENGLISH DRAMA

By J. A. Symonds. New Edition. *10s. 6d. net.*

SHAKSPERE AND HIS PREDECESSORS IN THE ENGLISH DRAMA

By F. S. Boas, M.A., sometime Professor of English Literature, Queen's College, Belfast. Fourth Impression. *7s. 6d. net.*

THE STUDENT'S ENGLISH LITERATURE

A History of English Literature and of the chief English Writers founded upon the Manual of Thomas B. Shaw. By A. Hamilton Thomson, B.A., of St. John's College, Cambridge. With Notes, etc. Fifth Impression. *9s.*

INTRODUCTION TO POETRY

Poetic Expression, Poetic Truth, the Progress of Poetry. By Laurie Magnus, M.A. Second Edition. *2s. 6d. net.*

By Ernest Weekley, M.A.

"Professor Weekley has a singularly happy knack of combining entertainment with erudition in the production of a popular book."—*Truth*,

WORDS ANCIENT AND MODERN

Crown 8vo. 5s. *net*.

The author of "The Romance of Words" recounts in some detail the lives of a number of words of which the etymology and fantastic changes of meaning are of special interest.

MORE WORDS ANCIENT AND MODERN

Crown 8vo. 5s. *net*.

A sequel to the above, dealing with *compound* words which have curious histories. It corrects some long-accepted derivations, and throws new light on the history of many familiar words.

A CONCISE ETYMOLOGICAL DICTIONARY OF MODERN ENGLISH

Crown 8vo. 7s. 6d. *net*.

This book is an abridgment of the author's *Etymological Dictionary of Modern English* published in 1921. The process of shortening has been carried out, not by omitting the less common words (for it is usually the uncommon word or the neologism that excites legitimate curiosity), but by making the explanations as brief as possible and by abstaining from the discussion of unsatisfying conjectures. It contains the whole of our literary and colloquial vocabulary, together with sufficient indications to show the origin of modern scientific terms.

AN ETYMOLOGICAL DICTIONARY OF MODERN ENGLISH Crown 4to. £2 2s. *net*.

The *magnum opus* from which the "Concise Dictionary" was compiled.

THE ROMANCE OF WORDS

Large Crown 8vo. Fourth Edition. 6s. *net*.
"A book of extraordinary interest."—*Observer*.

THE ROMANCE OF NAMES

Large Crown 8vo. Third Revised Edition. 6s. *net*.
"Full of fascination for the general reader. Packed with curious facts set forth in the most interesting way."

SURNAMES

Large Crown 8vo. Second Edition. 6s. *net*.
"Mr. Weekley has so artfully sprinkled his pages with odd and impossible names that we simply cannot help reading him."